"Joe LoMusio has developed a robust biblical theology of priorities. Only with God at the center can we really know him, allow him to transform us, and then understand how to balance the simultaneous responsibilities we have toward the other significant people God has placed in our lives."

—MARK L. BAILEY
Chancellor, Dallas Theological Seminary

"Life is relentlessly fragmenting. We are pulled in many directions while we strive to keep the main thing, the main thing. Too often we have been given a hierarchy of priorities only to discover that life doesn't cooperate with our lists and plans. Joe LoMusio helps us find a new perspective, showing us that it is possible to live without a competing set of imperatives that usually make us frustrated and constantly hitting a reset button. I believe you will go back to this book often as you seek to experience God in the center of your life."

—CLIFF MCARDLE
Far East Broadcasting Company

"For many years, I have wrestled with the idea that I need to live my life by a list of priorities: God first, wife second, family third, etc. In just a few pages, Joe LoMusio has revealed not only a better way to live but the biblical way! The sure way to follow, grounded in truth—the way of 'God at center.'"

—LARRY NIGGLI
San Diego Coalition for Men's Discipleship

"*God at Center* offers an excellent opportunity to calibrate thoughts about what is the core of our beliefs—that God not only relates to us in a personal way but is also the nucleus of our spiritual walk with him. There is great discovery in knowing that God is not only transcendent but can also be the glorious hub within our hearts and minds that can impact everything we do and everyone we encounter. The centrality of God goes beyond hierarchical and timebound limitations and frees the believer to radiate the boundless love of God, anytime and anyplace."

—ARNOLD HUNTLEY
Fellow, Colson Center for Christian Worldview

"I have reviewed many books and confess that some of them I skim. That is because of the quality of content and the book's ability to command my attention. But *God at Center* captured me—the quotations, the argumentation, the applications, the conclusion. I was captivated by the content, its structure, and the literary presentation. I read it carefully, applying its message to my thinking, and I challenge you to do the same."

—ELMER TOWNS
Cofounder, Liberty University

"Common sense tells us that to fulfill 'essential' tasks we must remove the 'unessentials' of life. Yet most of us agree that such knowledge does not predictably yield actions and habits that epitomize that knowledge. It seems that we need more than common sense. LoMusio highlights that prioritizing how we spend our time and placing God at the center of our lives is a daily choice; it's a choice that will ultimately determine how the rest of our relationships, responsibilities, and circumstances will unfold. The text is grounded in the attributes of God found in Scripture and is outlined according to the great commandment to love God and love others."

—MARY KAY PARK
Executive managing director, Far East Broadcasting Company

God at Center

Sierra—

God bless you Abundantly!

God Only and Always!

Matthew 22:37-40

[signature]

God at Center

Make Sense of Who You Are,
What God Wants You to Know,
and What to Do about It

Joe LoMusio

Foreword by Elmer Towns

RESOURCE *Publications* · Eugene, Oregon

GOD AT CENTER
Make Sense of Who You Are, What God Wants You to Know,
    and What to Do about It

Resource Publications
An Imprint of Wipf and Stock Publishers
199 W. 8th Ave., Suite 3
Eugene, OR 97401

www.wipfandstock.com

PAPERBACK ISBN: 978-1-6667-1988-8
HARDCOVER ISBN: 978-1-6667-1989-5
EBOOK ISBN: 978-1-6667-1990-1

AUGUST 24, 2021

Permissions

AMOREM DEO

~

CORAM DEO

~

CENTRUM DEO

Contents

x

Acknowledgments

Upfront, I need to acknowledge the late Dr. J. Grant Howard, professor of Pastoral Theology at Western Seminary in Portland, Oregon. While I have spent countless hours meditating on and formulating thoughts about this subject, the reality is that the core idea of "God at Center" originates, at least for me, with his book, *Balancing Life's Demands*. I found myself engaged by his wisdom and reasoning. His challenge to the church to embrace a biblically-based paradigm for keeping priorities was dynamic and it radically changed my perspective on how we should understand time management. I am therefore indebted to him for the insights gained and the opportunity to take and run with his thesis and make it an ongoing teaching goal of my own over many years of ministry.

Furthermore, I wish to thank the inestimable Elmer Towns, who in his late eighties and still keeping an international teaching and preaching schedule, nevertheless took the time to review my manuscript. His encouragement and comments were a Godsend. Providing the *Foreword* to this book has been a priceless gift that I will never forget.

I would also like to acknowledge my friend and colleague Larry Niggli. As the Area Director of the San Diego County Coalition for Men's Discipleship as well as the *Man in the Mirror* Area Director for San Diego County, Larry has been a good friend and a great encourager. His input and the sharing of ideas have been invaluable. He has provided helpful comments and editing suggestions every step of the way. I admire his desire to see men living for Christ with wholesome, balanced lives, as they seek to make God the center of their lives.

Lastly, I wish to acknowledge the loving support of my wife, my family, and my many friends and fellow believers, especially at The Rock Church of Temecula Valley. We are all on this journey together and none of us can do it effectively without the contributions we can make in each other's lives. We are to love God. We will love each other.

Foreword

CHOICES . . . YOU MAKE MANY choices every day. Some choices are inconsequential, like choosing to wear the blue shirt or the brown shirt. A few choices are life-defining, like will I go to college, which one, what major and how diligently will I pursue the demands to gain that degree . . . to gain that education . . . to gain that understanding of life. My choices will determine if I will be a dentist . . . a business owner . . . or an eight-hour-a-day factory worker.

Author Joe LoMusio wants you to put "God At Center" of all choices so you will "make sense of who you are, bring balance to your life, and know your purpose for living." LoMusio challenges you to realize there are two alternatives to living. First, there is the *Chronos Life*, which reacts to the time allotted to you which LoMusio describes as the quantity of time and opportunity and obligation of living. This Chronos is what each of us must do. But then the author describes *Kairos*, which is quality-time. This is life when we choose to put God at the center of our life so that He is our priority before we face our choices. God is the guiding force as we make our choice, and He is the focus and goal of our choices. The key to healthy living is "balancing all life" and we do this with God at the center.

You have got this book in your hand, that is a good beginning choice. Did you choose to purchase it, or did someone give it to you, or recommend it? Or did you just stumble across this book as you lived your *Chronos Life*? Maybe luck has put this book in your hand, and now you have a choice – what will you do with this book? Will you skim it? Read it through? Let it change your life?

Then you opened this book and now you have read at least the Foreword. That is a great start to reading the rest of this book. If you choose to read at least the first chapter, you will be faced with two challenging ways to live. You will learn that many people take life as it is dished out to them, i.e., *Chronos* time. That's you—me—all of life. But you will be faced with the possibility of *Kairos* time when you choose to balance the demands of life and you establish priorities in life, so that when you face the paradigm or solutions to every and all issues; you will know what to choose and what to do and how to react. You will learn to balance the competing demands of life.

As author LoMusio says, "Time is a tyrant," so he teaches us how to "redeem the time" according to the biblical answer to life's dilemmas. It is putting *God At Center*.

The whole thrust of the book will demonstrate to you that when God is at the center of our lives, then we can properly fulfill all our responsibilities, and balance all the demands on our life. With God at the center, we will properly love Him as demonstrated in Scriptures with all our hearts, minds, souls, and body. Then we can love others and minister to them. That includes our family, friends, maybe even our foes; so that we love our neighbor as ourselves.

LoMusio ends by reminding us we must be willing to *love* in five areas. *Love* the Lord constantly, unashamedly, and passionately. *Love* our family to demonstrate God is at the center of our life. *Love* being the church because it is who we are, rather than a place to attend. *Love* our job and invest spiritual value in it so that we do it to the glory of God. And *love* the world for whom Jesus died, so that we are a testimony to Jesus who died for them and we attempt to get them "reconciled to God."

I have reviewed many books and confess that some of them I skim. That is because of the quality of content and the book's ability to command my attention. But *God At Center* captured me—the quotations, the argumentation, the applications, the conclusion. I read it carefully, applying its message to my thinking, I challenge you to do the same.

Elmer Towns
Co-founder, LIBERTY UNIVERSITY

First Word

"It's Your Choice!"

OUR LIVES REFLECT THE CHOICES we make.

Every day we are confronted with a myriad of options. We know that life's obligations are not optional. We need to learn that things that matter most must never be at the mercy of things that matter least. How, then, can we know the difference between the mandatory and the mundane?

- What should be our priorities?
- Who gets our time, how much of it, and when?
- How can we balance all of life's demands?

Most will acknowledge that this is an old problem that does not have simple solutions in an ever-increasingly complex world. Those pursuing a Christian worldview can certainly ask—does the Bible offer any help?

The demands of life, and certainly for Christians, the demands of ministry and serving the Lord, are such that we are in constant need of "prioritizing" life. Balancing all the components of life—devotion, family, ministry, work, church, recreation, etc., can create conflicts and present real dilemmas which can result in less than healthy emotions and attitudes and a less than productive life.

Traditional approaches to establishing priorities are communicated in oft-repeated clichés and therefore often inadequate to reconcile the many demands and complexities of living in our modern world. The church for too long has simply parroted the traditional scheme of priority-keeping that relates more to the corporate business world than to a radical reordering of life, based on biblical principles. After all, why would anyone ever want to challenge the idea of putting God first and then everyone and everything else second, third, fourth, and so on?

But, as we shall see, this "life by the list" is not practical, logical, nor theological. Accordingly, we must pursue a different paradigm than traditional priority keeping; one that is completely biblical and consistently practical. And it must deepen our understanding of who God is, why we are, and how can we best serve others.

Is there such a radically different paradigm upon which we can build our lives?

Yes, there is!

Part One

When Is Priority?

A list of priorities doesn't make sense. It can't be intelligently explained. It can't be easily understood. It can't be logically lived out. no matter how you define and describe your particular approach if it is a sequential approach, it is loaded with contradictions, complexities, confusion, and chaos.

J. GRAND HOWARD

Teach us to number our days and recognize how few they are;

help us to spend them as we should.

MOSES
PSALM 90:12 (TLB)

This section aims to challenge the conventional method of priority-keeping and set forth an alternative in the form of a biblical paradigm offered in Matthew 22:36–40. Without much critical thinking on the subject, the church has for too long bought into the corporate model of time management and the structuring of priorities. It is time to follow the Bible's model.

One | Busy Here And There

Time Waits for No Man!

WE HAVE ALL HEARD THAT saying, haven't we? This axiom can be understood in several ways, but certainly, one way to understand it is that time is relentless.

Time is unyielding.

Time is unforgiving.

Time is uncompromising.

Time is inflexible and intransigent.

And the truth is, time in its rush forward does not care if you're not keeping up. As such, time is a Tyrant!

The Ancient Greeks knew that, so in their complex mythology they identified time as the god *Chronos* (from this word we get words such as "chronology"). Chronos was the un-aging king of the Titans and feared by all. He was viewed as a destructive, all-devouring force. He could not be diverted. He could not be defeated. He could not be resisted. He was unstoppable! And so, it is for us today. We still serve the god Chronos!

Instead of using time as an advantage, tenacious Chronos takes advantage of us. We become slaves of the clock—with his pointy hands and his ticking heart. And the sound of that ticking cannot be ignored, cannot be dismissed, and refuses to be muted.

Interestingly, the Greeks built into their cosmology that Chronos must be defeated. And so he was—by his son Zeus, in the Titan wars. This epic defeat of the god Chronos was understood to be a victory for the ancient Greeks. Even though it did not change anything, at least they figured out how to defeat big, bad Chronos. That was good news for the

3

ancient Greeks. The bad news for us today, however, is that we are not the ancient Greeks!

For a moment, let us turn from Greek mythology to Hebrew history. There is an interesting story, recorded in 1 Kings 20, where Ben-Hadad and the Arameans have invaded Israel, but they are defeated by King Ahab, not once but twice. And, of course, Israel has been granted victory on both occasions because of the Lord's intervention. In fact, after the second victory, the Aramean king is captured and brought before king Ahab, who curiously treats him as a friendly brother rather than a mortal enemy. Ahab, then, rashly agrees to a treaty with Ben-Hadad and allows him to go free.

This action by a faithless king displeases God, and a prophet is immediately sent to rebuke Ahab. The unnamed prophet devises an ingenious way to confront the king, disguising himself as a hapless, wounded Israelite soldier who allowed a dangerous prisoner to escape (1 Kgs 20:38–40). It occurs to me that the excuse that he offers in verse 40 has some relevance for us, at least regarding the topic we are pursuing. The excuse he offers is this, "While your servant was busy here and there, he was gone." The Contemporary English Version has him saying, "I got busy doing other things." And The Message paraphrases it, "I got busy doing one thing after another."

Sense The Relevance?

Can we not hear ourselves, at times, making that same lame excuse? Are we not having to ask ourselves periodically, "What have I missed out on by being too busy?" Our days are consumed with rushing to and fro, hither, and yon, back and forth, in and out. And, as a result, we find ourselves physically out of breath, emotionally out of sorts, and crucially out of time.

In our modern world (lightyears removed from Mt. Olympus) the tempo of our lives continues to increase and there are no signs of slowing down any time soon. Somehow, we have not learned, as Gandhi observed, that there is more to life than increasing its speed. As Christians, we must come to understand that hurry is almost always the enemy of a healthy and holy spiritual life.

The late Howard Hendricks, the inestimable professor for so many years at Dallas Seminary, offered an important observation that some people are actually compulsively active and rarely learn the lesson of what he called the *barrenness of busyness*. He wrote, "Activity simply becomes an anesthetic to deaden the pain of an empty life. And if we get off long enough, we discover we have activity without accomplishment."[1]

Commenting on our postmodern society, Rod;.ey Clapp offers this assessment: "The contemporary world, like an uncoordinated and loosely jointed giant, hurtles headlong down a steep slope, already off balance and stumbling, maybe facing an imminent—and disastrous—fall. We live in times of incredibly rapid and prolific changes. People, products, ideas, and culture meet, mingle, and mutate with dazzling speed."[2]

Pastor Mark Buchanan makes this pertinent observation: "We're busy people. The main experience of men and women and even children in North America is busyness, having far more to do any day, every day, all, than we can possibly get done. We simultaneously scurry and slog through breathless, breakneck schedules. We flounder in a welter of meetings and errands, demands and delays, expectations and obligations. It's joyless. It's endless."[3]

There is always a price to pay when we increase our speed in an attempt to overcome or out-race time. As in all competition, time then is more often an adversary than a friend. Time should be our ally, but instead, it is our enemy. We should master time, but instead, time becomes our master. We wish to harness time, but usually, we just end up being harassed by it. And then we wonder why we are left dazed, discouraged, and defeated.

The demands on our time continue to increase. Doug Sherman and William Hendricks in their helpful book, *How to Balance Competing Time Demands*, refer to the "relentless downpour of demands on our time."[4] The twenty-first century should be renamed after a hurricane. Some years ago, Tim Timmons captured this dilemma in his insightful book, *Maximum Living in a Pressure-Cooker World*. He wrote:

> Our modern world is an exhilarating place to live. We know more, we can do more, and we have more than any other society in the history of mankind. Just plug it in, push the button, and you have instant – everything! But along with having everything

1. Hendricks, *Taking A Stand*, 13.

2. Clapp, *Families at the Crossroads*, 17.

3. Buchanan, *Your God is Too Safe*, 100.

4. Sherman and Hendricks, *Competing Time Demands*, 21.

in an instant, we only seem to have it for an instant. Everything
is happening at such a breathless pace!... We are aboard a train
that is gathering speed, racing down a track on which there is an
unknown number of switches leading to unknown destinations.
No single scientist is in the engine cab and there may be demons at the switches. Most of society is in the caboose looking
backward. Everything is out of control. It's like having your feet
firmly planted in midair![5]

For the most part, let us not kid ourselves, Christians have been
running along with everyone else, trying to keep up. Os Guinness probes
the problem deeper and more creatively in his *Gravedigger File: Paper on
the Subversion of the Modern Church.* He sees the potential for spiritual,
moral, and intellectual schizophrenia amongst Christians, a result of having to juggle with "double, triple and quadruple-living, modular morality
and compartmentalization convictions (that become) as interchangeable
as Lego-like lifestyles." And "At the very least," he continues, "this frag-
mentation fosters the breathless, strung-out feeling characteristic of busy
modern Christians."[6]

Make no mistake, society is going to pay the price for our submission to the god Chronos. Virginia Brasier's lines, written some time ago,
are even more relevant in our day!

This Is The Age Of The Half-Read Page;
And The Quick Hash, And The Mad Dash.
The Bright Night With The Nerves Tight.
The Plane Hop With The Brief Stop.
The Lamp Tan In A Short Span.
The Big Shot In A Good Spot.
And The Brain Strain, The Heart Pain,
And The Catnaps Till The Spring Snaps—
And The Fun's Done![7]

A Tyrant Indeed!

Speaking of tyrants, I am reminded of the classic little book, written so
many years ago but still so relevant, *Tyranny of the Urgent*, by Charles

5. Timmons, *Maximum Living*, 15.

6. Guinness, *Gravedigger File*, 81.

7. Braiser, "Time of the Mad Atom," 1949.

Hummel. Just the title alone captures what most of us face every day. Hummel accurately suggests that we often live our lives in constant tension between the urgent and the important. He warned, though it seems most were not listening, that the greatest reoccurring danger (in time management) is letting the urgent things crowd out the important things.[8]

But things that matter most must never be at the mercy of things that matter least. Furthermore, we need to learn that the urgent and the important are not always the same thing! Sometimes we spend too much time on what seems urgent and not enough time on what is certainly important.

The Biblical answer to the tyranny of Chronos is stated by the Apostle Paul in one of the most important statements on time management found anywhere in the Word of God. In Ephesians 5:15–16, he writes, "See then that you walk circumspectly, not as fools but as wise, redeeming the time, because the days are evil."

What does Paul mean by *redeeming the time*? The word he chooses is significant—it is *exagorazo,* from the preposition *ek* ("out of") and the verb *agorazo*, which meant "to purchase." (The noun *Agora* was the marketplace in a Greek city where things could be purchased.)

Exagorazo appears four times in the New Testament, here in Ephesians 5:16, and the related statement in Colossians 4:5. The other two references are in Galatians 3:13, "Christ redeemed us from the curse of the Law," and again in Galatians 4:5 "He might redeem those who were under the Law." The two references in Galatians are significant and helpful because they show that when you redeem someone from slavery, as Christ redeemed us, you are purchasing them *out of* (exagarazo) their slavery. You are paying the price to take them out of a bad situation! A synonym would be the word "ransom."

But note this, in Ephesians 5:16 the reference to "redeeming" is not applied to people, but rather to time. So, the next important word in the verse is "time" ("redeem the time"), but what word does Paul use? Significantly, Paul does not use the word *Chronos*, but rather he uses the word *Kairos*. This is incredibly important! Both words refer to time, but not the same *type* of time.

And so now we must go back to Greek mythology to understand the difference. Like *Chronos*, *Kairos* was also personified as a god! In Greek mythology, Kairos was the personification of opportunity, luck,

---

8. Hummel, *Tyranny of the Urgent*, 4.

and favorable moments. The ancient Greeks saw Kairos as the god of the right moment, which could also be described as the fleeting moment. As such, this was time as it relates to a favorable opportunity.

The Greeks understood that such a moment must be grasped otherwise the moment would be gone and therefore could not be re-captured. That irretrievable moment is referred to in Horace Mann's compelling lines: "Lost, yesterday, somewhere between sunrise and sunset, Two golden hours, each set with sixty diamond minutes. No reward is offered, for they are gone forever."[9]

In the Preface to his book on *Time Management*, Ted Engstrom ponders if the pressure of time has blurred our perspective and the struggle to keep up dimmed our vision? He asks pointedly, "Are we slaves to cluttered desks? Are we so 'crisis-oriented' that opportunities pass by unrecognized?"[10]

We need to appreciate the difference between these two concepts of time. Kairos isn't about minutes, seconds, and measurement of time. Paul knew that Kairos time expressed the idea of the *right* time, the most opportune time, and not just Chronos time. Another way to distinguish the difference is to understand that *Chronos* is a quantity of time, while *Kairos* is the quality of time.

So, to "Redeem the time" (to *exagarazo* the *kairos*), you are purchasing out of "slavery" and bad use the fleeting opportunities with which you have been presented. In other words, you seize the moment. You take advantage of the fleeting opportunities. As the NASB renders Ephesians 5:16, "make the most of every opportunity", and the NIV has it, "make the most of your time."

No Time to Waste

And here is the reason why we must redeem the time, because, as Paul said, "the days are evil!" The reality is, we do not have time to waste.

Chronos is relentless in gobbling up time and people! Therefore, we always think of our time in a Chronos mindset. We have twenty-four hours a day, forty-plus hour workweek, and a list of things to do by such-and-such a time. But we also need to have a Kairos mindset. You

---

9. Mann, see NYT (1953) 29.

10. Engstrom and Mackenzie, *Managing Your Time*, 8.

only have a brief opportunity to spend meaningful moments with your spouse, to influence your children, to visit a friend in need.

A Kairos mindset understands that some moments are more valuable than others. Remember that Chronos does not care at all about that. For Chronos, all moments are just minutes! But for Christians, five minutes sharing the gospel with a friend is more valuable than five minutes you spend mindlessly scrolling through Facebook.

Do not let your obsession with Chronos obscure your attention to Kairos. Redeeming the time will always mean making the right choices. In fact, what gives Kairos its ultimate meaning is that when that opportunity comes, you will be faced with the unavoidable decision to seize that moment, or not. For the most part, that choice is always entirely up to you.

It is certainly not difficult to see how this plays out every day in our world. Our culture is overloaded with choices. We are often overwhelmed and sometimes even paralyzed by them. Alina Tugend mentions that "an excess of choices often leads us to be less, not more, satisfied once we actually decide. There's often that nagging feeling we could have done better."[11]

Tim Hansel has a great chapter entitled *Weary Servants of the Impossible* in his helpful book, *When I Relax, I Feel Guilty*. In it, he says that he is often dominated by "shoulds," "ought to's," and "musts." In fact, he admits that he is tyrannized by them. He then offers this insight, "The Western mind and culture leave little time for leisure, prayer, play, and contemplation. Hurry needs answers; answers need categories; categories need labeling and dissecting." He concludes, "In order to keep up my incessant activity, God was simply reduced to fit into my schedule. I suffered because he didn't fit."[12]

There is no getting away from it. Menus and options confront us constantly. Just go to a typical grocery store and you will be facing shelves that overwhelm you with choices. But deciding between brands of cereal at the market is one thing while deciding on family or career choices is far more critical. So, we need to be incredibly careful.

I often think back to that great sequence in *Indian Jones and the Last Crusade*, where the centuries-old Templar knight who is guarding the sacred chalice of Christ (the Holy Grail), remarks after the villain chooses

---

11. Tugend, "Too Many Choices," NYT (2010).

12. Hansel, *When I Relax I Feel Guilty*, 22.

the wrong cup and pays for it with his life. "He chose poorly" the old knight drolls. And then again, when Indian Jones chooses a chalice and it proves to be the correct one, he admits to Indy with an unmistakable glee, "You have chosen wisely."

Is God likewise concerned with the choices we make? Through the prophet Isaiah He declares to the children of Israel, "when I called, you did not answer; When I spoke, you did not hear, but did evil before My eyes, and chose that in which I do not delight" (Isa 65:12). Earlier, the Lord declared to those keeping His sabbath, to "choose what pleases me and hold fast my covenant" (Isa 56:4).

Choosing Wisely or Poorly?

In *Balancing Life's Demands*, J. Grant Howard wrote that in the battle of life, we are constantly up against options and at every turn and choices that we have to make. He spoke about obligations that pressure us and opportunities that would entice us. As a result, he knew that we would be infiltrated by feelings of guilt because we could not possibly respond to all the options. The challenge to keep up with it all is unrelenting. He writes, "We are bombarded with places to go, overrun with people to meet, pinned down with things to buy, fatigued with mail to read. We are being inundated on all sides by powerful forces that clamor for our time, talents, money, influence, wisdom."[13]

Whether the pressure of this struggle is constant or occasional it is nevertheless real enough. It is a battle that claims casualties by attrition. It matters little if the wounds are self-inflicted or come from dealing with others in the daily grind, the result is still damage and dysfunction. Dr. Howard writes:

> At times we are so pummeled with options that we contemplate surrender. We look in vain for a white flag to wave. Gradually we realize that we are under siege and that the siege lasts a lifetime. We can't surrender. We can't escape. We just keep on fighting. And the fight is carried on by making decisions. Some decisions involve only a minor skirmish; others are major. When we make the right choice, we win. If it's the wrong choice, we lose. There are no cease-fires, and tomorrow there will be more skirmishes.[14]

13. Howard, *Balancing Life's Demands*, 14.
14. Howard, *Balancing Life's Demands*, 14.

It is helpful to identify the options confronting us. Howard suggests that there are seven categories of options and he lists them as choices that are:

1. Necessary (such as eating and sleeping).

2. Postponable (not so demanding: wash the car, write a letter).

3. Bad (immoral: cheat on a test, lie to your spouse, drink and drive).

4. Good (moral: tell the truth, flowers for wife, cook favorite dish).

5. Expanding (progress: cell phones, computers, autos).

6. Enticing (the tempting things of life, luxuries we may not need).

7. Motivating (personal growth, work-overtime, exercise, diet).

His list seems to cover thoroughly the complex choices that confront us, either individually, or in some cases, teaming up against us. Not wanting to add to the seven categories, I did, however, think it would be adventurous to restate them, and so I offer them as:

1. Demanding options

2. Debatable options

3. Dangerous options

4. Decent options

5. Diverse options

6. Deceptive options

7. Driving options

So, we have to choose, don't we? And often. Because we are not pre-programmed robots, it is our privilege and our prerogative to decide. Choosing something, especially something that may be vitally important to ourselves as well as our loved ones, is one of our greatest blessings in life as well as being one of our greatest burdens. The blessing is the privilege and ability to choose. The burden is you better make the right choice!

Turning to The Word

So, what do we do? Where do we go? To whom do we turn? The answer is we turn towards God. We must turn to His Word. That God wants to guide us in decision-making is something He offers to us constantly.

As did David, we too should pray, "Show me Your ways, O Lord; Teach me Your paths. Lead me in Your truth and teach me, For You are the God of my salvation; On You, I wait all the day" (Ps 25:4–5). And God answers, "I will instruct you and teach you in the way you should go; I will guide you with My eye" (Ps 32:8). And then His Word affirms, "The humble He guides in justice, And the humble He teaches His way. All the paths of the LORD are mercy and truth, to such as keep His covenant and His testimonies" (Ps 25:9–10).

The well-known exhortation from Solomon in Proverbs 3:5–6 deserves our attention: "Trust in the Lord with all your heart; And do not rely upon your own understanding. In all your ways, acknowledge Him; And He shall direct your paths." Eugene Peterson's paraphrase in The Message is noteworthy: "Trust God from the bottom of your heart; don't try to figure out everything on your own. Listen for God's voice in everything you do, everywhere you go; he's the one who will keep you on track. Don't assume that you know it all."

This great proverb, rich in Hebrew parallelism, presents keywords and clauses that, when unpacked, provide a clear path to God's will for our lives as we seek to make the right choices in life. And it starts with the word "trust." The word in Hebrew is *batach* and it is purposely placed first in the sentence for emphasis. It is a word that describes confidence and the sense of surety and safety. Solomon wants us to know that the one in whom we have faith, is the one on whom we can trust. This word *batach* is seen many times in Scripture: "Commit your way to the Lord, *trust* also in Him, and He shall bring it to pass" (Ps 37:5). "The Fear of man brings a snare, but whoever *trusts* the Lord shall be safe" (Prov 29:25). "Every word of God is pure; He is a shield to those who put their *trust* in Him" (Prov 30:5). "Blessed is the man who makes the Lord his *trust*" (Ps 40:4).

The question we must ask ourselves, even while we claim to have faith in God, is do we really trust him? They are not necessarily the same thing! Faith is a belief in someone or something without logical proof. Trust is a firm reliance on the character or integrity of another. Because I have faith in God, I can now trust him to *be* God.

Faith comes first, then trust. My faith in God makes it possible for me to trust God. Because I know him, I have come to learn that I can rely upon him, that I can trust in him. Faith in God precedes trust, and it will be our trusting in God that confirms our faith. Trust is a demonstration of Faith. Trust is faith in action. Faith is something you possess. Trust is something you perform.

Next Solomon tells us that we should not rely upon our own understanding. The term can mean a supporting on and/or a depending upon something, hence a "leaning" upon. It is the antithesis of the first statement. We are not to depend upon—rely upon—trust in ourselves. The implication is that God knows better.

Why would I want to rely upon what I think I know rather than upon what he certainly knows? That would be pretty foolish, would it not? In Proverbs 28:26, Solomon would warn, "He who trusts in his own heart is a fool, but whoever walks wisely will be delivered." We should know that God knows the answers and we do not even know the questions! He knows the facts, has all the facts, and we pretty much have none of the facts. The great Vance Havner once remarked that our efficiency without God's sufficiency results in a deficiency. Now, that is a fact!

This leads then to his next challenge in verse 6—to acknowledge God in all our ways. Once again Solomon simply uses a common word, translated "ways," which is the word for *path* and can also mean "journey." I think he means that we are to acknowledge God in the course of our life. Again, he uses a common verb—"to know," but here in the imperative.

An old English grammar states that imperative verbs do not leave room for questions or discussion. What Solomon is talking about is not an option. It is imperative that we acknowledge God in all our ways. The word "acknowledge" comes from two middle-English words—*knowledge* and *admit*. To acknowledge is to "admit knowledge." Here then it must mean that we admit to the knowledge of God, which is far superior to ours.

And what is the result of this? God promises that he shall direct our paths. In a life full of choices and the decisions that we must make daily, surely this is what we want. Decision-making is committing to path-taking. And when it comes to going down one path or another, we are ill-equipped and often misinformed to know which path is the right one. Jeremiah knew that much, he wrote "O Lord, I know the way of man is not in himself, it is not in man who walks to direct his own steps" (Jer 10:23).

Proverbs 3:5–6 is one of the most instructive passages in the Bible, compelling us to honor God's will and way for our lives. It is his eternal promise to lead and guide us through the complexities of life. It must be his will and his way because there is no other will that we can trust and no other way that we can follow.

Having spent numerous hours studying and meditating on this great passage, I thought I would attempt to paraphrase these dynamic Hebrew verses. This is what I wrote: "Actively have confidence in the Lord, the One on whom you believe, and that with everything that is in you. Do not depend on your knowledge as an alternative to God's. Always acknowledge him and his will in the course of your life at all times and in every way. And God will intentionally and effectively take charge and lead you in the fulfillment of his will for your life."

What's Next?

In our culture, people theorize and fictionalize, capitalize and compartmentalize, glamorize and accessorize, but what we need to do considering all the options facing us is prioritize. But what does prioritizing mean? And, considering the above comments about time, is prioritizing an unavoidable acknowledgment of the rule of Chronos, or is it the necessary adjustment needed to utilize Kairos? One can be merciless, the other is priceless. I agree with Ted Engstrom who wrote that "Time, as measured, is the enemy of time as lived."[15] Wow!

As Christians, do we simply follow what I call the "corporate model" of prioritizing? You know what I mean—we put something first, followed by something second, then third, and so on. It is what J. Grant Howard called *Life by the List*.

But is a sequential list of priorities the best way to order our lives? And, if it is not, then is there a better way? And more importantly, for Christians, is that way better suited for an obedient biblical lifestyle? Is there a method in the Word that is better than the model set forth by the world? Are we going to follow Wall Street or God's will?

If we are to borrow anything from the corporate world in the ordering of our spiritual lives, it would be what most young executives are told

---

15. Engstrom and Mackenzie, *Manage Your Time*, 22.

regarding their structure of priorities—that they must keep their focus on the big picture! Having said that, for Christians then, our main goal and focus is not a picture, but a Person. The big picture for us is our big God!

With that obvious challenge, then, we would be told that means putting God first on our list. Who would argue with that? However, the problem with a list, any list, even if it is a list that has God in first place is that it is not practical and may not be biblical. In reality, we do not live our lives sequentially, but rather situationally, and God wants to touch every situation of our lives.

Doug Sherman and William Hendricks combine forces seeking the validity of a sequential list of priority-keeping (which they refer to as the *Two-Story view* of life and work) by questioning how does a list of priorities helps us balance the many commitments that compete for our time? And their answer? *It does not.* The reason it does not, according to the authors of *How to Balance Competing Time Demands*, is that this type of priority-keeping is not found in the Bible. "Instead, the Bible gives us not a list of priorities, but a set of categories that we must balance under Christ's Lordship. It's not family versus career, but family *and* career; not church versus work, but church *and* work; and so on. God is not simply the top priority in a list of responsibilities. He's the Lord of life who must be brought in on *everything* we do."[16]

So, is there a different, more biblical way to prioritize our lives? The answer to that is yes. There is an alternative paradigm that positions God in the center of our life—*God at Center*. This is not just so much semantics, it is a dynamic re-ordering of how we prioritize our lives. God as Center. God at the center of my life, which is a far more strategic positioning than even God as being in first place in my life.

The next chapter will seek to make a practical and biblical argument to prove it.

---

16. Sherman and Hendricks, *How to Balance*, 53.

Two | Life By The List

EVERY DAY WE ARE FACED with choices. Think of all the choices you made just today. At the beginning of a sermon one Sunday, I remember sharing something I wrote with my church congregation. I entitled it, *Choices You Had to Make Today*:

> What to wear, and how to fix your hair!
> What shoes for your feet, and at breakfast, what to eat?
> And even before that, the choice entered your head,
> Whether to get up, or just spend the day in bed!
> Then, of course, you had to choose
> To stay home today, or head for the pews!
> Oh wait, we have no pews! But still, you had to choose,
> Didn't you?

Well, okay, most of those "choices" are not all that critical, but some days, some choices are. The point is, the incessant options and choices that are before us, along with the pressure of having to make wise choices, can certainly wear us down, especially when you factor in the more critical issues of life.

In the last chapter, I distilled J. Grand Howard's seven categories of options facing us every day to those that are Demanding, Debatable, Dangerous, Decent, Diverse, Deceptive, and Driving. Each day we are on a collision course with any number of these. It may be head-on, we might be rear-ended, and the worst is when we are blind-sided. Anything we can do to avoid these collisions, at all costs, is worth paying.

Therefore, in response to the myriad of options awaiting us like dangerous curves on a slippery mountain road, we commit ourselves to do what we have been told will save us; we commit ourselves to the task of prioritizing. So, what is prioritizing? What is a "priority"?

The word originates in the late fourteenth century from a medieval Latin word, *prioritatem*, which conveyed the idea of a "condition of being prior." The word *prior* itself is a Latin adjective indicating precedence or rank. It came to be understood as meaning that which is "before." It could also be understood as that which comes next, and classically, was used to identify the next ranking monk in the monastery, to the Abbot. Accordingly, that monk was called the *Prior*.

A *priority* then became the word to describe that which we placed before something else, due to its perceived importance. The issue before you possessed rank and therefore has precedence over another issue. Once identified, we then might say it becomes our "top priority," (which interestingly, of course, is rather redundant, given that "top" and "priority," in this context, mean the same thing).

Not only that but intriguingly, the original word in Latin was only singular. It seems that, originally, there was no plural form for this word. Why is that? Well, apparently, there would have only been *one thing* that was thought worthy enough to be given precedence. It is not until the chaos and complexities of modern-day did English was there a need to adapt and allow for a plural form so that multiple tasks could now be prioritized. We now have *priorities*!

Make a List and Count It Twice

The basic and well-accepted definition of "priority" is, "The fact or condition of being regarded or treated as more important." Simply put, a priority expects that something is more important than something else.

In our faced-paced world, where *Chronos* ticks off the minutes, you must make choices immediately. You are the one who must decide which something is more important than your something else. Certainly, to do this, you have to be able to discern the trivial from the substantial and have the discipline to not allow one to threaten the other.

We cannot allow what matters most to be superseded by what matters least. We must realize that not everything that is competing for our attention is of equal value and importance. Clearly, this is what Paul meant in Ephesians.5:15-16, at least in part, when he challenged, "See then that you walk circumspectly, not as fools but as wise, redeeming the time, for the days are evil."

Somewhere along the way of that walking, we were told that prioritizing was the way to prove that we were being circumspect. That is all fine and good, but instead of seeking a deeper meaning of keeping our priorities aligned biblically, we bought into a shallower, more worldly model of priority-keeping. Without questioning it, and without thinking there might be another way, we began creating our lists and ranking things in terms of their perceived importance. And that list, by its very nature, must be in sequence. We were trapped. We must now live life by the list!

Admittedly, this list will look different depending on the life and values of the one creating it, but for Christians, it would generally mean something like this:

1. God

2. Family

3. Work

4. Church (Some might insist on rearranging priorities three and four.)

5. Ministry

6. Self

Now, we must be critically introspective and completely honest, because, upon inspection, this listing of priorities can present as many problems as we think it solves. When we analyze this sequence of the things we deem important, we need to ask some serious questions.

Let us start at the top—what does it mean to have God in first place? Does it mean, for instance, that you give him the "first" of your time, and that at the beginning of each day? And would that time be measured in quantity and or quality? Furthermore, what qualifies as fulfilling this prioritized commitment? In other words, would it be time spent in prayer, minutes reading the Bible, hours attending church, and then how often?

Perhaps it means that you think of God first, before you think of anything else first, or before you think of someone else next? Does it demand that you think of him first, talk to him first, do something for him first before you do something (anything) for someone else?

And then, how would you maintain that priority throughout the day? Or is it, having thought of God first at the beginning of the day and therefore fulfilling that requirement, you don't have to concern yourself with thinking of him for the remainder of the day? After all, you made him that top priority, and, as J. Grant Howard warned, isolated him in first place!

Let's move on to priority number two in our list—the Family. Now how do we prioritize between our spouse, our kids, our extended family, including our in-laws? First, we must tell them they are *not* "first" (that, of course, is God's spot). They are *Second*. Have you ever stopped to consider if that is an encouragement to someone to know that they are second? Do you think your wife is edified to know she is not first in your heart? (Oh, I know we have a pat answer for that, and one that sounds very spiritual, but I will tackle that later on.)

Let's get back to our family in second place. Is that also measured by the clock? Is it a matter of time? Does it demand we apportion time to give to our family, and if so, how much? If we are living life by the list, then it demands less than God, but more than work (or church, depending on which one you have occupying slot number three).

And then, once again, is it okay if it is "quality" time if it cannot be in fact quantity time? After all, we have to go to work, and so we don't always have quantity time for family. But wait, that is not right, because we prioritized family *before* work. Now what?

That brings us then to Work / Church. Let us be honest, for most of us, our work is certainly not third or fourth in terms of time spent on the job. Most people spend more time at work than they give to God, family, and church combined! And then, do not forget, we complicate things relative to "work" when we factor in stay-at-home parents. Isn't that work? Twenty-four/Seven!

When considering church as a priority, how is that proven? Does that mean attendance, and how often? Surely it must mean giving (and that would mostly mean giving money!), and it should also mean serving and sharing in the ministry of your church, locally and globally.

And then, after you have somehow tried to accommodate all your meaningful priorities to other people and other things, what about yourself? Where do you come in? When does taking care of your personal needs and wants become a priority?

We have been told that it is biblical to think of ourselves "last." That is, do I even have any time left over for myself? But wait a Chronos minute! If I sleep eight hours a day, that's almost certainly more time than I am giving to my spouse and kids, and probably second only to my work. I better get my priorities straight!

Life by the List

Okay, I know I am guilty of exaggerating (a little), but it was well-intended hyperbole to make an important point. And the whole point is this—when we analyze life by the list, we realize how impractical and illogical it is. And why is that? Because a sequential list followed literally means that you must pay attention to one thing at the neglect of another.

A "list" of priorities may work well for managing things, but it does not work very well at maintaining relationships. My argument is not with the proverbial "*To Do*" list. We all know the benefit of structuring a prioritized project list for getting tasks accomplished, whether on your job or in your garage. My argument is when we try to use that same template of *To-Dos* with our spouses, families, friends, and neighbors. People! Should we not acknowledge a difference between people and projects?

Yet we have been told to dutifully make our lists and then, as Christians, we anoint our prioritized list by making sure God is at the top. God must be first and that, we are sure, will justify everything. Think of it, we add God himself to our *To-Do* list of life, a list that may include quite any number of people, but as long as he is first on the list, we're good. Perhaps we think it's okay to "do" people, after all the Bible does say, "Do unto others as you would have others do unto you." But then, should we not ask—how do I *do* God? And if that is what I am doing, is that not patronizing him?

Still, we try to *do* God, by ensuring that we do him first (whatever that means). But then here is another soul-searching question, which is a by-product of prioritizing people on our list; ask yourself, does it bring glory to God if you pay attention to him but neglect your family?

Bob Pierce, the founder of World Vision, spent ten months of every year away from his wife and children. Think of that. He was an amazingly gifted man who served the cause of world evangelism tirelessly. In certain areas of Asia, he is thought of as almost a god. But read his daughter, Marilee Dunker's book on her father. She has no recollection of her father when she was a child. Bob Pierce gave virtually his every waking moment to realize his vision for World Vision, but it cost him his own home and his family? He ended up with his life shattered, his family fractured, divorced from his wife, and his eldest daughter committing suicide!

I have no intention of casting a pall on the ministry of this man, but I must ask, in all seriousness, do you think for one minute that that is the price God expected Bob Pierce to pay by putting God first on his list?

Does it edify your children to know that they will always and only be in third place on your priority list? Tell your wife you love her with all your heart, but she will always be in second place in your life. See how that works for you?

What is the alternative? Is there another way? Is there an alternative to life by the list?

Yes, there is!

The Priority Paradigm

I am convinced that the Bible sets forth a paradigm that clearly and convincingly sets forth how we are to prioritize our lives. And, it is not following a sequential list, even if you put God in first place.

While there are several passages in Scripture that address the ordering of our lives, none is more important than Matthew 22:36–40. It is the Bible's premier priority passage. It offers the most powerful paradigm for the ordering of our lives. The passage begins with a Pharisee who is going to question Jesus, seeking to test Him. He asks, "Teacher, which is the great commandment in the law?" To this, Jesus replies, "'You shall love the Lord your God with all your heart, with all your soul, and with all your mind.' This is the first and great commandment. And the second is like it: 'You shall love your neighbor as yourself.' On these two commandments hang all the Law and the Prophets."

This text is loaded with theological truths and practical repercussions that need to be carefully and accurately interpreted and then applied! We can easily apply basic Biblical hermeneutics to assist in unpacking this passage. Hermeneutics is the science of accurately interpreting a text. Essentially it involves three key steps: *observation, interpretation,* and then the all-important *application.*

So, let us make an initial observation, which is that the pharisee asked for one commandment and Jesus gave him two. Is that significant? We will find out that it must be. Jesus quotes Deuteronomy 6:5, "You shall love the Lord your God with all your heart, with all your soul, and with all your mind," and then affirms in the next verse, "this is the first and great commandment."

But he does not end with that, he adds this, "and the second is like it, you shall love your neighbor as yourself." He then concludes, in verse 40, with the crucial observation, that "on these two commandments hang all the law and the prophets."

We must notice that the lawyer asked Jesus to give him the one commandment that was the most important of all the commandments and in answering, Jesus gave him two commandments. And not only that but Jesus also referred to them as "first" and "second," yet with this all-important caveat; he said that the second was "like" the first.

Observing that crucial statement in verse 39, and allowing it to be a bridge between the two commandments, we can now question further, how is "first" and "second" to be understood? In what way (or ways) is the second commandment like the first?

As we try to understand what Jesus was saying, it does not appear that his reference to "second" means second in importance, for these two commandments are not being ranked, only listed. In our western mind and culture, as soon as we hear ordinal numbers like "first" and "second" we immediately assume a ranking. Granted, that could certainly be the case, but now, in the interpretation phase, we can do some basic word study to determine if that is, in fact, the case.

The word "first" is the Greek adjective *protos* which can have a variety of meanings ranging from "above all else" or "foremost" or that which is "prominent." It can describe that which is "chief," that which is "principal," and that which is in a "position of honor." The word "second" is also an adjective, *deuteros*, which carries the obvious meaning, but it can also mean "again." The fact is, there is nothing remarkable about either of these two words. There is nothing mystical or mysterious about them to assist in our interpretation of them outside of their normal understanding of something prominent and something else which is also prominent again.

I believe that the key to interpreting how Jesus intended for us to understand them lies in another word associated with them. And that would be the word "like" (remember Jesus said that the "second is like the first"). This keyword, which will unlock this passage, is the Greek adjective *homoios*, which means something "resembling, the same as, similar in appearance or character, of equal rank." Well now, we have something that demands we probe deeper.

When Second is First

We must ask, in what way is the second commandment like the first? And the text itself gives us six solid answers:

1. It is "great" (vs. 38)
2. It is "first" as in "foremost" (vs. 38)
3. It involves "love" (vss. 37, 39)
4. It involves "self" (vss. 37, 39)
5. Both are in the Old Testament (vs. 40 see also Deut 6:5, Lev 19:18)
6. Both focus on someone beyond self ("God and Neighbor")

You cannot avoid the resulting interpretation—the word "like" links the two commandments together as being of equal and related importance. Matthew 22:36–40 teaches us about priorities by telling us that we have two, and they are of equal importance, and they are not necessarily in sequence. In this critical passage, Jesus is not outlining sequential priorities, regardless of how much we think he is. Rather, he is establishing basic, biblical responsibilities. In fact, what he is teaching is *the* most basic responsibility we all have. What is it—or, better, what are they?

That brings us now to the application phase of our hermeneutic. As Christians, we have two priorities and they are of equal importance and they are not necessarily in sequential order! In observing what the passage says, also notice what it does not say!

It does not say "God *then* Neighbor." What it says is "God *and* Neighbor." Jesus is telling me that I am to love God *and* my neighbor. And I am to do them both, do them both now, and do them both all the time! But that is not all. I am to love myself as well (remember Jesus said, "Love your neighbor as yourself"). In this Biblical paradigm, is "self" last? Actually no it is not. Again, take note of what the passage does *not* say. It is not "God *then* neighbor *then* self." It is "God *and* neighbor *and* self."

One Commandment

The Great Commandment, while in two parts, is yet one Commandment. The great commandment's two parts cover three essential entities—God, Neighbor, and Self. And any reference to either of these three parts individually is a reference to and an affirmation of all three collectively. We must get this. This is crucial to our hermeneutical process. This is critical to our interpretation. As such, we should expect biblical support. We need proof, and here it is: "For all the law is fulfilled in one word, even in this: "You shall love your neighbor as yourself" (Gal 5:14). "Bear one another's burdens, and so fulfill the law of Christ" (Gal 6:2). "Owe no one anything except to love one another, for he who loves another has fulfilled the law. For the commandments, 'You shall not commit adultery, you shall not murder, you shall not steal, you shall not bear false witness, you shall not covet,' and if there is any other commandment, are all summed up in this saying, namely, 'You shall love your neighbor as yourself'" (Rom 13:8–9).

It is important to note that in both the quotes from Galatians, Paul does not even mention loving God, yet he is saying we are fulfilling the commandment. And again, in the quote from Romans, there is no mention at all of Deuteronomy 6:5 and the "first" commandment. Why is this? Because Paul knew that the "first" commandment was being fulfilled by the "second" commandment. That is what being "like" means. You do one, you have honored the other. You enact one, you have effectively engaged in the other.

Matthew 22:36–40 could not be crafted any more cleverly or compellingly. We often rush through these verses however and miss the depth of meaning that Jesus intended. There is yet one more proof that the two are considered one, and it is unmistakable. In Mark's Gospel the Great Commandment is stated thus:

> Which is the first commandment of all? Jesus answered him, "The first of all the commandments is: 'Hear, O Israel, the LORD our God, the LORD is one, and you shall love the LORD your God with all your heart, with all your soul, with all your mind, and with all your strength.' This is the first commandment. And the second, like it, is this: 'You shall love your neighbor as yourself.' There is no other commandment greater than these" (Mark 12:28–31).

Observe that last sentence. Do you notice anything strange—grammatically? We know that nouns, verbs, and pronouns, should agree in gender and number. If the noun is singular, then the verb will be singular, and the antecedent pronouns will also agree in gender and number. As we look again closely at the final sentence in Mark 12:31, how is it stated?

The noun "commandment" is singular, even though two are listed. The verb is singular as we would expect—"There *is* no other..." But look at the pronoun: it should read "There is (singular verb) no greater commandment (singular noun) greater than *this one* (which would be singular in agreement with the noun and the verb)." But that is not what it says! It says "than *these*." The demonstrative pronoun in this verse is a plural form. Do you think that this is just a grammatical error? Did the Lord Jesus Christ not know proper grammar? Are we saying there are grammatical errors in the Word of God?

If two commandments are being ranked first and second, and they are to be understood as being separate commands, then we should expect the text to read: "There are no other commandments greater than these." That would be the "correct" grammatical form, with the verb ("are"), the noun ("commandments"), and the pronoun ("these"), all in agreement.

But if the two commandments are equal and are to be understood as being one Commandment, then a unique grammatical structure would be needed to demonstrate that. The seeming grammatical error is therefore intentional and it is verified that way in the Greek text. The verse reads just as you see it: "There *is* (singular) no other *Commandment* (singular) greater than *these* (plural)." A grammatical oddity for sure, but a biblical certainty indeed.

This unique construction is affirmed in numerous versions of Scripture. For instance, the Good News Translation renders Mark 12:31 "There is no other commandment more important than these two." Yes, the unsearchable riches of the Word of God. This is a stunning revelation.

Why is this so important? Our observation has led to an interpretation, which now allows for an accurate application. The precise interpretation of this passage yields the revelation that God is *not* saying put me first and everyone else second, and make sure you remain last. It challenges me to confess this spiritual reality, that God is big enough, great enough, secure enough, loving enough to say—Put me first, *and* put your wife first, *and* your husband first, *and* put your children first, *and* put your neighbor first because when I do that, I have proven and demonstrated that I love him with all my heart, soul, and strength!

That, my friend, is what Jesus is teaching us. That is what the Apostle Paul was affirming. It is not living your life following some sequential listing of priorities, it is living your life following the demands of love. Loving God, loving your neighbor, loving yourself. And you can do that, at any time, all the time, and in each and every situation of life. It acknowledges the incontrovertible fact that we live our lives situationally and not sequentially.

It is the situations of life that will determine who gets what time and when. It is the situations of life that will determine the distinction between the Chronos clock and the Kairos opportunities. Matthew 22 affirms the reality that we will live our lives situationally and not sequentially.

The only way this paradigm falters is when we do not love God with all our heart, all our soul, and all our strength because then, if we do not, loving our neighbor is futile, and loving ourselves is foolish! Repeatedly, the Bible exhorts us to love God. There is nothing greater you can do. But then at the same time (and do not miss this), God's Word also says that we are to love our neighbor. And again, not only that, while you're at it, do not forget to take care of yourself as well.

God, You, and Your Neighbor

God. You. Neighbor. These three. And, if you look carefully, the only one who is in question is—You! What do I mean by that? There is no question that God loves you. There is no question that God loves your neighbor. What God wants to know is do you love him? And what God wants to know is do you love your neighbor? What God wants to know is will we love others for him? Because what God wants to do is love others through us!

In light of this, consider anew the somewhat controversial (and perhaps a little confusing) account of Jesus questioning Peter on the shore of Galilee after His resurrection. How do we understand what Jesus was doing in restoring Peter in John 21? You know the dialogue that takes place. Jesus asks Peter a simple question, "Peter, do you love me?" Peter answers with a similarly simple answer, "Yes, I love you." The response Jesus gives Peter is significant. Does he say, "That's good Peter, I was beginning to wonder?" Or, should he have said, "Okay then, if you love me, fall down and worship me." Maybe some would have wished he replied, "Okay, you've got my permission to be the first Pope and have people bow down and serve you."

Of course, Jesus did not respond in any of those imagined ways. But notice what Jesus says to Peter. Take note of what Peter is told to do because Jesus knew the doing of it would validate the declaration of love. The Lord replied to Peter, "Feed my sheep."

Bible students and scholars want to make a big deal about the dialogue between Jesus and Peter. Had Peter given up and gone back to his old lifestyle? Did Jesus ask three times because Peter denied Him three times? And why does Jesus use one word for *love* and Peter uses another? And so, we are wearing out our Greek lexicons trying to get to the deeper meaning of the whole thing. Now there may be some significance to those issues, but the reality is, we are missing the most basic truth this passage is presenting to us. Which is this—If you say you love Jesus, you will feed His sheep.

Do you love Him? Yes! Feed his sheep. Do you claim to follow him? Yes. Well, then you will serve people, nurture others, care for others for whom he died. Do you love God? Yes! Love your neighbor. The truth we should take away from this is that doing one proves the other. One fulfills the other. They are, on the authority of the Son of God, one and the same. That is to say, the second is *like* the first.

Just as compelling as what Jesus told Peter on the shore of Galilee is what the Apostle John tells us: "If anyone boasts, 'I love God,' and goes right on hating his brother or sister, thinking nothing of it, he is a liar. If he won't love the person he can see, how can he love the God he can't see? The command we have from Christ is blunt: Loving God includes loving people. You've got to love both" (1 John 4:20–21 MSG).

Alternative to the List

Earlier in this chapter, I affirmed that there is an alternative to the conventional, corporate model of priority-keeping which is so ingrained in our thinking. "Life by the List" is not practical, and it is not even biblical. So, the alternative we seek must be thoroughly biblical, and practical.

With the myriad of options before us and the challenge to make the right choices confronting us every day, we see the need to prioritize those demands on our life. We know that we have to balance them somehow. Undoubtedly that is what motivated J. Grant Howard to write his book *Balancing Life's Demands*. He was convinced that "Life by the List" is not the way to do it. "A list of priorities doesn't make sense. it can't be intelligently explained. it can't be easily understood. it can't be logically lived out. no matter how you define and describe your particular approach if it is a sequential approach, it is loaded with contradictions, complexities, confusion, and chaos."[1]

Life by the list means life in sequence, and we rarely live our lives that way. Life is lived in situations, and so we should not sequence our priorities, but rather we need to situationalize them. There is an alternative to prioritizing our lives with a list of First, Second, Third, Fourth, and so on. Yes, there is an alternative to God being First on your list. (Heresy! You say?)

Well, what about this—God at the Center of your life?

Challenging the idea of "God first" probably does seem heretical. But we need to understand that the Bible calls for something even better, which I believe is *God at Center*. For some, this may seem like an exercise in semantics. In some respect, it might appear that "God at Center" is saying the same thing as "God first." But read on, because really it is not.

The next chapter should bring the distinction into a clearer focus. There is a difference, and it just may be a life-changing development for you. It will certainly provide a whole new orientation and, I am convinced, one that is more biblical. Dr. Howard understood that and saw that this reorientation took priorities off of a list and wrapped them around a life. "When God is at the center of your life, (now) any (and every) situation can potentially involve God . . . unless you insist on isolating him in first place!"[2]

Have you ever had an episode of BPPV? That is Benign Paroxysmal Positional Vertigo. There are numerous related conditions, all with serious-sounding names, Peripheral Vestibular Disorder, Multi-Sensory Deficit Syndrome, Disequilibrium, and so on. All of these relate to one overriding issue—balance.

Losing one's balance, consistently, clinically, is no laughing matter. One site refers to vertigo as a *disabling, relentless, terrifying, unpredictable, paralyzing hell*. Studies have shown that vertigo, dizziness, and balance-related conditions are among the most common health problems in adults and that some forty percent of adults in the United States will experience vertigo at least once in their lifetime. I did, years ago, and it was not pleasant. The room I was in was spinning around me and it knocked me to the floor. Any attempt to move caused immediate feelings of nausea. It *was* disabling and paralyzing! I had to lay on the floor,

---

1. Howard, *Balancing Life's Demands*, 37.

2. Howard, *Balancing Life's Demands* , 33.

immobile, for hours until it finally passed, and then that only allowed me to get up off the floor and relocate my weakened condition to my bed for the rest of the day.

Living life *will be* exhausting and trying to maintain your balance and stay upright and coherent is not always easy. When your life is out of balance, when emotional vertigo has gripped you, the result *will be* disabling and paralyzing. Our society is full of people who are out of balance. Dizziness and dysfunction are everywhere! I have often thought about how the Scriptures offer relief as we see numerous references to having our feet on solid ground. God knows life can get shaky and out of balance. Several Scripture texts attest to this: "He alone is my rock and my salvation, my fortress; I shall not be shaken" (Ps 62:6 NRSV). "My feet stand on level ground." (Ps 26:12a NIV). "He set my feet on solid ground and steadied me as I walked along" (Ps 40:2b NLT). "Look! I am placing a foundation stone in Jerusalem, a firm and tested stone. It is a precious cornerstone that is safe to build on. Whoever believes need never be shaken" (Isa 28:16 NLT).

It seems clear that pretty much every reference to God as our Rock and sure foundation is intended to provide us the security and stability that we so desperately need in a world that is whirling around us and spinning out of control. Do not fail to take advantage of this truth. Do not allow yourself to get out of balance. Victory over vertigo can be achieved by a well-ordered life based on sound biblical principles. A life out of balance due to the dizzying array of demands placed on your life will not be best served by following the corporate world's template of managing life's priorities. The Bible has a better idea.

We need to get up off the floor!

Three | God At Center

As STATED IN THE PREVIOUS chapter, Matthew 22:36-40 provides the biblical paradigm for creating and applying priorities, which cannot be based on a sequential list, but rather, as I shall demonstrate, a circle of responsibilities, based upon the three main components of the passage.

The three entities of the Great Commandment are God and Neighbor and Self. If we are going to map out the Great Commandment, perhaps the best way to do it is with a series of three concentric circles:

The placement of God would be, of course, in the center circle. That is the biblical position, and that is the alternative position to putting Him in "first place" on your list of priorities. Now we need to decide where to place the other two—Neighbor and Self.

The prevailing teaching on *self*, which expects self-denial, would suggest putting yourself as far down the list as you can, or in the case of our circle, as far outside the circle as possible. But that does not align with what Jesus said. He said you are to love yourself. As the construction of this biblical paradigm would suggest, there is only one legitimate place for self to be, and that is strategically positioned *between* God and your neighbor. So, "Self" goes in the middle circle of the three concentric circles.

That leaves the positioning of "Neighbor" in the outer circle, which now completes what will comprise our "Circle of Responsibilities" (a term which I much prefer over a "list of priorities").

God in the Middle

God should be, no, he must be, the Center of our life! The Scriptures offer numerous pictures of this truth, especially if we consider the oft-used phrase "in the midst," wherein the idea of "midst" (middle) usually implies "center." Consider a couple of references: "The disciples were afraid of the Jewish leaders, and on the evening of that same Sunday, they locked themselves in a room. Suddenly, Jesus appeared in the middle of the group" (John 20:19 CEV). "And after eight days, again the disciples were inside and Thoma was with them and Yeshua came when the doors were barred; he stood in the center and he said to them, 'Peace be with you'" (John 20:26 PHBT).

The position Jesus prefers is not on the fringe. He is not content to be a person on the perimeter. He is not interested in occupying the extremities or being confined to the boundaries. He seeks to be in our midst, the very middle of us, the center of the action, or, as we might say, the heart of the matter. He is not interested in the outer limits of our life. He seeks the inner sanctum.

Furthermore, elsewhere in Scripture, this centering of God in His creation is attested to on numerous occasions:

- Genesis 2:9 (the Tree of Life is in the center of the Garden.)
- Deuteronomy 23:14 (God walks in the center of the camp.)
- Psalm 46:5 (God is said to be in the center of the City of God.)
- Zephaniah 3:17 (The LORD in the center of Jerusalem.)
- Revelation 7:17 (The Lamb occupies the center of the Throne of God.)

As we replace a Life by the List with a Circle of Responsibilities, we obviously must start at the center, where God is.

But First, Another First

We know that the Great Commandment as presented by Jesus was two commandments that are inseparable and thought of as one. In the previous chapter, we dealt with how those words, "first" and "second" need to be understood, and that the two commandments are equal in importance and application.

There is, however, another well-known passage that uses the word *first* and it must be considered next. I refer to Matthew 6:33, where Jesus said, "But seek first the kingdom of God and His righteousness, and all these things shall be added to you."

A cursory reading of the passage, especially when removed from its context, does seem to suggest that it is a priority passage. It seems that Jesus is telling us that in the ordering of our lives, the *first* thing we do is seek God, his kingdom, his righteousness. But is that what he is saying? If it is, then we are immediately reminded of the difficulty in defining what it means to put God in the "first" place.

- How is that defined? What demonstrates that you have done it?
- Is it first in time? (Chronos—quantity? Or Kairos—quality?)
- What proves that you have achieved seeking God's kingdom first?
- Is it proven by prayer? How is that gauged? The length of your prayer?
- Is it solidified by Scripture reading? How many passages? Are they memorized?
- Is it confirmed by church attendance? Worship, Giving, serving?

In breaking down Matthew 6:33, once again, we need to ask some important questions. If something is being listed as "first," then that presupposes that there will be a "second," and maybe a "third," perhaps a "fourth," and so on? Rules of outlining tell us that you cannot have a "1" without a "2," or an "A" without a "B." If Something is being listed as "first," then it must follow that there will be a "second." We must allow for the interpretation that by stating we should seek 'first' the kingdom of God and his righteousness, it could be understood that Jesus is perhaps permitting us to seek other things as well, just as long as the first thing we seek is God's kingdom and righteousness.

In other words, is Jesus saying in effect, "you are being anxious about a lot of things, and you're going to be seeking after what the gentiles seek after—just make sure your priority is to seek God and His stuff first." Do you think that is really what He meant?

And before you answer that, consider that the same passage as recorded in the Gospel of Luke does not even have the word "first" in it. Luke has Jesus saying, "But seek the kingdom of God, and all these things shall be added to you" (Luke 12:31). Now that would be a serious omission by Luke if a priority list was supposed to be the focus of what Jesus was telling us to do?

I would offer that Matthew 6:33 is not just saying that God's kingdom is the "first" thing we should be seeking, I believe it is saying that God's Kingdom is the *only* thing we should be seeking! Now just pull over and park for a moment and think about that. And as you ponder what I have just said, here is a question—Is *seek only* better than *seek first*? Roll that around in your mind for a moment. Is the reality that we seek something only more meaningful than seeking it first?

Let me illustrate the distinction by making the comparison analogous to saying that the Bible is our *final* authority when there is a more precise, more theologically engaging way to say what we should mean. And that would be that the Bible is our *sole* authority.

In other words, saying the Bible is your final authority can just mean that you have referred to numerous sources, but you are willing to rely upon the Bible as your final source of authority. Sounds good, I guess. But when I say the Bible is my sole authority, I am affirming that I am not interested in any other so-called sources of authority except the Word of God. Granted, you may disagree with that process, but you cannot disagree with the distinction that is created.

Tell me, which one do you think honors God more—that you arrive at His Word last or that you affirm His Word solely? If you see the difference between "final" and "sole," do you not also, then, see the difference between "first" and "only?"

Let me put it this way. For you men, go ahead and tell your wife you love her first, or, tell her that you love her only. Which one do you think she would choose? The difference would be that you love your spouse first (among others?) or you love your spouse only and there are no others! Should it not be clear which one is more effective and more convincing?

And that is the way I think Jesus is using the word "first" in Matthew 6:33. For Jesus, "first" means foremost, not almost. "First" implies "one time only" and there is nothing else that even comes in a close second. There is no second, or third, or fourth, there is just first, as in "One." There is only—ONLY!

God Only!

I can say I am seeking God's Kingdom first, but the real challenge of Scripture is that I am seeking God's Kingdom "only" and nothing else matters. Nor will anything else really help.

As the process of hermeneutics always affirms, context is essential to interpretation. Look at the context of Matthew 6:25–34. Jesus is not outlining our priorities in seeking the things we need to get on with our lives—food, clothing, mammon, etc. He was not creating a list of priorities and then topping it off with God in the necessary first slot.

There is no first slot. There is only one slot. And that is God. Seek him, and his righteousness, only! There is no seeking God's Kingdom first, so that, presumably, you can then seek something else second, and then something other than that third. Eugene Peterson, in his paraphrase of Psalm 16:5, has David say, "My choice is you, God, first and only . . . " That certainly does capture the best of both ideas, does it not?

William Law (author of the classic *A Serious Call to a Devout and Holy Life*, published in 1729) challenged us that if we do not choose the Kingdom of God for our lives then it really does not matter what you choose instead.

Precisely.

Augustine said that Christ would not be valued at all if he was not valued above all. Those are compelling words to hear and they do indeed challenge us. But we must admit that we find ourselves a little uncomfortable around them because they seem so simplistic, yet stern. We want some wiggle room. We want the liberty to value him when it is convenient and the leeway to avoid feeling guilty when we do not. Does it have to be all or nothing? Must it be that we are always "All In?" Must he be above all or not at all?

The context of Matthew 6 is clear, Jesus is saying seek God and his Kingdom and that is it. All the other stuff you will discover along the way. He is telling us not to sweat it . . . don't stress about it . . . don't worry about it! The unsaved Gentiles seek after all those things (vs. 32), but Jesus says the children of God do not have to seek after that which will be provided them by their Heavenly Father. The implication of Matthew 6:33 is why seek after that which is already being provided for you. So, Jesus says the only thing you need to seek after is a greater and deeper understanding of the Kingdom of God. Now that makes perfect sense, doesn't it?

That is ultimately the message of this famous passage, in its immediate context as well as in the greater context of the Sermon on the Mount (Matthew 5–7). You have a Heavenly Father who feeds the birds, he will feed you. You have a Heavenly Father who clothes the fields with flowers, he will clothe you?

In *The Divine Conquest*, Tozer tells us that "The believing man is overwhelmed suddenly by a powerful feeling that only God matters. A mighty desire to please only God lays hold of him. Soon he learns to love above all else the assurance that he is well-pleasing to the Father in heaven."[1]

One Priority

So, we have one priority. (The medieval Latin mystics were right, that's why they had no plural form for the word priority—it implied just one thing of importance.) That one priority, in the language of Matthew 22, is the Great Commandment. Again, it is to "Love the Lord your God with all your heart and all your soul and all your strength and to love your neighbor as yourself." That one priority, in the language of Matthew 6, is to "Seek God's Kingdom always and only."

And all of this translates, practically speaking, to God inhabiting his rightful place in your life. It is the only place He wishes to be—at the center. And, when he is the center of your life, he can now affect and touch anyone around you, through you. It can be (and at any time) spouse, children, extended family, friends, church, at work, at play. It can be coming in and going out. It may be in season or out of season—whatever the situation!

1. Tozer, *The Divine Conquest*, 42.

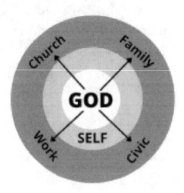

A. W. Tozer, who always saw things more clearly than most, remind-ed us that when God is exalted in the right place in our lives, a thousand problems are solved all at once. I believe that God's rightful place in my life is at the center of my life. God *in* the center of every waking mo-ment of my life. This is what he offers. This is the great trade-off, what the Bible would describe when we purposefully and intentionally replace self-centeredness with Christ-centeredness.

The seventeenth-century monk, Michael Molinas in his book *The Spiritual Guide* (which, by the way, received a papal ban in 1687), wrote about this centermost part of our being, which he referred to as the *su-preme region*, "it is the sacred temple of the Spirit . . . the place where God delights to abide. It is there he manifests himself to the one he created. He gives himself in a way that transcends both senses and all human under-standing. It is in this place that the one true Spirit—who is God, domi-nates the soul and masters it, instilling into it his own enlightenment."[2]

The Scriptures will reveal that God at center yields a blessing, a benefit, and a burden, and all at the same time! The *blessing* of God at Center is peace. It is rather instructive, that when Jesus shows up, he brings peace, his peace. "When therefore it was evening, on that day, the first day of the week, and when the doors were locked where the disciples were assembled, for fear of the Jews, Jesus came and stood in the middle, and said to them, 'Peace be to you'" (John 20:19 WEB). "Jesus came, the doors being locked, and stood in the middle, and said, 'Peace be to you'" (John 20:26 WEB).

Jesus' calling card is peace, after all, He is Sar Shalom, The Prince of Peace. Listen to what he offers: "Peace I leave with you; my peace I

2. Molinos, *The Spiritual Guide*, 123.

give to you. Not as the world gives do I give to you. Let not your hearts be troubled, neither let them be afraid" (John 14:27). I saw a clever sign one day that exhibited a creative word-play with a life-changing message:

KNOW JESUS—KNOW PEACE.
NO JESUS—NO PEACE.

There is a *benefit* of God at Center, and that would be security. The link between God's presence and God's protection is unmistakable in the Bible: "God is in the midst of her (Jerusalem), she shall not be moved" (Ps 46:5a). "God is our refuge and strength, a very present help in trouble" (Ps 46:1).

But then, there is also a *burden* of God at Center, which is holiness. When we are committed to allowing God to be at the center of our very lives, there will be a responsibility and accountability that comes with that. Moses wrote, "Because the Lord your God walks in the midst of your camp, to deliver you and to give up your enemies before you, therefore your camp must be holy, so that he may not see anything indecent among you and turn away from you" (Deut 23:14 ESV). If God is in the center, He expects holiness—"For God did not call us to be impure, but to live a holy life" (1 Thess 4:7 NIV).

I certainly agree with Martyn Lloyd-Jones who believed that holiness is not something we do so that we may become something; rather it is something we are to do because of what we already are. Holy living is a choice. Holiness is not something God forces on us, but it is something he expects from us. We are his sanctified children. We are to act like it. We are to be who he expects us to be. "I am the Lord your God, you shall be holy; for I am holy" (Lev 11:44). "As He who has called you is holy, you also be holy in all your conduct, because it is written, 'Be holy, for I am holy'" (1 Pet 1:16).

Notice these texts are not saying, "Be *as* holy as I am holy," but "Be Holy *because* I am Holy." We are not going to be as holy as is God, but He still expects holiness in our lives. We are not going to be sinless, but, as Christians, we are supposed to sin—less!

Strategy of the Circle

Back to our *Circle of Responsibilities*, once again, we must consider the strategy involved in our circle of responsibilities. It makes perfect sense to have God at Center, and it makes strategic sense to have "self" next.

It shows us that God can touch all those around us and that he will do that through us. God's grace comes *to* you, but He also expects it to flow *through* you to someone else. We are to be conduits of his grace and mercy to a lost and dying world. A world that is all around us.

I have often illustrated that truth by referring to the two "seas" in Israel. I have traveled to Israel several times and never tire of being around the Sea of Galilee. It is beautiful and historic. The Jordan River, which originates at the base of Mount Hermon, flows south into the Sea of Galilee, but then it does not stop there. It flows *through* the Sea of Galilee as it continues its winding journey south depositing itself into the Salt Sea less than one hundred miles away.

The comparison of the two bodies of water is instructive. The water of Galilee is pure and clean and full of life. There is plant life and fish, and plenty of boating and water-skiing and sail-surfing. In contrast, the water of the Salt Sea is anything but. There is no life, no plants, no fish, no sporting activities unless you deem floating a sport. One body of water is full of life, but the other is not. It is virtually just the opposite. No wonder it is called the *Dead Sea*!

In comparing the two bodies of water, there is only one explanation. The Jordan runs to and through the Sea of Galilee, but it only runs to but never through the Dead Sea. There is no flushing, nor rushing of life. There is no conduit, no passageway, there is only a closed-off container that can only result in stagnation.

The two seas of the Holy Land are the supreme and suburb parable of our lives. You are either going to be a Sea of Galilee Christian or you are going to be a Dead Sea Christian. We are going to receive the life-giving grace of God into our lives and then allow it to flow through us to bless someone else, or we are going to receive that graceful flow and somehow choke it off and think we can keep it all to ourselves. It is our choice. One lifestyle leads to growth and the other leads to decay. We can be full of life, or we can be lifeless.

Will we allow God to touch others through us? Will we permit him to bless others because of us? But that's not all. Consider a corollary truth in the same circle chart—you are strategically positioned between *God* and *Neighbors* so that your neighbors can see God through you. They have an opportunity to see God in you! It is supposed to work both ways. God touching your world through you and your world seeing the goodness and grace of God in you!

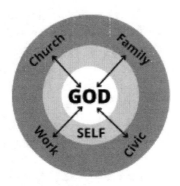

This is a powerful image, would you not agree? This is an amazing reality and responsibility. I have to ask myself repeatedly, "Can they?" "Will they?" I have to own the possibility that there may be someone who will only have the opportunity to catch a glimpse of God because of me. I have to realize that in seeing me, will they just see me, or will they be able to discern in me the God whom I love and serve? I often reflect on this by recalling a simple poem I once heard:

> *Others may be stained glass of rainbow hue.*
> *I choose to be a window pane for the sun to shine through.*
> *A clear pane, a clean pane, is that I would be,*
> *unconcerned with temperament and personality.*
> *I would have light shine through me, so that my friends might say,*
> *Not, what a lovely pane, but what a lovely day!*[3]

Can those around you see through you to God? God at Center. What a privilege. What promise and power. Think of the possibility, and yes, the accountability. Maybe that's why so many Christians shy away from this. We are content to have Jesus in our lives as *Resident* but not necessarily as *President*. We will keep Him (intentionally or not) at the perimeter. He is the friend at the fringe of our lives.

We make sure he does not get too close to the epicenter of our lives. We adeptly keep him, to quote J. Grand Howard again, isolated in First Place. But I believe that we must meet Him in the center, or we have no chance of living a fuller, deeper life.

I love how Calvin Miller touches on this in his book, *Into the Depths of God*. In the book, he has a chapter entitled *Centering: Avoiding Sterile Fascination with God*: "God is not honored by our sterile fascination with

---

3. Collins. *Morning Light*, n.d.

him. The whole idea of centering is not to talk about the inner life but to actually move into it. Centering is more than conversation fodder for our next Bible study. It is a serious call—an ardent methodology—for moving into a profound relationship. It is the serious pursuit of God."[4]

Most of us live our lives on the periphery of God's empowering. We need to get to the center, which is certainly a spiritual journey, and not a geographical one. Calvin Miller believes that this can only be achieved through prayer. It is certainly more than that, but it starts with prayer, an obsession with communicating with God. It is, it would seem, what the Apostle Paul described as *praying without ceasing*. It is a constant obsession. It is also, a constant challenge.

Again, Calvin Miller: "Centering prayers are interested in relationship, not answers. Centering prayer wants God alone—all of God—more of God—only God."[5]

God at Center

God *at* Center. God *is* the Center of your life. There is his rightful place. And the only place where he can make a difference in your life and any of the lives around you.

As such, we need to know more about him. We all need to write a personal version of J. I. Packer's book: *Knowing God*. Therefore, in the next few chapters, we need to do just that. We need to *know* the God who is there.

The God who is where? In the Center. It is, as Tozer said, God's rightful place. It is, as Michael Molinos said, the supreme region where God dominates and masters our soul. Molinos wrote that it is where God reigns upon his throne, with rest in that place, and that "Whatever the Lord sends into your life, there is no disturbance in that place."[6]

This is the God we must know, the One who can master our soul and bring peace to our spirit. This is the God with whom we can have a relationship; redemptive and real. Gary L. Thomas introduces his book *Thirsting for God*, with this simple yet insightful statement, "The

---

4. Miller, *Into the Depths of God*, 104–105.

5. Miller, *Into the Depths of God*, 109.

6. Molinos, *The Spiritual Guide*, 49.

foundational issue is our relationship to God. If we center our life on Him, every other area will fall into place as well."[7]

Centering your life on God is to make God the center of your life. I have heard countless Christians say, "I want to be at the center of God's will"! I am convinced that can only happen if one has made God the center of their life. The prophet Zephaniah provides this (with my parenthetic commentary):

> The Lord your God in your midst (in your center), The Mighty One, (the One who) will save; (the One who) will rejoice over you with gladness, (the One who) will quiet you with His love, (the One who) will rejoice over you with singing (Zep 3:17).

So, how well do you know the One who you are to love with all your heart, soul, strength? Are you convinced that it is his Kingdom which is the *one* and the *only* thing you should seek after? Do you have a relationship with this God? Do you know Him? And if you do not, would you like to know him? And if you already know him, would you not like to know him better?

Well, then here is the good news . . . the great news . . . the glorious news—you can!

---

7. Thomas, *Thirsting for God*, 13.

Part Two

Who Is God?

A right conception of God is basic not only to systematic theology but to practical Christian living as well... I believe there is scarcely an error in doctrine or a failure in applying Christian ethics that cannot be traced finally to imperfect and ignoble thoughts about God . . . For this reason, the gravest question before the Church is always God Himself, and the most portentous fact about any man is not what he at a given time may say or do, but what he in his deep heart conceives God to be like.

A. W. TOZER

This is what the Lord says: "Let not the wise boast of their wisdom

or the strong boast of their strength or the rich boast of their riches,

but let the one who boasts boast about this: that they have the understanding

to know me."

JEREMIAH

JEREMIAH 9:23–24A (NIV)

This section aims to challenge thinking regarding the person of God. If God is to be the center of our lives, then it is vitally important that we know and understand God as to his essence and his attributes.

Four | Knowing The God Who Is There

Until a man has found God and been found by God,

he begins at no beginning and works to no end.

So WROTE H. G. WELLS, the prolific British writer, acclaimed to be the "father of science fiction," and who was also acknowledged as a prophetic social critic. He seemed to possess keen insight, not only into ideas that become great novels but also into the philosophical and mental makeup of man in general. It was in that light, no doubt, that he penned this well-known observation.

I would say that he was pretty insightful, wouldn't you? Perhaps he was inspired by the more well-known and widely-believed statement in the Westminster Shorter Catechism, produced by a synod of English and Scottish theologians in 1646, which declared: "Man's chief end is to glorify God and to enjoy him forever."

I would propose that we cannot glorify God properly, nor enjoy him fully unless we know him practically and profoundly, and that, *positionally* he is at the center of our lives. If God is only at the fringe of our lives, then he will only be known theoretically. Our knowledge of God will be, in general, by hearsay and even just conceptually, but rarely dynamically. It is only when God is at the center of our lives that we can know him experientially, empirically, emphatically! We must settle for nothing less. God desires this and nothing less for us.

> This is what the Lord says: "Don't let the wise boast in their wisdom, or the powerful boast in their power, or the rich boast in their riches. But those who wish to boast should boast in this

alone: that they truly know me and understand that I am the Lord." (Jer 9:23–24 NLT).

Having made a case for shifting our priority paradigm from a list to a circle and understanding that circle to represent our lives with our world surrounding us and our God at the center of us, it is now time to parse each of those entities. It is time to shift our study from the time-related issues that dominate our lives, and which dominated our attention in the first three chapters, to the substance of the three entities of Matthew 22 that now drive our biblical priority paradigm. I need to know more about God, Self, and Neighbor.

Why is that important? If I am going to order my life with God at the center of it, I need to know God more fully and transformationally. If I am going to love my neighbor as myself, I need to know myself more affirmingly and self-assuredly. And, if I am going to love my neighbors, I need to know who they are, why they are, and how I can actively and intentionally connect with them lovingly and relationally.

God at Center, First

So then, first, we come to consider the mind-stretching concept and reality of the Person of God. Who is God? What is God? Why is God? When is He? Where is He? How is He?

In his book, *The Divine Conquest*, Tozer refers to the unconditioned priority of God in his universe, and that it is a truth celebrated in both Testaments. He believes it to be a truth so necessary to all right thoughts about God that it cannot be emphasized strongly enough. He writes, "For all things God is the great Antecedent. Because He is, we are and everything else is. He is that 'dread, unbeginning One,' self-caused, self-contained and self-sufficient."[1]

How important is it that we know God, albeit imperfectly and with our finite understanding? Frankly, it will be the most important thing you will ever know. J. I. Packer authored an entire book on the importance of *Knowing God*. He wrote: "The world becomes a strange, mad, painful place, and life in it a disappointing and unpleasant business, for those who do not know about God. Disregard the study of God, and you sentence yourself to stumble and blunder through life blindfold, as it were,

---

1. Tozer, *The Divine Conquest*, 20.

with no sense of direction, and no understanding of what surrounds you. This way you can waste your life and lose your soul."[2]

Later in the book, Packer asks a series of pertinent questions, all similar and all with the same convincing and convicting answer: "What were we made for? To know God. What aim should we set ourselves in life? To know God. What is the eternal life that Jesus gives? Knowledge of God (John 17:3) 'Now this is eternal life: that they know you, the only true God, and Jesus Christ, whom you have sent.' What is the best thing in life, bringing more joy, delight, and contentment, than anything else? The Knowledge of God."[3]

This pursuit of the knowledge of God must become the full-time quest of the church. In the middle of the twentieth century, the Lord called a Christian and Missionary Alliance pastor to articulate what it meant to pursue the knowledge of God profoundly and deeply. A. W. Tozer produced numerous books, preached hundreds of sermons, spoke at countless conferences, and always with the same unequivocal challenge to believers to quit their shallow thinking of God and know Him better and pursue Him deeper.

The single most important and impactful book I have ever read, after the Bible, is *The Knowledge of the Holy* by A. W. Tozer. In his Preface, he states that the modern church has too often entertained a low view of God, which has resulted in a loss of the sense of majesty as well as the loss of awe and a consciousness of the divine Presence. This decadent concept of God, utterly beneath the dignity of God, for Tozer, amounted to a moral calamity for many professed believers.

Essentially, *The Knowledge of the Holy* is a study of the attributes of God, and while there are numerous books on that subject by eminent theologians, I respect that Tozer wrote the book, as he said, "not for the professional theologians but for plain persons whose hearts stir them up to seek after God Himself."[4] I've read many of those heavy theological tomes and Tozer's small paperback book provides a more stirring, awe-inspiring glimpse of the Divine Presence than all of them. He begins his quest, accordingly, with a chapter entitled, *Why We Must Think Rightly About God*, and in the very first sentence declares that the thoughts we entertain about God in our minds will be the most important thing about

2. Packer, *Knowing God*, 14–15.

3. Packer, *Knowing God*, 29.

4. Tozer, *Knowledge of the Holy*, 6.

us. I understand from that, that what I think of God and how I think it will mold and shape who I am.

God Himself

Tozer challenged us that the most profound (*gravest*) question before us is always God himself! But it is only six short paragraphs into his first chapter that you discover Tozer's thesis for this invaluable and highly practical book. He states, "A right conception of God is basic not only to systematic theology but to practical Christian living as well."[5]

That is our goal—theological truth that transforms our lives. Without that knowledge, and in specific, a knowledge of God himself, we will encounter barrenness of soul and famine of spirit. We dare not replicate the spiritual famine described by the Prophet Hosea, where the people were destroyed for a lack of knowledge. And what lack of knowledge was it? "There is no truth or mercy or knowledge of God in the land" (Hos 4:1).

In America today, this prophecy is being re-lived (which only goes to validate the maxim that if we do not learn from history, we are doomed to repeat it). The level and depth of knowledge of God are shrinking to all-time lows, and most alarmingly, it is that way in the church. Rivaling the dumbing down of the American culture is what may prove to be even more catastrophic—the dumbing down of the American church. It seems that if we are thinking about the nature of God at all, it is not very deep, nor critical, nor life changing.

The truth of God is often subverted in our secular culture, but when that subversion creeps into the church, there will be a wavering among the faithful as they assimilate the "uncertain sound." Pastors, priests, polity, and programs are fair game for being attacked, but the Enemy knows it is the Person of God that is the real target. Subtle error can sneak it, be disguised, and do damage, but no one will realize it until a generation later, and then it will undoubtedly be too late.

So, we have a whole generation today that has heard that God's Love is *Reckless* and his Grace is *Ridiculous*, but what is reckless and ridiculous is the carelessness with which we think we have artistic license to portray the Person of God. It is exactly what Tozer warned us about decades ago.

---

5. Tozer, *Knowledge of the Holy*, 8.

Make no mistake, the church is paying the price for this lack of knowledge, as society drifts farther and farther away from God.

James Emery White, in his book, *The Rise of the Nones*, details the decline of religious affiliation in America. Who are the "Nones?" They are the people who check the box for "None" when asked to identify their religious preference. In essence, they are claiming they follow no God, but in truth, they are simply revealing that they do not know (any) God.

When Jesus Returns

I've often pondered a statement Jesus makes, recorded in Luke 18:8, where he asks a searing question: "When the Son of Man returns, will He find faith on the earth?" What did Jesus mean? To what "faith" is he referring? Most commentators suggest that he means faith as a transitive verb and therefore the ability to exercise faith in something. Others see it in an adjectival sense, as in someone being "faithful."

Grammatically, there seems to be a problem with both the verb or adjective interpretation. The word Jesus uses is *pistin,* which is not the verb form of faith, but rather the noun form. And not only that, *pistin* is an "articular noun," as it preceded with the definitive article. A variant reading (a literal reading) therefore has Jesus asking, "Will the Son of Man find *the* Faith on the earth?" I realize that this is a controversial rendering, but it is not without precedent.

Alfred Plummer acknowledges several views regarding this interesting verse of Scripture and the use of the articular noun form. It could be *the* faith that perseveres in prayer or *the* faith that demonstrates loyalty. But Plummer argues that the faith in question in the verse refers to *the* faith in Jesus as the Messiah and Savior. In agreement with this is well-known and highly respected Professor Robert H. Stein, who notes that the use of the article before faith suggests that this question should be translated, "Will he find *the* faith?" Rather than, "Will he find faithfulness?"[6]

Is it possible that Jesus was questioning whether there would even be Christian faith extant on earth when He returns? It is a startling thing to consider, especially since we know Jesus promises the church protection from the powers of hell (Matt 16:18). However, some might see that as protection from attacks without, and so a legitimate question would

6. Stein, *Luke,* 447.

be—what about disintegration from within? Following that line of reasoning, there are those who would remind us that Christianity has always been only a generation away from extinction!

"No way!" you say. Well, are you so sure it cannot happen?

The reality is, it is probably already happening. If not literally as an entity, Christianity is, at the very least, being marginalized in today's culture to the point of being—pointless. Gene Edward Veith, Jr., in his insightful and prophetic book, *Postmodern Times: A Christian Guide to Contemporary Thought and Culture*, questions why Christianity is almost invisible in contemporary culture. "Contemporary Christians," he writes, "… often seem to be at peace with an ungodly culture, lack staying power, spiritual commitment, and fidelity to Biblical moral standards." He warns that Christianity is facing a "cultural extinction," and observes, correctly, that "Christianity has been excommunicated from the culture at large— systematically excluded from schools, the intellectual establishment, and the media."[7]

If the church ceases to be culturally relevant, if Christianity is marginalized to the extent that it ceases to have any significant impact on the culture at large, would that not result in some form of de facto extinction? The process has already started. It's been ongoing for years. Stay tuned!

Still hesitant to think it cannot happen. Let us approach this possibility from another angle. A startling reality is that it has happened before. As the book of Judges opens, we read in Judges 2:7 that, "The people served the Lord all the days of Joshua, and all the days of the elders who outlived Joshua, who had seen all the great works of the Lord which He had done for Israel." But then, Joshua dies, and then that generation that stormed the Promised Land passes away as well. What we read next is startling!

> When all that generation had been gathered to their fathers, another generation arose after them who did not know the Lord nor the work which He had done for Israel. Then the children of Israel did evil in the sight of the Lord and served the Baals; and they forsook the Lord God of their fathers, who had brought them out of the land of Egypt; and they followed other gods from among the gods of the people who were all around them, and they bowed down to them; and they provoked the Lord to anger (Judg 2:10–12).

7. Veith, Jr., *Postmodern Times*, 209–210.

Should we not be stunned by this?

The Book of Joshua is full of victories; as the children of Israel occupy the Promised Land, but the very next book, Judges, is full of miseries, as the next generation forgot who gave them that land and why.

As a result, the outcome is inevitable. The victories of Joshua become the tragedies of Judges, and they are repeated time after time. And by the time you get to the end of the book, the postscript, almost as an excuse states: "In those days there was no king in Israel, and everyone did what was right in his own eyes" (Judg 21:25).

Think of the implication of that statement. Think of it scripturally, but then think of it culturally as well. The history of Israel recorded by Judges states that the "generation that arose that did not know the Lord," became the "children who served other gods and did evil in the sight of the Lord." The link between the two is unmistakable. The nation that forgets God will invariably turn to evil.

It occurs to me that if we are going to use the generations of Israel that acknowledged God and passed along his Word and will to future generations, thereby being a positive example for the church (e.g., Ps 145:4 "One generation shall praise Your works to another, And shall declare Your mighty acts"), then we must also see the generations who did not acknowledge God and forgot all his mighty works—and they are also an example to us (albeit not a positive one).

Can It Happen Again?

So, here is the piercing question, the hard question, the one question we cannot afford to overlook or ignore—can what happened in Israel in the fourteenth century BC, happen in the church in the twenty-first century AD?

Is that why Jesus is questioning? Is that what Jesus is asking? Knowing Hebrew history, was he suggesting the possibility of whether anyone will be found on earth who still holds to *the faith* once delivered to the saints?

And if you feel this may be too far-fetched, let me remind you what the Apostle Paul said about the second coming of the Lord, "for that Day will not come unless the falling away comes first" (2 Thess 2:3). The New Century Version has it, "That day of the Lord will not come until the turning away from God happens." J. B. Phillips, in his translation, refers to this falling away as a definite rejection of God.

The whole point of this is to point out the possibility that a whole generation that finds itself bankrupt relative to righteousness and faith arrives at such a sorry state of affairs because they have forgotten their God. And that started with the erosion of knowledge about the person of God. Hosea is right in telling us that the famine is a result of the loss of knowledge about God. And that lack of "knowledge" is not only knowledge *about* him, but also the inability to *know* him.

It is not an issue of forgetting dogma and doctrine, it is an issue of forgetting the divine being of God himself. The problem does not occur because we will have forsaken creeds and canons, it is because we will have cast off a personal relationship with the one true God. There is always the reality that some may know *about* God, but never really know God. There is a difference.

The very thought of this possibility uncovers the peril that will come along with it. Imagine that before Jesus returns there is the possibility that there will not be a generation that believes in him as Savior and Lord! It happened in Judges, could it happen again?

There are a considerable number of authoritative voices who see the possibility:

- The former Archbishop of Canterbury, Lord Carey, has said that Christianity in Great Britain is just a generation away from extinction.

- The Archbishop of York, Dr. John Sentamu, highlighted the gravity of the dying church in England by telling clergy they need to Evangelize or Fossilize.

- The Anglican Church in Canada is disappearing. Canadian apologist Dave Kalamen, the founder of Kelowna Christian Center Society, warned that the church has lost the power of the Gospel and is at risk of creating a post-Joshua generation "who do not know the Lord or even the work He has done" (Judg 2:10).[8]

- In America, a major poll indicated that two-thirds of young people will leave the church once they start to live on their own.

- Writing that "Christianity [itself] is never more than one generation away from extinction," Steve Rabey, in his book, *In Search of*

---

8. Kalamen, *One Generation Away*, (2018).

Authentic Faith, said, "this generation is falling through the cracks of Christendom and the modern church is sleep-walking their way to oblivion."[9]

Another book, co-authored by Britt Beemer (America's Research Grp) and Ken Ham (Answers in Genesis), is entitled *Already Gone*. This is their assessment:

> The abandoned church buildings of Europe… are graphic symbols—warnings to those of us who are seeing the same trends in our local congregations: we are one generation away from the evaporation of church as we know it. Slowly but certainly the church of the future is headed toward the morgue and will continue to do so—unless we come to better understand what is happening and implement a clear, biblical plan to circumvent it.[10]

As we look at our current culture in America. The signs of erosion are all around us, are they not? Recent riots amid nationwide protests for police reform were startling in the scope of anarchy and godlessness. The accompanying threat of violence and the loss of freedom grips us as we watch our nation in free-fall.

Ronald Reagan, in one of his memorable speeches, said that freedom is never more than one generation away from extinction. He said we do not pass freedom to our children in the bloodstream, but that it must be fought for, protected, and then handed on for them to do the same. He warned that if we do not, then one day we will spend our sunset years telling our children and our children's children what it was once like to live in the United States where men were free.

President Reagan was right (in a political context) and by way of application, there is the possibility that the history of *Judges* can happen (in a spiritual context). I think the two are related. Our freedoms will fall in America if Christianity is forgotten in America. If the coming generations throw out God, God will certainly throw off America! When God's only begotten son becomes God's only *forgotten* son, then none should blame God for forgetting about America.

English historian Edward Gibbon is best known for his mammoth work, *The History of the Decline and Fall of the Roman Empire*, published in six volumes between 1776 and 1788. In his conclusion, He listed five overriding reasons why the great Roman empire collapsed, they were:

9. Rabey, *In Search of Authentic Faith*, 27.
10. Beemer and Ham, *Already Gone*, 17.

- The rapid increase of divorce and the undermining of the sanctity of the home.

- The spiraling rises of taxes and extravagant spending.

- The craze for pleasure and the brutalization of sports.

- The building and financing of gigantic armaments and the failure to realize that the real enemy lay within the gates of the empire in the moral decay of its people.

- The casting off of religion and the fading of faith into a mere form, leaving the people without any guide.

To this historical point, Francis Schaeffer agreed. In his classic work, *How Should We Then Live (The Rise and Decline of Western Thought and Culture),* he wrote, "Rome did not fall because of external forces, such as the invasion by the barbarians. Rome had no sufficient inward base. The barbarians only completed the breakdown—and Rome gradually became a ruin."[11]

We are living in a time in America where the barbarians are not so much at the gate as inside the gate already. The Vandals are the vandals we see looting and burning on our nightly news. Anarchistic groups like Antifa and the new Visigoths. America is burning in more ways than one, and if we do not reclaim our connection to God it will only be a matter of time, that like Rome, our great country will become a ruin. And if and when that happens, it won't take much to see that the five reasons for the fall of the Roman empire offered by Gibbon, almost point for point, will be engraved upon the tombstone of America.

Christianity's enemies are legion and they are to be found attacking both from without and from within. Similarly, America has many enemies as well, inside and out, and one thing is certain, if Christianity fails, America is doomed. The strength of America is its Christian heritage and foundation. The reason America exists and thrived can only be understood in terms of its Judeo-Christian ethos. Casting off that heritage dooms us.

The only reason for Christianity to exist is in its relationship with the God who is there, the God who can be known. If we fail to know our God, we will fail at the most crucial and basic level of our being. Therefore, nothing is more important than knowing the God who is there. The God who would be at the center of our lives and the center of our world.

11. Schaeffer, *How Should We Then Live?* 29.

We need to know God. But first, and this is crucial, we need to be convinced that there is a God to be known.

Five | There Is A God To Be Known

GERMAN THEOLOGIAN AND SCHOLAR, LUDWIG Köhler, in his text on Old Testament Theology, asserted that in the Hebrew Scriptures the existence of God is entirely a foregone conclusion; always presupposed, never denied, nor even questioned. And then to that, he added this: "The assumption that God exists is the Old Testament's greatest gift to mankind."[1]

Yet today, there are plenty who do question his existence. How do we know there is a God? We know that this is a question that must be answered. We affirm that there is something that is not just quite right with the universe until we can know the answer. Somewhere deep inside us, we know that if we can only prove he exists, everything will then make sense, and if we cannot, then nothing makes sense. If he is, then there is a reason why we are, and if he is not, then there is no reason for why we are as well.

Theologian Henry Clarence Thiessen accurately stated that a belief in the existence of God was necessary. Thiessen insisted that if we deny God's very existence, the result would be perpetrating violence against the very laws of our nature.

Opening the Bible, we are confronted immediately with the reality that God makes no argument for His existence. Genesis 1:1 declares rather tersely "In the beginning God . . . " And that is it! Notice, it does not say, "In the beginning, this is where God came from," or "This is the beginning of God," or "In the beginning, God became." No, it is just—"In the beginning God"!

1. Köhler, *Old Testament Theology*, 19.

The Bible begins with a statement and not a question. And from that moment to this, we are left to try and comprehend the incomprehensible. To express the inexpressible. To explain the inexplicable. To define the indefinable. Somehow, we must attempt to formulate an understanding of that which is beyond our capabilities to understand!

Tozer saw the issue clearly, and so he wrote, "The human mind, being created, has an understandable uneasiness about the Uncreated. We do not find it comfortable to allow for the presence of One who is wholly outside of the circle of our familiar knowledge. We tend to be disquieted by the thought of One who does not account to us for His being, who is responsible to no one, who is self-existent, self-dependent, and self-sufficient.[2]

So, our inadequacies and inabilities are rather apparent. It is like trying to create a two-dimensional map of a three-dimensional form. The limitations become rather obvious. We are at a disadvantage before we even start. Nevertheless, we try.

God Does Exist!

So how do we know there is a God to be known? Theologians, philosophers, and historians have set forth numerous arguments to explain the existence of God. Numerous arguments to explain God's existence have been developed, of which at least five have become the most prominent.

Timothy Keller asks an important question in his book *The Reason for God*, he asks, "How can we believe in Christianity if we don't even know whether God exists?"[3] Attempting to prove that God exists is a discussion, the arguments of which have been set forth, debated, believed or refuted, for millennia. For those of us who would approach this discussion from a faith-based position, we know that several pertinent proofs argue for the reality and existence of God. Keller prefers to call them *clues* and believes them to be "divine fingerprints" that can be discovered in many places.

Where are these clues to be discovered? How many arguments can be set forth to prove the reality of God? Some, like Alvin Plantinga, suggest there might be as many as three dozen! Perhaps there are more. Why not? Conventionally, however, and for the sake of our investigation, let

2. Tozer, *Knowledge of the Holy*, 33.
3. Keller, *The Reason for God*, 131.

me set forth the five more well-known and time-tested arguments that have been set forth.

The Prime Mover

The first argument is what I refer to as the *Prime Mover* argument. In theological and philosophical circles this is the classic Cosmological Argument. The Greek word *cosmos* provides the basis for developing this discussion, as the word is understood to mean an "orderly arrangement."

As it relates to the created world, it argues for the reality that what we see must have been created by, set in motion by, someone outside of that which was created. Others refer to it as the *Prime Mover* or *First Cause* proof that God exists. Scriptural validation comes from the many verses that present God as Creator, starting, of course, with Genesis 1. Another statement that has a direct bearing on the idea inherent in the cosmological argument comes from Hebrews 3:4, where we are told, "For every house is built by someone, but He who built all things is God."

One needs only to go outside on a still, starry night and look up and behold the wonder. Where did all of what you see come from? And consider, not just the presence of it, but the perfection of it. Try to take in, not just the massive details of it, but the orderly arrangement of it. Has it all happened by chance? Is what we see his arrangement or just a cosmic accident? I like how Keller argues the point: "If there is no God, and everything in this world is the product of (as Bertrand Russell famously put it) 'an accidental collocation of atoms,' then there is no actual purpose for which we were made—we are accidents."[4]

No, we are not accidents and the world around us has not come into being by accident. The chances of that are remote and absurd to a degree that can hardly be calculated. I agree with historian and Old Testament scholar Dale Patrick, who argued that the idea of a self-generating cosmos would be in and of itself, a contradiction. Frances Schaeffer would agree, "No one has presented an idea, let alone demonstrated it to be feasible, to explain how the impersonal beginning, plus time, plus chance, can give personality."[5]

---

4. Keller, *The Reason for God*, 138.
5. Schaeffer, *How Should We Then Live?* 95.

The Perfect Designer

We can now see how this cosmological argument then moves almost seamlessly into the next argument for the existence of God. A second argument has been referred to as the *Teleological Argument,* which I call *Perfect Designer*.

The word "teleological" is derived from the Greek word, *telos,* which means "end, goal, conclusion." In this context, it refers to the end-product of something. This, then, is your classic argument from design, or as some have put it, the *Watchmaker* argument, that is to say, the existence of a watch proves there is a watchmaker.

Similarly, as previously noted, all of what we see around us did not just happen. The intricacies of the observable universe are stunning in their complexities. The odds of all this just happening by chance are beyond calculable. Someone described the utter remoteness of that possibility by comparing it to a tornado touching down on a junk yard and producing a Boeing 747.

Virtually no one denies that the universe seems to be designed. Albert Einstein, whose very name is synonymous with "genius," may have rejected the God of his Jewish heritage because of the presence of evil in the world, but he never rejected the notion of God's existence. And why? Because as one of the greatest physicists who ever lived, he understood well the implications of cause and effect. He saw that the universe was an effect and therefore it had to have a source. He saw that the universe was designed and so it must have had a designer.

The same was true of Voltaire, who was often divisive and critical when it came to matters of faith and practice but demonstrating an abject honesty, persuaded by sheer reason (which he was known to champion), he was forced to admit that if a watch proves the existence of a watchmaker but the universe does not prove the existence of a great Architect, then, he said, "I consent to be called a fool."

The purposeful ordering of a complex universe is readily seen everywhere, and that life is possible due only to that fact. So intricate is this design can be seen in the fact that to sustain life, the earth must be just the right size and its rotation around and distance from the sun must be precisely measured, its degree of tilt on its axis, with only slight variations that result in seasonal changes, and its land-water ratio maintained in a critical balance.

The *Divine Fingerprints* are everywhere! "The heavens proclaim the glory of God. The skies display his craftsmanship" (Ps 19:1 NLT).

Purposeful Knowledge

The next argument I call *Purposeful Knowledge.* In scholarly circles, this is referred to as the *Ontological Argument,* derived from the Greek present participle which can be translated as "being." This may be the most philosophical argument of all, as it sets forth the reality that the very idea of God is proof that He exists. Do you get it? God is real because if he were not, you would have no idea of him. The reality of God—the being of God—is explained by the "idea" of God.

I often think that this argument is best understood by what can be referred to as man's "intuitive knowledge" of God. Where did our intuition about God come from? What is its origin? When I did my PhD dissertation research, my focus was upon ancient Near Eastern pantheons and an explanation that the reason why whole civilizations created polytheistic systems of belief was that mankind is innately religious.

Ancient man knew, intuitively, that there is a God, and in a void of revelation and knowledge, he created gods to satisfy that intuitive curiosity. Paul encountered that reality in Athens where the polytheistic Greeks had created an altar to the "Unknown God" (Acts 17:23). Driven to honor all the gods they could think of, they were haunted by the unacceptable thought that they might have overlooked one. And so, up went an altar(s) to appease that unknown, overlooked deity.

Many of us will remember the Authorized Version's rendering of what Paul said to the Athenians, that he perceived them to be "in all things too superstitious." Of course, we have updated English versions now which are quick to tell us that the translation should have Paul saying they were "serious about their religion." That may be, but I still like that word "superstitious." Interestingly, the word Paul used (which is rather cumbersome in English at 19 letters) is *Deisidaimonésteros* combining the word for deity with the word for dread. Now that is a curious combination. Incurably religious indeed.

So, the question again is, where did this knowledge of, dread for, desire to appease a deity come from? The deeply philosophical (and religious) answer is—If there were no God, we could not possibly have an idea of God.

Positive Influence

That brings us to a fourth argument, which I call *Positive Influence*. You will recognize this as being the argument from *Conscience*. As with the previous topics, key questions help us focus on the issue at hand. With this argument, the key question can be stated this way: "Where does our sense of right and wrong come from?" Most people know when they have done something bad, so why is that? What is it in our makeup that triggers this sense of guilt when we know we have done wrong?

The argument from conscience would offer that the very fact that we have a conscience is proof of a divine creator who built into us a sense of good, having been created in his image. We should then ask, how is it that there is good? A world enslaved by natural selection and random chance could hardly produce goodness, let alone any sense of guilt that would result from not doing good.

I call the argument from conscience the positive influence argument because there is only one way to explain where the good and positives of life came from. The Influencer is God himself. The very fact that I possess a conscience is because of the positive influence created in me by God, who is holy and good.

Hans Küng was correct when he said that conscience makes theists of us all. That truth is reflected in the Apostle Paul's comment in Romans when he wrote, "people demonstrate that God's law is written in their hearts, for their own conscience and thoughts either accuse them or tell them they are doing right" (Rom 2:15 NLT).

The reality of good and therefore the acknowledgment of goodness, especially in contrast to evil, is an important corollary issue to this argument. When we talk about conscience, we are talking about something that only works because of a moral standard to which we seem genetically predisposed (if you believe Paul) to maintain. When we do not, we feel a sense of guilt. That is, at least, we are supposed to.

Guilt occurs because of a violation of the good, and good is understood in contradistinction to evil. If we have guilt it is because there is good, but where did that *good* come from? This argument would insist that good is the result of God. If there were no God, there could be no good. And, if there were no good, there would not be any "conscience." Indeed, there would be no need to remind us of when we do bad.

This line of reasoning, then, leads us to consider the reality of the bad, and where does evil come from. There are plenty of teachers out there telling us that the presence of evil is proof that there is no God. After all, they say, if there is a God, and he is just and good, why would he allow evil into his world?

I would suggest the contrary, however, that the presence and problem of evil are not arguments against God they are arguments that prove his existence. Why is that so? We only know evil because it is the absence of good, and good can only be possible because there is a God. The reality is, if there were no God, there could be no good. If there was no good, we could not be aware of evil. If we follow this logic, evil, therefore, validates that there is good. If that is so, then we also know that good validates the existence of God.

Practical Sense

An appeal to logic is an appropriate segue into our final argument, which I call *Practical Sense*. This fifth and final argument is often simply referred to as the *Logical Argument*. At the core of this conclusion is a thoughtful recognition that considering all the evidence (and indeed, as presented in the above-stated arguments) the most logical explanation for the existence of everything that we see and know—is that there is a God. Thiessen states it this way: "The belief in the existence of God best explains the facts of our mental, moral, and religious nature, as well as the facts of the material universe: therefore, God exists."[6]

Paul writes in Romans 1:19, "But the basic reality of God is plain enough" (MSG). It is indeed. I agree with Keller who concludes his chapter on the Clues of God by stating that belief in God is unavoidable. He argues the theory of a God existing is better attested with all the evidence we see than embracing a theory that there is no God.

This final proposition then is a simple, yet powerful argument that appeals to reason and logic. It is more reasonable to affirm a divine creator once confronted with the complexities of the cosmos than to admit to all of the intricacies of creation having occurred by chance. It is more logical to believe in God, given the divine fingerprints witnessed everywhere, than to deny his existence as if those clues lead to nothingness (which, of course, then results in hopelessness).

That "logical" idea needs only *Theos* before it to make sense of it all. It is now theological. It is both logical and theological truth. The antithesis

6. Thiessen, *Systematic Theology*, 31.

of this argument is illogical and therefore futile. It reminds us, as the very Scripture declares, that it is "The fool who has said in his heart, 'There is no God'" (Ps 14:1).

God's Whereabouts

Do people who claim they do not believe in God, really believe that? Sherwood Eliot Wirt, in his book, *A Thirst for God*, agrees with Professor John Baillie of Edinburgh, who made a persuasive argument that people who insist that they do not believe in God, really do, in the "bottom of their hearts." When, as Christians, we are in company with the psalmist and are confronted with those who scoff at us and ask, "Where is your God?" Wirt believes that we do not have to bring up all these arguments to prove God. He then wrote wryly, "Apparently God's existence is not the issue. His whereabouts is what really concerns people."[7]

There is some important insight in that assessment. There is so much "proof" that God exists, it hardly needs arguing or defending. The issue is not that people do not believe in God because they do not believe He exists, they do not believe in God because they have not seen him, heard him, experienced him in any concrete way. And, of course, that is where we, as Christians, come in. Is it not part of our missional calling to make God known to those who lack any knowledge of Him? Are we not challenged to make God's whereabouts noticed by those who need to see it? Meeting God and experiencing his fulness changes our lives. We can now tell someone who God is, where God is, and what he has done. Like the psalmist, we can say, "Come and hear, all you who fear God; let me tell you what he has done for me" (Ps 66:16 NIV).

God is active, his actions can be witnessed, his whereabouts can be known. Those of us who know him (and not just about him), should be able to tell others who do not know him. Those of us who have had a life-changing encounter with Jesus, need to testify of that to those who are still dead in their trespasses and sins. Thomas Carlyle, the great nineteenth-century Scottish historian once said that what England needed was someone who knew God other than by hearsay.

The truth of that statement, as it might reflect our day, should give us pause. Do we "know" God, and know him personally, purposefully, powerfully? Or are we more like the seven sons of Sceva and only know "a

7. Wirt, *Thirst for God*, 34.

Jesus whom Paul preaches" (Acts 19:13–15)? It is a valid question, and it demands an honest answer. Do you only know a Jesus whom your pastor preaches? Do you only know a God that someone told you about, and therefore you only know him by hearsay?

The greatest question confronting each of us is—do I know God for myself? Have you affirmed, for yourself, that he exists? Have you heard, for yourself, his voice? Like David, have been able to say that you have tasted and seen him for yourself? Is your faith personal, or is it by proxy?

Often, we seem to be more interested in what others are saying about God rather than personally discovering what God may have said about himself. We each have our version of *First, Second, and Third John.* No, not that John—but John Calvin, John MacArthur, and John Piper (to quote Gary L. Thomas' observation in *Thirsting for God*).

Monumental Task

I believe that to realize God in the center of our lives is to commit to knowing him more completely and more clearly. If not, then we have little chance of living a fuller, deeper life. J. Grant Howard saw that and wrote: "Christians who don't have an expanding, deepening knowledge of God are like players who have no coach, no rule book, no game plan, no schedule, no playing field, no training program. They are depending on one thing only—uniforms."[8]

The task of knowing God is monumental. It can be arduous. David, in Psalm 42:2, likens his soul's thirst for God to a deer panting after much-needed, life-giving water. I fondly remember, as a young pastor, meeting Sherwood Eliot Wirt at a writer's conference in Portland, Oregon. The conference was held on the campus of Warner Pacific University, where the godly Scottish pastor, Ralph G. Turnbull was Professor of Religion in Residence.

I remember Dr. Turnbull inviting us into his campus study, lined with shelves full of books, many of them old and priceless. There Wirt spied an old dusty commentary on the Psalms. He was at the time working on revising his book on Psalm 42, which he titled appropriately *A Thirst for God.* Finding the out-of-print treasure, he begged profusely that Dr. Turnbull loan him the book for his further research. This the old professor was reluctant to do, but finally gave in to the impassioned

8. Howard, *Balancing Life's Demands*, 79.

pleadings. It would seem on reflection, that Wirt put into practice the theme of his study on David and his pleadings with God to make Himself known.

This pursuit of God will take you the rest of your life. Paul's great comment to the Christians in Philippi regarding his relationship with Jesus ("that I may know Him . . . " Phil 3:10) needs to be appreciated in context. Paul wrote that statement some twenty-five years following his Damascus Road experience when he first met Jesus. Think of that! Here is a man, who in those two and half decades experienced more life-altering moments of faith and practice than probably all of us combined, and yet here he is, still admitting to a yearning and a passion to know Christ more.

If Paul, years into his relationship with Christ, is still pursuing with passion the knowledge of God, why do we stop? Why must we slow down? Paul was captured by the idea of knowing Christ in all His fulness—His life, His sufferings, His death, and yes, gloriously, His resurrection power (see Phil 3:8–11). There is no greater pursuit than that. There is no bigger idea than that. Oliver Wendell Holmes once said that some ideas are so great that when they once find entrance into a human mind, they permanently stretch it, and leave it forever afterward bigger.

Knowing Who is There

There is no bigger idea than the reality of God. There is no greater privilege than to know the God Who is There. And that the idea of God—the enormous, mind-blowing, monumental idea of God—and the challenge for you to know Him personally, purposefully, and powerfully, will permanently stretch you and leave you forever afterward bigger.

Old Testament scholar Dale Patrick could not have said it any more forcefully: "The biblical God insists on being the only God, and the world created by this God is presented as the only true world."[9] Belief in this God of the Bible, then, results in an acknowledgment of His presence and power everywhere. This awareness is unavoidable.

It also demands that we are "all in" on our commitment to know Him, follow Him and ascribe to Him the honor He deserves. It is to acknowledge, as Paul wanted the Athenians to understand, that in this God "we live and move and have our being" (Acts 17:28).

9. Patrick, *Rendering of God*, 117.

In *The Message*, Eugene Peterson paraphrases this by saying that we cannot get away from God! Wherever you go and whenever you get there, God will be there. Patrick explains the deeper implication: "God to be present in a given moment in time at a given place and to participate in a given action, he must be present in every time and place and participate in every action."[10]

Anything less than that does not explain the God of the Bible. It does not account for, nor fully comprehend the God who is there. I believe this is the reason that Francis Schaeffer reminded us in *The God Who is There*, that regardless of what man's systems might be, he still must live in a world created and owned by God. The God who is there is the God who has always been there, before man was, as well as before anything else was, that man knows anything about. God exists, has always existed, and will always exist. The late, great James Brown may have sung, *This is a Man's World*, but the truth is, this is God's world, and always has been and always will be. The old hymn says it best:

> *This is my Father's world,*
> *And to my listening ears*
> *All nature sings, and round me rings*
> *The music of the spheres.*
> *This is my Father's world:*
> *I rest me in the thought*
> *Of rocks and trees, of skies and seas;*
> *His hand the wonders wrought.*[11]

10. Patrick, *Rendering of God*, 120.
11. Babcock, *This is My Father's World*, 1901.

Six | Your God Is Too Small

In *The Christian Man*, Patrick Morley states that there is a God we want and a God who is and that they are not necessarily the same. He reminds us that our task is not to change God (into someone we want or wish him to be), but rather that we would allow God to change us. That is timely advice and it comes with his observation that "the turning point of our lives is when we stop seeking the God we want and start seeking the God who is."[1]

The God who is is the God who was, and the God who will be, or as Scripture puts it, "the same yesterday, today, and forever" (Heb 13:8). We are to live our lives each day in recognition that each day is ordered by the Lord, for every day is a day that he has made. Things start to get complicated, however, when we allow the current "day" (as in our culture, the *day* in which we live), to shape our beliefs and our worldview. God does not change, but our view of him does. The danger occurs when we go from "This is the day the Lord has made," to "This is the Lord the day has made"!

I am reminded of the witty invective by Voltaire, who said, "The Bible says that God created man in His image and now man has returned the favor." So, that is the choice—the God the day has made, or the day God has made. He is either your Creator or your creation.

One thing is certain, the God the day has made will not be the God of the Bible. The Jesus of our modern culture will look nothing like the Jesus of the gospels. Tozer warned "Left to ourselves we tend immediately to reduce God to manageable terms. We want to get Him where we can

1. Morley, *The Christian Man*, 45.

use Him, or at least know where He is when we need Him. We want a God we can in some measure control."[2]

Some years ago, Canadian scholar, John G. Stackhouse, Jr. wrote an insightful article entitled, *The Jesus I'd Prefer to Know*. In the article, he discussed how most representations of Jesus reflected characteristics of the day and the scholar who was doing the research. A phenomenon he referred to as "scholarly self-indulgence." But the Jesus of the Bible will not be dismissed or dismantled so easily. Stackhouse correctly observed that "The biblical presentation of Jesus refuses to remain nicely confined to any of our containers."[3]

The Jesus the world wants is an emaciated Christ. The effeminate, long-haired, *Lily of the valley* and *Rose of Sharon* Savior. (It should interest you to know that neither the lily nor the rose was intended to be portrayals of the Messiah, regardless of some of the old hymns.) In one of his memorable sermons, Peter Marshall cried out in exasperation that we have had enough of the emaciated Christ, the pale, anemic, namby-pamby Jesus, the gentle Jesus, meek and mild. He demanded that we should see the Christ of the gospels, striding up and down the dusty miles of Palestine, sun-tanned, bronzed, and fearless!

And, of course, it is that Jesus who cannot be controlled—by the Pharisees, or the pseudo-religionists and sociologists today. Stackhouse implies in his article that Jesus isn't the *nice guy* the world wants him to be, and the proof of that is the Cross! "Why would anyone crucify the reasonable Jesus of the Enlightenment? Why would anyone crucify the dreamy poet (Jesus) of Romanticism? Why would anyone crucify the Law-abiding, mild-mannered rabbi of revisionist Jewish scholarship? Why would anyone crucify the witty, enigmatic, and marginal figure of the Jesus Seminar?"[4]

The late American Jewish scholar, Jacob Neusner commented on the various views of Jesus, admitting that many Theologians created the figure that they could admire the most and cost them the least. Again, as if to address that indictment, Stackhouse concludes: "The Cross stands amidst each such easy path, each attempt to avoid the heart of the matter and the cost of discipleship. The Cross remains a stumbling block for all

---

2. Tozer, *Knowledge of the Holy*, 16.
3. Stackhouse, Jr., *The Jesus I'd Prefer to Know*, 68.
4. Stackhouse, Jr., *The Jesus I'd Prefer to Know*, 69.

who encounter this Jesus. He is perhaps not the person we want, but he is surely the person we still desperately need.[5]

A God the Day has Made?

Patrick Morley is right, the choice is between the God we want, the creation of our imaginations, or the God who is—in actuality, reality, and revelation. Will you settle for just the God you want? He will be the Lord the Day has made. He will not be so big that you cannot contain him. He will not be so powerful that you cannot control him. He will not be so miraculous that you cannot manage him. He will not be so smart that you cannot outsmart him (so some may think). He will just be a God who is alright, but not who is awesome.

Years ago, a popular song in the church was *Our God is an Awesome God* by the late Rich Mullens. We sang the words, but do we know why he is an Awesome God? How is he an awesome God? When is he an awesome God?

And before we set out to even try to discover how awesome God is, we need to consider this in the context of our core premise, that God is to be at the center of our lives. Take a moment and consider the amazing paradox of God at Center. A God so "big" (as we are about to discover) occupying a space so small (that is our lives). How are we to contain the uncontainable? How are we to house the infinite God who knows no borders? What mystery is this? How miraculous is this? How majestic is this?

Is it possible, however, that not fully appreciating the mystery nor completely owning the miracle, we find ways to limit the majesty? After all, as Neusner said, he becomes the God of the *least cost*. In 1953, New Testament scholar J. B. Phillips published a small book entitled: *Your God is Too Small*. It is an intriguing book, but the first thing we should notice is not to misunderstand his title. He was not asking a question he was making a statement. His challenge fits our purpose:

> Let us fling wide the doors and windows of our minds and make some attempt to appreciate the "size" of God. He must not be limited to religious matters or even to the "religious" interpretation of life. He must not be confined to one particular section of time nor must we imagine Him as the local god of this planet or even only of the Universe that astronomical survey has so far

5. Stackhouse, Jr., *The Jesus I'd Prefer to Know*, 69.

discovered. It is not, of course, physical size that we are trying to establish in our minds. It is rather to see the immensely broad sweep of the Creator's activity.[6]

It should occur to us that even talking about God being "big" or "small" is pointless and borders on the absurd. Both terms—big and small—are quantitative and God is beyond being defined quantitatively. There is nothing in the sphere of our human knowledge and understanding that we can adequately compare to God. There is nothing, regardless of the quantity of it, that can be brought alongside God with which we can measure Him.

As one of our most popular worship songs reminds us—*He has no rival! He has no equal!* And those two phrases only begin to demonstrate how *Awesome* he is.

Whom Can Compare?

As we might expect, the Bible declares the truth about the awesomeness of God and that he is unequaled and unrivaled in numerous places. One of the most engaging, as well as amazing, is the fortieth chapter of Isaiah. At the core of this great chapter is the challenging question set forth by God himself, "'To whom will you compare me? Who is my equal?' asks the Holy One" (Isa 40:25 NLT). Isaiah 40 is an experience like no other, brimming with startling images and amazing analogies, all to prove the truth of these two rhetorical questions.

Isaiah never would have asked the question "How small is your God?" For the great prophet, it is not an issue of how small is God, but how small are we in comparison to God. The illustrations that he lists, revealed to him by the Spirit, are intended to inundate us in the immensity that is God.

First, (in Isa 40:12a) we are asked this question: "Who has measured the waters in the hollow of his hand?" What are the waters being referenced? The oceans? Are they the lakes, rivers, and streams of the earth? We know that almost three-quarters of the Earth's surface is covered by water and ninety-seven percent of all that water is ocean water. It has been estimated that the oceans combined total some 320 million cubic miles of water. That is a lot of water!

6. Phillips, *Your God is Too Small*, 65.

And Isaiah tells us that God holds all that water, *not* in his hand, but the "hollow" of his hand. The hollow of your hand is the small, cupped indentation in the center of your palm. The average human hand can hold about half of a tablespoon of water in that spot (I checked), God's hand holds over 320 cubic miles of water!

And then with that same hand, Isaiah says he has "Measured heaven with a span" (Isa 40:12b). The Hebrew word implies a measurement that is taken by spreading the thumb and little pinky. That is a *span*. The NIV says God "with the breadth of his hand marked off the heavens." So, the image we are supposed to imagine is from one end of the hand (the thumb) to the other end (the pinky finger).

Whenever I think of the span of a hand, I often think of palming a basketball. Have you ever been able to do that? Pretty cool if you can, but then, God palms the universe! (And just how impressive is that? Sit tight, we'll come to the size of the universe in a moment.)

The prophet then asks some penetrating questions in verses 13–14: "Who has directed the Spirit of the Lord, Or as His counselor has taught Him? With whom did He take counsel, and who instructed Him, and taught Him in the path of justice? Who taught Him knowledge, and showed Him the way of understanding?"

These seven questions all speak to God's omniscience. They are, of course, all rhetorical. They all demand the same answer, and immediately. So, the obvious answers are; no one directs his Spirit, no one counsels or teaches him, no one instructs him, no one teaches him knowledge, and no one can show him the way of understanding.

Do you recognize that God has never had to learn anything, discover anything, or has he ever uncovered anything by surprise? Isaiah wants to make sure we understand that God does not need to be taught anything, shown anything, nor have anything explained. Tozer puts it this way: "Because God knows all things perfectly, He knows no thing better than any other thing, but all things equally well. He never discovers anything. He is never surprised, never amazed. He never wonders about anything nor (except when drawing men out for their own good) does He seek information or ask questions."[7]

Having compared some of creation's wonders to the Creator, Isaiah now reminds man how truly small he is in comparison. He continues his masterful descriptions: "All the nations of the world are but a drop in

---

7. Tozer, *Knowledge of the Holy*, 62–63.

the bucket. They are nothing more than dust on the scales..." (Isa 40:15a NLT).

Take a moment and think of all the "great" nations in history. Consider the great ancient empires—Egypt, Babylon, Persia, Greece, Rome. And then, so we are up to date, let's include modern history—England, Germany, Russia, China, America. Great nations, dynasties, empires, but collectively, compared to God, they are just a "*drop in the bucket*." As an idiom, this means *really* small. Just the bucket alone in comparison would be small, but this not the whole bucket, but just a drop. It is but a tiny, almost unnoticed *drip* from the bucket!

The prophet is not done with the comparison, he says next that the nations "are nothing more than dust on the scales" (Isa 40:15b). If you weigh something on scales, you want an accurate reading. That means that the scales must be clean and free of any debris or leftover produce. The scale must be free of any of those particles that might result in an inaccurate measurement. But wait, Isaiah is not talking about dirt or debris or leftover produce, he is just talking about dust. The minuscule, virtually unseen dust that might settle down on a surface. That is what the nations are, all of them, in comparison to God!

Isaiah shifts to yet another comparison: "He picks up the whole earth as though it were a grain of sand" (40:15c). The surface of the earth measures out at 200,000,000 square miles. All the dirt and sand that make up the surface of the earth are, individually quite small. Scientists define sand as grains that measure from 1/400 inch. And Isaiah's comparison is not "grains" of sand, but A grain of sand! One grain, no larger than a four-hundredth of an inch in size. That is what the earth is. Now, if you want to blow your mind, think of yourself in comparison to the size of the earth upon which we live, and then, using Isaiah's measurement, compare the size of the earth to God.

After reading just these few verses in Isaiah 40, we are left to ponder that the collective brilliance of human empires and nation-building accumulating over some 5000 years of recorded human history equals no more than a drop of water, a speck of dust, and/or a grain of sand!

And Isaiah is only getting started! Again, now in verse 18, he challenges, "To whom can you compare God? What image can you find to resemble him?" Evidently, Isaiah believes we need more convincing, so he continues with a mural of God as the one, "Who stretches out the heavens like a curtain, and spreads them out like a tent to dwell in" (Isa 40:21–22b).

This description of creation is unique, and it gives us a mental image whereby we might be able to comprehend how big is the known Universe. This is a task that is daunting regardless of how you approach it. We must start somewhere, so let's start small—with the distance between Earth and our Sun, which is a mere ninety-three million miles. Our Solar System is comprised of eight (or nine?) planets and is located near the outer edge of our galaxy (called the *Milky Way*). If our Solar System was the size of a quarter, in comparison, our galaxy would be the size of the North American continent. Can you locate that quarter?

Not a little Overwhelming

Here is one way in which we can think of these distances. If you make the thickness of a single piece of paper equal to a measurement of ninety-three million miles, (the distance of the earth to the sun), it will take a stack of paper 310 miles high to reach the edge of our galaxy. And that is just our galaxy (the Milky Way). What about the observable universe? It would demand a stack of paper thirty-one million miles high!

Astronomers estimate the observable universe is ninety million light-years across. While the numbers can be a little overwhelming, we must try somehow to understand this, in terms of distance and size. A light-year is the distance light covers in one year traveling at 186,000 miles per second. In one second! Consider it this way—repeat this sentence out loud right now: *The speed of Light covers a distance of 186,000 miles per second.*

Reading that sentence just took you five seconds to say, and in those five seconds, a beam of light traveled 930,000 miles. In those five seconds, that beam of light would have traveled around the earth 372 times!

Consider the math that can be calculated in Isaiah 40:22. Light travels 186,000 miles per second, which totals 11,160,000 miles per minute, which then totals a whopping 670,000,000 MPH. As we keep adjusting our estimate upwards, we come to six trillion miles per year! And that is the distance light will travel in just *one* light-year. But our Universe is ninety million light-years across. Do the math if your head has not exploded yet. Six trillion times ninety million. You do not have enough time or zeroes to write it out. And then get this, many astronomers believe and admit that the Universe is expanding. That means the number is ninety million and counting!

It is interesting to note that scientists can only measure the observable universe in finite terms. We can only use scalable measurements utilizing finite values—miles, kilometers, light-years, etc. Famed astronomer Edwin Hubble admitted these measurements were only distance indicators and that he favored a term (he coined), which is the Universe is "sensibly infinite."

So, if the Universe is "infinite" (has no limitations regarding time or space), it could only have been created by an infinite Being, who is "bigger" (more immense) than it is! "Bigger" in the sense that he is outside of it. If the universe is "sensibly infinite," it is because our Infinite Creator God flung it into space as he spoke it into being. Isaiah says that God hung it all out there like we would draw open a curtain. "He stretches out the skies like a piece of cloth and spreads them out like a tent to sit under" (Isa 40:22 NCV). No wonder Solomon wrote, "Behold, heaven and the heaven of heavens cannot contain You" (1 Kgs 8:27). The Message paraphrases this, "The cosmos itself isn't large enough to give you breathing room!"

All by Name

Astronomers are often amazed at the size of the Universe and that has led many of them to embrace the idea, that on grounds of size alone, there must be other life out there, somewhere. Accordingly, we now have astrophysicists and astrobiologists, who along with astronomers, are eagerly scanning the heavens for some sign of sustainable life. They are convinced, given the size of the Universe, that if the Earth is all there is (in terms of supporting life), then the Universe is over-sized. For them, therefore, it is logical to assume that there must be life elsewhere.

Ego-centered scientists rarely stop to consider that this whole thing is not about us, but about him who created it all. The reason the universe is super-sized is that the super God is displaying his Glory. Isaiah 40 is a showcase for showing forth his Greatness. That is what makes this passage of Scripture so compelling; it is unveiling God's majesty, demonstrating his enormity, and just flat out proving his awesomeness.

"The heavens are telling of the glory of God; And the expanse of heaven is declaring the work of His hands" (Ps 19:1 AMP). The Universe is showing off God, and that has nothing to do with us. The Universe is praising God, even if we do not. Psalm 148:4 declares, "Praise him, you highest heavens, and you waters above the heavens!"

Look at the images of the far-flung galaxies across the heavens. What are all those multiplied billions of stars doing out there? Are they just floating around bumping into each other like some cosmic bumper car track? They have been created to showcase the Creator of the Universe. They come into existence praising God and they go out of existence with their dying breath in praise to God.

Isaiah would have us consider all these stunning images of stars and clusters of stars. He writes, "Lift up your eyes on high, and see who has created these things, who brings out their host by number; He calls them all by name, By the greatness of His might and the strength of His power; Not one is missing" (Isa 40:26).

The reference to the "host" is a reference to the starry heavens. Let's do some biblical stargazing. How many stars do you think there are? The numbers are astronomical. One billion? A trillion? Some estimate that the stars in the sky are equal to the grains of sand on all the beaches on planet earth. Just in our Galaxy alone, astronomers estimate the number to be 100 billion. And then what about all the other galaxies in the known universe?

In October of 2016, "Deep Field Images" from the Hubble Space Telescope caused astronomers to start adjusting *up* their estimates of the number of galaxies in the observable universe. They are now saying that there may be as many as two trillion galaxies out there! And that's based on the data from our most powerful telescope. Now how many of you think the universe probably exceeds the distance that our most powerful telescope can see?

Certainly, some astronomers believe that and so they are saying now that the Universe may contain ten trillion galaxies. Multiply that by the average of the Milky Ways' 100 billion stars and the total amount of stars in the universe exceeds one septillion (that is a one followed by twenty-four zeroes)! And Isaiah says that God created them like hanging a simple curtain.

This is mind-blowing stuff. And we are still not finished with Isaiah 40. There is more. The prophet declares that God knows all the stars by name. He calls them all by name! We are told that the average person can remember about 150 names. And then as we get older, we start to forget the ones we knew. God has no such problem.

Awesome God

Our God is indeed an awesome God, but "awesome" is not an awesome enough word to describe Him. *Stupendous* is not stupendous enough of a word to describe our God. *Amazing* is not amazing enough of a word to describe our God. *Incredible* is not credible enough to describe our God. *Incomprehensible* is not comprehensible enough to describe our God.

This is the God who is to be at the center of my life. This God, who is the circumference of a Universe so vast as to be incalculable, yet would "occupy" the center of my tiny, finite life. J. B. Phillips was right to declare *Our God is Too Small*, but I have a hunch that what he meant was that none of us can fathom how big God truly is, and if we try, we will come up short. The best our finite understanding could imagine would still be too small in comparison. Imagine that. Phillips wanted to emphasize that we must see God in all his greatness, all his vastness, all his "bigness." And so he would say that we can never have too big a conception of God.

Overwhelmed as we should be by all of this, yet the question can be asked—what does this have to do with us in a practical sense? We need to go back to Isaiah 40 and see that Isaiah, in comparing our smallness to God's greatness, reveals a special truth that we should all apply. Do not miss the transition between Isaiah 40:26 and verse 27. The prophet turns his attention to Israel, the people who are supposed to know their God. Recall, as we noted above, that verse 26 concludes by telling Israel that God calls all the stars by their name and that by the greatness of his might and the strength of his power, "not one is missing." The word used here can also be translated, "to fail," or "to fall." Eugene Peterson renders this, "He never overlooks a single one!" (MSG).

What occurs next then, in verse 27, is intended to be a comparison, which when made by the children of Israel, would result in encouraging them and something by which they could take great comfort. So Isaiah asks, "Why do you say, O Jacob, that God does not see you, that you are hidden from the Lord, and that He is not concerned with what you are going through?" Consider again, *The Message* paraphrase: "Why would you ever complain, O Jacob, or, whine, Israel, saying, 'God has lost track of me. He doesn't care what happens to me.'"

Do you see that? Isaiah tells them that God never forgets a star, that he knows them all and none of them are missing. And, therefore, he will not forget you when you go through trying times. When you look up into the night sky and see the multitude of stars, all twinkling their light, you should be reminded that God knows every one of those stars and not one of them fails, not one of them winds up missing. Then take comfort in knowing that God has created you, and you are of much more value to him than any star. Take heart and be encouraged. You will not fail. You will not wind up missing!

This truth then leads Isaiah to declare one of the most memorable paragraphs in the entire book. It continues to provide encouragement and strength to all who believe it:

> Have you not known? Have you not heard? The everlasting God, the Lord, The Creator of the ends of the earth, neither faints nor is weary. His understanding is unsearchable. He gives power to the weak, and to those who have no might, He increases strength. Even the youths shall faint and be weary, And the young men shall utterly fall, but those who wait on the Lord Shall renew their strength; They shall mount up with wings like eagles, they shall run and not be weary, they shall walk and not faint (Isa 40:28-31).

Count of God

What is it that you might be facing today or tomorrow? Do you think it is beyond God's ability to handle whatever confronts you? Do you think it is too difficult for him to figure it out? Is it more complex than creating a Universe that is so large, we are hard-pressed to understand the math? But he created the Universe, and he created the math, so you can rest assured your financial issues do not tax Him. He named the stars and never forgets their names nor forgets where they are. Are you not more important to him than so many glowing masses of hydrogen and helium? He cradles the oceans in the hollow of his hand but also promises his hand to us. "Don't be afraid, for I am with you. Don't be discouraged, for I am your God. I will strengthen you and help you. I will hold you up with my victorious right hand" (Isa 41:10 NLT).

The psalmist tells us in Psalm 2 that God sits in the heavens and laughs at the raging of the nations. The collective threat and rage of the nations would be intimidating for us, but they are just a drop in the bucket and counted as less than nothing to God. But what about us? How do we stack up against the nations? He sent his son to die for us. We are not counted less than "nothing," we are counted more than anything! Jesus proved that upon the Cross.

What amazing, astronomical grace. What more can he do to prove his love for us? This incredible, incomprehensible, all-powerful, awesome God loves us! He loves me. He loves you. If that does not blow your mind, it should at least capture your heart.

He knows us, and still loves us! And why? I do not know! Nor do you. But at least we are in good company with David, who in Psalm 8:3–4, also wondered in amazement: "When I consider Your heavens, the work of Your fingers, the moon, and the stars, which You have ordained, what is man that You are mindful of him, And the son of man that You visit him?"

If we learn anything at all from Isaiah 40, it should be this—the God who cannot be compared to anything measurable tells you to compare your smallness to His greatness. And then to remember that he will never forget you or misplace you, no matter how small you may actually be.

This is the God who desires to be the "priority" of your life, first and foremost of your faith, the only and sole authority of your world. This God is the one who would be at the center of who you are. You can count on him when there are not enough numbers to calculate him. You can believe in him when everything about him, in the eyes of the world, is unbelievable. You can hope in him when things around you appear hopeless, helpless, and hapless. And you can rest in him and wait on Him when everyone else is restless, impatient, out of breath, and out of strength. You can wait because you know God will never be late.

Whatever real problems you might be dealing with, and I would not belittle any of them, the fact (and faith) remain, run them through the filter of Isaiah 40. They are not bigger than God. Whatever they are. No matter. Unless that is, your God is too small.

Recently I came across a book that was published in the early 1960s by Robert W. Spike entitled *To Be A Man*. As the title suggests, the author's quest was to expose every man's quest to know God and thereby in the knowing, become a man, a real man, the man God wants you to be. This need to know the real God so that I can become a real man is vitally important. Spike's observation is compelling and applicable to all, men and women: "The primary experience that men have of God is that He is different from man. He is High. He is Holy. He is Mysterious. He is Awful in imagination and to be feared. Otherwise, he is not God; he is a little convenient household idol we have set up so we won't be scared of the dark. God, the Ancient of Days, our Creator, Redeemer, and Defender, can never be cozied up to. We worship him. We ponder the mystery of his creation and our part in that creation."[8]

I think that is what Isaiah would have said to us as well. The God of Isaiah 40 cannot be cozied up to. He can only be worshiped in abject humility and awe. He is the Creator. We are His creation. There is absolutely nothing that can be compared to Him, great or small.

8. Spike, *To Be A Man*, 25–26.

Seven | Inexpressible God

PASTOR AND AUTHOR MARK BUCHANAN was challenged by reading J. B. Phillips' book, *Your God is Too Small*. Responding to what he believed to be a call to return to the true God of mystery, sovereignty, and intimacy, Buchanan authored his book, *Your God is Too Safe*.

Early on Buchanan uses the term *borderland* as a metaphor for the place in which many Christians find themselves, a place where there is "inner deadness . . . spiritual sleepwalking . . . chronic stuck-ness."[1] It reminded me of how some Christians respond to revelation (borrowing from the title of an old hymn) when they go to church *just as they are*, sing a few stanzas of *Just As I Am*, and then go home *just as they were*. The point is, for the most part, not much ever changes.

Mark Buchanan sees the issue as one of whiling away our days in borderland, keeping God safe as we seek to winnow out all mystery. He is right of course. We are uncomfortable with the unknown and mysterious. There is nothing safe about trafficking in those regions. Tozer's comment is worth repeating as he reminds us that "The human mind, being created, has an understandable uneasiness about the Uncreated. We do not find it comfortable to allow for the presence of One who is wholly outside of the circle of our familiar knowledge. We tend to be disquieted by the thought of One who does not account to us for His being, who is responsible to no one, who is self-existent, self-dependent, and self-sufficient."[2]

1. Buchanan, *Your God Is Too Safe*, 21.
2. Tozer, *Knowledge of the Holy*, 33.

We can say that God exists, but that does not mean we can understand his divine nature. We can say, "*God is!*" but then we have to ask, "God is . . . *what?*" What is God in terms of his Being? The *Being* of God is what we might commonly refer to as God's *Essence*. And we need to understand that we are only referring to *Who* God is and not *What* God does. What God does is understood as his divine attributes (which we will discuss in the next chapter). What God is, refers to his divine essence. Most theologians pursue an understanding of God in terms of his essence (the life-existence he has in himself), and his attributes, (the characteristics and workings of God as he relates to his creation).

Defining God is not easy to do and can hardly be exhaustive. We should not want a God that we can define absolutely. There must remain with him that which cannot be explained and that which cannot be expressed. Our attempts to define can lead to our desire to confine. Once I think I know everything there is to know about God then I can exercise a certain measure of control over him. As Mark Buchanan warned, it is the way we keep God safe.

Coming at this danger of trying to define God from a different angle, Don Heberling wrote an article entitled *God in a Box*. He writes, "While we grow in our experience of life and expand our mental horizons, our ideas of God often remain on the level of an eight-year-old. These limited ideas of who God is and how He works hinder us from grasping by faith what He is doing."[3]

Heberling compares our systems of theology and our attempts at defining God to creating two-dimensional maps of a three-dimensional form. They might be helpful, but we have to remember that they cannot possibly explain everything there is to know about God. "The map is not the territory. Likewise, our conceptions of God are not the reality. There is still a mystery to be explored; no one holds the corner on the knowledge of God, we can never exhaust our knowledge of God. He is bigger than all our boxes."[4]

Pursuing an understanding of who God is and what God does must come with an understanding that we are limited in that pursuit. We can offer definitions, but these definitions usually only describe his attributes. We can say that God is omniscient, omnipotent, omnipresent, holy, perfect, pure, wise, etc., and we can try to understand these concepts, but

3. Haberling, *God in a Box*, 18.
4. Haberling, *God in a Box*, 19.

that does not mean we are accurately describing the essence of who God is and what he does.

But this is to be expected because God is essentially different from who and what we are. He is *wholly other*. He is not a physical being as are we. He is not limited to space and time as we are. He is different. He is not the same as us. So, when we describe him, we can only describe him in ways with which we are familiar even if these descriptions can never be sufficient.

Wholly Other and Beyond

God's essence is who he is in himself. The word *essence* comes from the Latin *esse* which means "to be." So, we can also say that it means "being." God's essence is the *Being* of God, it refers to his very nature, to his substance. It is hard for us to say exactly what all that means. Why? Because God's essence is beyond us. We cannot comprehend it. There is not even very much we can say about it. God's essence remains a mystery to us, inaccessible and so wholly other that we only have a name for it but not much else.

The church has struggled with this for centuries. For example, in the fourth century, Basil of Caesarea (St. Basil the Great) said that we may know God from his energies (his term for attributes), but that we do not undertake to approach his essence. He acknowledged that God's energies are revealed to us, but his essence remains beyond our reach.

The early church fathers knew, that while we can appreciate God's attributes as immanent, God's essence is transcendent and therefore beyond our ability to fully understand it. They would acknowledge that maintaining the unknowability of the essence of God was important, as he would not be much of a God if we could say that we know everything there was to know about his very essence.

Furthermore, we must not confuse God's essence (who he is in himself) with his attributes (what he does because of who he is). As it pertains to God's essence, we can know some things, but hardly can we know everything about the divine nature. What can be known about God's divine nature is certainly enough to both instruct and inspire us.

We start first with the recognition that the nature of God is immaterial, incorporeal, and invisible (Rom 1:20, Col 1:15). The first two are virtually identical in meaning and both as realities would result in the third.

Immaterial and incorporeality mean that God has no physical body and is without any material substance. Moses reminded the children of Israel of this truth in emphasizing the first two Commandments: "But be very careful! You did not see the Lord's form on the day he spoke to you from the heart of the fire at Mount Sinai. So do not corrupt yourselves by making an idol in any form—whether of a man or a woman" (Deut 4:15–16 NLT).

That God is a spiritual being, without bodily form is presented in both Testaments, and we are reminded of Jesus' declaration in John 4:24, that "God is Spirit." While God is immaterial, incorporeal, and invisible, that does mean he is impersonal. This would explain, then, the only exception to this truth, which is the Incarnation. The coming of Jesus Christ, the Second Person of the Godhead, remains the single most incredible miracle ever!

Outside of Creation

God is *self-existent* which means He has the ground of existence in himself, and this is what sets him apart from his creation. God is outside of his creation, detached from it, and in need of nothing from it. Everything created needs to rely upon something or someone to exist. Not God. He needs no one else to exist. He is not dependent upon anything outside of himself. God is self-sufficient. God lacked nothing before creation, and he depends on nothing from creation.

When discussing God's self-existence, theologians use the term *Aseity*, which refers to an existence originating from and having no source other than itself. R. C Sproul explains it this way:

> In contrast to self-creation, there is the idea of self-existence, or what is called in theology the concept of aseity. That is an obscure and esoteric term. Yet, that one little word captures all of the glory of the perfection of God's being. What makes God different from people, from the stars, from earthquakes, and from any other creaturely thing is that God—and God alone— has aseity; He alone exists by His own power. No one made Him or caused Him. He exists in and of Himself. This is a quality that no creature shares. People are not self-existent; neither are cars or stars. Only God has the concept of self-existence.[5]

5. Sproul, "The Self-Existent God," (2018).

Scripture attests to this truth, for instance in Revelation 4:11, "You are worthy to receive glory, honor, and power, for you created all things, and by your will, they were created and have their being." The Apostle Paul says of Christ, "He existed before anything else, and he holds all creation together" (Col 1:17 NLT).

God's transcendence means that God is greater and superior to anything in the finite, created world. And from the basis of that transcendence, we can learn from other statements about the self-existence of God, that is to say, God is said to be eternal, infinite, and immutable.

Perhaps here I need to explain that I do not see concepts such as the eternality of God or the immutability of God as being attributes, at least not in the conventional sense. I make a distinction between God's attributes and His essence. By that I mean, God's attributes are what we know about him in terms of what he does (especially concerning man), but his essence is who he is, in and of himself. So, the *essence* of God refers to who he is, and the *attributes* of God refer to what he does. If I am correct in this theological distinction, then I am compelled to align his eternality as being part of his divine essence, in that God does not *do* eternal, God *is* eternal. Additionally, God does not *do* immutability, God *is* immutable. Immutability, like his eternality, is part of God's divine essence of being.

The fourth question posed in the Westminster Shorter Catechism asks, *What is God?* And then answers: "God is a spirit, infinite, eternal, and unchangeable, in his being." While the WSC may not be making as fine a distinction between God's essence and his attributes as I am, it is noteworthy that the well-respected statement aligns God's infinitude, eternality, and immutability with his being, just as I am suggesting.

From Everlasting To Everlasting

God is Eternal. God is without beginning or end. He is free from all succession of time and he is the cause of time. Isaiah claims, "He is the One who inhabits eternity" (Isa 57:15). Moses, in Psalm 90:2, uses the unique Hebrew prepositional combination of *min . . . ad* (meaning "from . . . to/ until") with the noun *'olam*, which results in the English translation as "From everlasting to everlasting." The verse is a powerful testimony for the eternality of God. "Before the mountains were brought forth, or ever You had formed the earth and the world, even from everlasting to everlasting, You are God." The New Century Version renders is, "You have always been, and you will always be."

God's eternality is what separates him from us, for he only is eternal. I know there is some confusion here, especially when we think of the concepts of eternal and everlasting as being synonymous. But I believe there is a distinction. Everlasting means just what it says—lasting forever, and the emphasis is on the tail end as it does not say anything about the starting point. My starting point is that God created me, and I will live forever.

The idea of being eternal, I believe, is a reference to both the starting point and ending point, in the sense that there is no starting point, nor will there be an ending point. God only has no starting point, but we do, as his creation. God also will have no ending point. So, God only is eternal. I am not. I am an everlasting being, but technically not an eternal being (as I had a definite starting point of existence). God only is eternal.

Tozer captures the mystery and majesty of this truth as he sees the unique grammatical equation in Psalm 90:2 as this: "From vanishing point to vanishing point." He writes: "The mind looks backward in time till the dim past vanishes, then turns and looks into the future till thought and imagination collapse from exhaustion, and God is at both points, unaffected by either."[6]

In *The Divine Conquest*, Tozer is even more descriptive as he refers to God as "The Eternal Continuum," and describes the eternality of God as only he can: "Begin where we will, God is there first. He is Alpha and Omega, the beginning and the ending, which was, and which is, and which is to come, the Almighty. If we grope back to the farthest limits of thought where imagination touches the pre-creation void, we shall find God there. In one unified present glance, He comprehends all things from everlasting, and the flutter of a seraph's wing a thousand ages hence is seen by Him now without moving His eyes."[7]

Without Limitations

The infinitude of God means that he is not limited by space, dimensions, or barriers. While eternal relates to matters of time, infinite relates to matters of space. That God is eternal means he is not affected by time,

6. Tozer, *Knowledge of the Holy*, 45.
7. Tozer, *Divine Conquest*, 21.

and that he is infinite means he is not limited by space. Both concepts however relate to the sense of going on and on, endlessly. The psalmist declares "Great is our Lord and mighty in power. His understanding has no limit" Psalm 147:5 (NIV). In the King James version that clause is translated, "His understanding is Infinite."

Once again, as this is essential to understanding God's essence (who he is), he is the only infinite being there is. Infinitude is unique to God and him alone. We are, on the other hand, as his creations, finite beings. We have limitations, God has none. We know boundaries and borders, God does not. We are surrounded by walls and ceilings; God cannot be so contained. God is unconfined, unbounded, illimitable, inexhaustible.

This dynamic of the essence of God is a difficult concept for us to fully grasp. God's infinitude means he has no limitations, but we certainly do, and one of our limitations is just this—a finite mind cannot possibly grasp the infinite, unlimited Being of God. Once again, Tozer states the issue accurately: "To say that God is infinite is to say that God is measureless. Our concept of measurement embraces mountains and men, atoms and stars, gravity, energy, numbers, speed, but never God!"[8]

It is unavoidable that we use terms we can understand in our attempts to define and understand the essence and nature of God. Yet the reality is, we are using "creature" words to describe the Creator. We are "measuring" him with descriptive terms even though he remains outside of our measurements and beyond our calculations. Tozer continues, "We cannot speak of measure or amount or size or weight and at the same time be speaking of God, for these tell of degrees and there are no degrees in God. All that He is He is without growth or addition or development. Nothing in God is less or more, or large or small. He is what He is in Himself, without qualifying thought or word. He is simply God."[9] God only is Eternal. He only is Infinite. And still, there is one more undeniable truth about his essence.

Unchanging and Unchangeable

Immutable means not changeable. That God is immutable means God does not change. Typically, most theology books will list immutability as being one of God's attributes, but I think it should be listed as an essential part of his essence. The divine essence is who God is, and God is immutable. It is part of his divine Being.

Some theologians claim that God's immutability defines all his other attributes, so; God is immutably good, immutably wise, immutably merciful, his love never changes, and so forth. This assertion would seem, therefore, to prove my prerogative that immutability is part of God's divine nature and essence, rather than being just one of his many attributes. God's immutability then allows for him to act mercifully or graciously in an unchanging capacity. While we experience what God does which then helps us understand who God is, we must understand that it is who God is that drives what he does.

God is unchanging in his character and will. To be mutable means liable to change, and change is a "creature" word. We change, God cannot. "I am the Lord, I change not" (Malachi 3:6). God will not change, nor can he change, and if he did change, he would have to deny himself and his eternal and infinite perfections. So, James writes, "He never changes or casts a shifting shadow" (Jas 1:27 NLT). "He is not a man that He should change His mind" (1 Sam 15:29).

The immutability of God provides comfort and stability to all those who will believe in him and follow him. In a world where change happens rapidly and sometimes without warning, we who love the Lord know that we can trust in him and his word as a sure foundation. That God is unchanging in his character and will is a great blessing to us. Imagine if he was a capricious God, a fickle God? Any sense of stability for our lives would be on shaky ground indeed. But he is immutable, and his word is forever "settled in Heaven" (Ps 119:89).

Speaking on the relevance of the Immutability of God for our lives, J. I. Packer sees it as the one thing that binds believers today with believers in the Bible. Our commonality is grounded in the reality that God does not change. Packer writes: "Fellowship with Him, trust in His word, living by faith, 'standing on the promises of God', are essentially the same realities for us today as they were for Old and New Testament believers. This thought brings comfort as we enter into the perplexities of each day: amid all the changes and uncertainties of life in a nuclear age, God and His Christ remain the same—almighty to save."[10]

God's character, being perfect, has not changed. God's attributes being the perfect actions of his will are the same today as they were in the

---

10. Packer, *Knowing God*, 72.

day of Abraham, Isaac, and Jacob. Was he powerful then? He remains so today, there has not been any erosion of his omnipotence. Was he merciful then? His mercy and grace continue this day in undiminished splendor. Was he wise and omniscient then? He is unchanged in his wisdom now and knows as much now as ever. His omniscience remains untaxed. His omnipresence remains ever-present. His omnipotence continues unrestrained.

All creatures change. We are ever-changing, God is never changing. Spurgeon writes, "Man, especially as to his body, is always undergoing revolution. But God is perpetually the same. He remains everlastingly the same. There are no furrows on his eternal brow. No age hath palsied him; no years have marked him with the mementos of their flight; he sees ages pass, but with him, it is ever now. He is the great I AM-the Great Unchangeable."[11]

Such a God as This

This then is the very *essence* of God. He is self-existent and self-sufficient. He is transcendent, wholly above and wholly beyond His creation. And what is true about Him cannot be true about any other being in the universe he created.

God is *Eternal* and therefore not bound by time.
God is *Infinite* and therefore not barred by space.
God is *Immutable* and therefore not burdened by change.

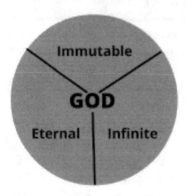

---

11. Spurgeon, Sermon, No. 1, (1855).

While we read these theological truths concerning the Person of God, and know they can only apply to God himself, there remains the need for us to affirm them and benefit from our relationship with such a God as this.

This is the God who we are to give center stage in our life. We are not eternal as is he, but we are everlasting, and that life comes from him. We are not infinite as is he, but being finite puts us in a position of humility and reliance upon his infinite goodness. We are not immutable as is he, but we can place our trust in the God of stability and never-changing love.

God gives us everlasting life.

He leads us with infinite wisdom.

He loves us with unchanging grace and mercy.

In *Knowing God*, J. I. Packer accuses Christians of looking at God too often with the wrong end of a telescope. This, he suggests, reduces God to pigmy proportions which result in producing pigmy Christians. He writes, "The modern way with God is to set Him at a distance, if not to deny Him altogether . . . and the irony is that modern Christians, preoccupied with maintaining religious practices in an irreligious world, have themselves allowed God to become remote."[12]

It is the goal of this study to turn that telescope around and see God in all his fulness, in so far as his fulness is revealed to us. We desire him to be at the center of our lives. That is his rightful place. We need to know him, who he is, what he does, and why he does it. Understanding something of his essence is a starting point. Next, we turn the telescope on the divine attributes, so that we can gain a greater appreciation for the mighty workings of God. It must be our prayer that this God of such dynamic *doings* is doing His will in and through us and touching the lives of all those around us.

---

12. Packer, *Knowing God*, 6.

Eight | From Beyond To Before

NINETEENTH-CENTURY BRITISH PASTOR AND PREACHER Charles Haddon Spurgeon knew well the importance of knowing God. In a sermon he delivered in 1855, he proclaimed this:

> The highest science, the loftiest speculation, the mightiest philosophy, which can ever engage the attention of a child of God, is the name, the nature, the person, the work, the doings, and the existence of the great God whom he calls his Father. There is something exceedingly improving to the mind in a contemplation of the Divinity. It is a subject so vast, that all our thoughts are lost in its immensity; so deep, that our pride is drowned in its infinity.[1]

How do we even begin to pursue this *Knowledge of the Holy?* In the previous chapter, I attempted to define that which is inexpressible and inexhaustible—the very essence of God. We now move from the God who is beyond us to the God who is *before* us. We go from the God who we cannot possibly understand fully, in terms of his divine essence, to the God who we cannot possibly ignore or avoid because his divine attributes are constantly before us.

God is alive, and he displays characteristics of his existence. We refer to them as his divine *attributes*. It is these characteristics that help us understand the life of God—who God is, what he does, and how he does it.

Theologians have as their lifetime pursuit the task of mapping out the attributes of God as revealed in Scripture. This task is inevitable, given

1. Spurgeon, Sermon (No. 1) Jan 7, 1855.

the reality that the Bible is a virtual catalog of those characteristics. His divine attributes are on display from Genesis to Revelation. Even as we start, we are met with two critical prerequisites. The first is to acknowledge the hidden dangers in attempting to define anything about God. And by that I mean the inherent danger that defining something seeks to exert control. If I can define it, I believe I can control it.

This may well be a carryover from the ancient practice of naming something or someone. To name someone gave you authority of that person. For example, notice how this plays out in the story of Jacob wrestling the Angel of the Lord in Genesis 32:22–30. Take note of how each of their names plays an important role as to who is in control. And, of course, add to that the spiritual reality that God renames the believer according to Revelation 2:17. (Indeed, as the old hymn says, we have "a new name written down in glory!")

Another concern is that defining looks for completeness. Its goal is to box something in, to know something from start to finish. Again, defining leads to confining. But any listing of divine attributes must not be thought of as exhaustive of the person and character of God. It would be foolish to think that we can know everything that can be known about God.

The second prerequisite is that we will be helped in this pursuit of identifying and defining the attributes of God if we make some important distinctions about them. The attributes of God are usually divided into two categories. The key difference in distinguishing those two categories are attributes that are unique and possessed by God only and those attributes that he possesses but also allows us to share in their exercise. Typically, theologians refer to them as either *Moral* and *Non-Moral*, or *Objective* and *Subjective*, or most commonly as *Incommunicable* and *Communicable*. I have never really thought these terms were very clear and helpful and would rather refer to them simply as being either *Exclusive* or *Inclusive*.

God's exclusive attributes would be those that only he possesses. They are "exclusive" to him and him only. The inclusive attributes of God are those which he possesses but also allows us to share in the exercise of them, therefore we are "included" in their use.

Accordingly, the exclusive attributes reveal God as he is in himself, apart from us. As an example, God is omniscient, which means he knows all, everything there is to be known, all the time. Omniscience is unique to God only, and even though you might think you know it all, you do not!

The inclusive attributes reveal God as he is in relation to man. With these, we see how God interacts with us and then to a lesser extent how we can interact with each other. As an example, God is merciful, and showing mercy is a characteristic in which we can share. We can be merciful, as well, to those around us.

Journey Like No Other

Attempting to catalog all the attributes of God, in whatever way you are going to categorize them, is a theological task like no other. It is a journey of the finite into the infinite realm. It is trafficking in truth that demands we slow down and notice every signpost. It is a study of the height, depth, and breadth of the Godhead, in so far as we can possibly comprehend those divine dimensions. And then, we are still left with questions that allude answers and a knowledge that can only proceed as far as our faith will take us. Lewis Sperry Chafer wrote: "The attributes of God present a theme so vast and complex and so beyond the range of finite faculties that any attempt to classify them must be only approximate as to accuracy or completeness."[2]

Dr. Chafer was right, the pursuit of the attributes of God can be a complex endeavor, especially in that we can hardly agree on just how many there are and then what they are. Consulting any number of books out there on the subject by Theologians past and present, and or logging on to the myriad of online resources that would similarly discuss the attributes of God, you will be confronted with list after list that is similar, yet different; identical, yet varied; broad, yet narrow; orderly, yet random. In short, we are all over the map when it comes to identifying the attributes of God.

One of the most thorough research websites on biblical topics and study is the *Precept Austin* website, the work of Dr. Bruce Hurt of Austin, Texas. He has done a masterful job of collating thousands of pages of commentary, word studies, Hebrew, and Greek grammar, etc., from scholars and preachers both past and present.

When you open up the page on the Attributes of God you are met with a well-planned out chart presenting as exhaustive a list of attributes

2. Chafer, *Systematic Theology*, 189.

as you could imagine in a dizzying array of boxes, columns, headings, descriptions, Scripture references, and even links to Christian hymns that relate to the given attribute. And then, after all of that, what appears at the very end of this seemingly exhaustive presentation is this:

DISCLAIMER

Although the purpose of this page is to give an overview of the Attributes of God, I must apologize because this table is not even "the fringes of His ways and how faint a word we hear of Him!" (Job 26:14) As Horner has written, "There can be no condensed learning of God; the very thought is an insult to His transcendent majesty." Rather we have to learn . . . what it is to slow down and meditate on the truth of His Being, to ruminate over, to ingest and digest the revelations concerning His holy character, to wonder overwhelmingly, to "be still [cease striving] and know that I am God" (Ps 46:10).

Did you get that? I commend him for this acknowledgment. In one of the most amazing resources available to us on the topic of the attributes of God, we are overwhelmed by the amount of material offered, including lists created by Charles Haddon Spurgeon and Arthur W. Pink, all of them related and all of them different, and all of it not exhaustive!

So, now I am compelled to offer my disclaimer, as we dive headlong into this all-important chapter on the attributes of God:

The attributes that I will cover will not be at all exhaustive of who God is and what God can do. I think the best thing to do is to present a number of the attributes that are the most obvious, and the ones that get the most exposure in Scripture.

Furthermore, this book is not intended to be a heavy theological tome, so I will keep my descriptions brief and hopefully touch on aspects of these amazing attributes of God that will be both instructional and inspirational.

Without the authority of the Bible, our attempts at defining an attribute of God would amount to being merely an opinion. And it's not "opinions" about God that we need, it is a revelation. We must have, therefore, knowledge of the character and conduct of God as revealed in His Word.

Of one thing we can be certain, some attributes are unique only to God, what I am referring to as his exclusive attributes. And there are attributes that he possesses in full and perfect measure, but that can be experienced by us as well, albeit in a more limited, imperfect measure. These are the inclusive attributes.

God's Exclusive Attributes

We start with the three *Omni's* (the Latin prefix meaning "all" or "every") and affirm that God is *Omnipresent* (All-present), *Omnipotent* (All-powerful), and *Omniscient* (All-knowing).

First, that God fills all of his creation with his immensity and presence is his omnipresence. This attribute unique to God is attested to throughout the revelation of the Word of God. "The eyes of the Lord are everywhere, keeping watch on the wicked and the good" (Prov 15:3 NIV). "Where can I go from your Spirit? Where can I flee from your presence?" (Ps 139:7 NIV). Eleventh-century French theologian Hildebert of Lavardin stated this attribute elegantly: *God is over all things, under all things; outside all; within but not enclosed; without but not excluded; above but not raised up; below but not depressed; wholly above, presiding; wholly beneath, sustaining; wholly within, filling.*

That God fills all his creation with his power and authority is his omnipotence, and as with the revelation of his omnipresence, it is attested throughout Scripture. "I am almighty God" (Gen 17:1). "O Sovereign Lord! You made the heavens and earth by your strong hand and powerful arm. Nothing is too hard for you" (Jer 32:17 NLT). Tozer provides this explanation: "Since He has at His command all the power in the universe, the Lord God omnipotent can do anything as easily as anything else. All His acts are done without effort. He expends no energy that must be replenished. His self-sufficiency makes it unnecessary for Him to look outside of Himself for a renewal of strength. All the power required to do all that He wills to do lies in undiminished fullness in His own infinite being."[3]

And then, thirdly, that God fills all his creation with his wisdom and knowledge is referred to as his omniscience. "Our Lord is great and very powerful. There is no limit to what he knows" (Ps 147:5 NCV). "For I am God, and there is no other; I am God, and there is none like Me, Declaring the end from the beginning, and from ancient times things that are not yet done" (Isa 46:9–10). And once again, the description of this attribute from the pen of A. W. Tozer is invaluable: "God knows instantly and

---

3. Tozer, *Knowledge of the Holy*, 73.

effortlessly all matter and all matters, all mind and every mind, all spirit and all spirits, all being and every being, all creaturehood and all creatures, every plurality and all pluralities, all law and every law, all relations, all causes, all thoughts, all mysteries, all enigmas, all feeling, all desires, every unuttered secret, all thrones and dominions, all personalities, all things visible and invisible in heaven and in earth, motion, space, time, life, death, good, evil, heaven, and hell."[4]

Making the Complex, Simple

Over the years I have meditated upon and studied these three exclusive attributes of God, which are constantly on display everywhere in Scripture. Respectfully, I have attempted to craft definitions of each of them. I admit each statement is simple, yet I trust, meaningful. One night in a Bible study, a friend of mine, prayed "Lord, make that which is complex—simple. And make that which is simple—a revelation." So, here is my attempt at just that:

> God's Omnipresence: *All of God is everywhere and anywhere and there is nowhere where he is not.*
>
> God's Omnipotence: *God can do anything he wants to, anytime he wants to, anywhere and everywhere he wants to.*
>
> God's Omniscience: *God knows all there is to know, everything there is to know, at any time, in any time, at the same time, all the time.*

Let us affirm that these are God's Exclusive Attributes. He possesses them, we never will. We must be everlastingly grateful for a God who possesses such amazing, all-encompassing, all-consuming, all-embracing, all-important characteristics. He is our all-powerful, all-knowing, ever and everywhere present God. With King David, let us cry out, "There's none like you, God, no God but you, nothing to compare with what we've heard with our own ears" (1 Chr 17:20 MSG).

Yet, God is more than just the sum of his Exclusive Attributes. There are also his Inclusive Attributes for us to consider. Once again, these are the characteristics he possesses, but also allows us to possess, to a lesser extent. The lists of the attributes of God are numerous with the attributes mostly grouped with not many distinctions. Words and concepts like

4. Tozer, *Knowledge of the Holy*, 62.

Eternal, Immutable, Love, Holy, Truth, Righteousness, Mercy, Infinitude, etc., are all just thrown together as if they are all on the same equal plane.

It is my conviction, however, that some important distinctions are warranted. For instance, I am convinced that a distinction should be made between his Essence and His Attributes as noted earlier. Once we affirm such a basic distinction, then we can also see the need to understand one further distinction within the listing of God's attributes. That distinction would be between those attributes which He possesses only and solely and those attributes which we share with him.

God's *Inclusive* Attributes

I believe that these attributes should also be divided into two categories, with the distinctive feature being those which have as their basis either the holiness of God or the love of God. We should recognize that the characteristics of God which he possesses and also allows us to participate in are rooted in either his holiness or his love. Take special care to appreciate that these two concepts—holiness and love—are not in opposition to each other or in competition with each other, but that they are always in perfect harmony in God.

Perhaps we can chart out these two important distinctions within the Divine Nature. As mentioned above, I am not trying to present an exhaustive list, but present the attributes of God that are perhaps the most well-known.

GOD'S	
HOLINESS	**LOVE**
RIGHTEOUSNESS	GOODNESS
JUSTICE	GRACE
TRUTH	MERCY
FAITHFULNESS	KINDNESS

What I am suggesting, as this chart demonstrates, is that God's attributes of righteousness, justice, truth, and faithfulness (and those like that) are driven by his holiness, and his goodness, grace, mercy, and kindness (and those like that) are likewise driven by his love. As stated above, neither of these will violate the other. They will not contradict nor compete with each other. God does not set aside his holiness so he can be loving, and he does not forego his love when he acts in holiness.

That God is a God of holiness and a God of love is true of him all the time at the same time. One attribute does not outweigh the other, nor does one take priority over the other. They are held in perfect balance in the perfect nature of the perfect being of God. And yet each has a separate and special form and function within the divine nature of God.

This twofold distinction should present itself as logical, and I trust, theological. Consider the significance of God's holiness and God's love and that, as I believe, it is often demonstrated in Scripture that they lead to all the other inclusive attributes of God.

For example, do you think it possible to lead a life of holiness and not be *right, just, truthful,* and *faithful*? Is it possible for me to love like God loves and not be *good, gracious, kind,* and *merciful*? If I try and think of all these separate attributes and how I can meet the requirements and demands of all of them, it becomes overwhelming. It is virtually impossible. So, eventually, I quit. I give up.

But wait. What if I just focus on living a life of holiness? Just that—holiness. Separated, consecrated to God's word and will. Will I not be "just" in all my dealings, if I just do that? Will I not also manifest a life of *truth, honesty,* and *integrity*? Would not holiness demand that of me and produce that in me? Does this make sense to you? It does to me. And once it starts to make sense, it begins to be life-changing!

And, what if I focus upon God's love, his *agape*? Will I not demonstrate a life of sacrifice, steadfastness, and service (all characteristics of *agape*)? Will I not evidence *grace* and *goodness* and *kindness,* and if I do not, would that not prove my life of love is a fraud?

Read the books, visit the websites, consult the charts, many of which show two dozen or more attributes of God (at minimum). Which ones work for you, which ones do not? Which ones are easy, which ones are hard, which ones do you understand, which are the ones about which you do not have a clue? Which ones do you think you can be, which ones do you know you will never be? But, put all that aside for a moment and just dedicate yourself to owning and pursuing these two Scriptural commands—this one: "You shall be holy, for I am Holy" (1 Pet 1:16), and this one: "Let us love one another, for love is of God; and everyone who loves is born of God and knows God" (1 John 4:7).

You will not be neglecting a pursuit of all the other attributes by just focusing initially on these two, you will be engaging all the others. Why? How? Because all the other inclusive attributes intersect at the juncture of holiness and love. I think of them as two great headwaters from which flow all the other tributaries of godly living. Without them, I venture to say, all the other attributes would dry up. There can be no real righteousness, justice, and truth apart from the holiness of God. There will be no goodness, kindness, and graciousness without the love of God.

The HOLINESS of God

God's holiness is referred to over five hundred times in Scripture, but to attach several references to it doesn't do it justice. Many theologians believe that the holiness of God occupies the foremost rank within the hierarchy of God's attributes. Some theologians, like A. A. Hodge, taught that holiness should not be thought of as just one attribute among the others. Robert Lewis Dabney wrote, "Holiness is to be regarded not as a distinct attribute but as the result of all God's moral perfection together."[5]

The holiness of God has that unique quality where it can be both noun and verb. God *does* holy deeds, but that is because God *is* holy. Nothing or no one can even approach the holiness of God. "God's holiness is not simply the best we know infinitely bettered. We know nothing like the divine holiness. It stands apart, unique, unapproachable, incomprehensible and unattainable. The natural man is blind to it. He may fear God's power and admire His wisdom, but His holiness he cannot even imagine."[6]

Moses declares "Who is like You, O Lord. Who is like You, glorious in holiness" (Exod 15:11). The psalmist sings, "Exalt the Lord our God, and worship at His holy hill, for the Lord our God is holy" (Ps 99:9). In Isaiah 6:1-3, the prophet's beatific vision remains one of the most well-known scenes in Scripture. Like a pristine portal welcoming us into the glories of the book of the great Hebrew prophet, we hear him describe what he saw and heard: "In the year that King Uzziah died, I saw the Lord sitting on a throne, high and lifted up, and the train of His robe filled the temple. Above it stood seraphim; each one had six wings: with two he covered his face, with two he covered his feet, and with two he flew. And

---

5. Dabney, https://www.goodreads.com/author/quotes/904468.

6. Tozer, *Knowledge of the Holy*, 111.

one cried to another and said: "Holy, holy, holy is the Lord of hosts; The whole earth is full of His glory!"

Commenting on this passage, R. C. Sproul offered this insightful observation: "The Bible says that God is holy, holy, holy. Not that He is merely holy, or even holy, holy. He is holy, holy, holy. The Bible never says that God is love, love, love, or mercy, mercy, mercy, or wrath, wrath, wrath... (but) It does say that He is holy, holy, holy, the whole earth is full of His glory."[7]

The words used in either Testament (one Hebrew and one Greek) each describe the idea of being *separated* and as they apply to God refer to him being, as a result, totally good and entirely without evil. And in all of creation, he is the only One who is Holy (Rev 15:4).

God is holy and no one else is as holy as he is. No one and not one thing even come in as a close second! John Piper describes it this way: "His holiness is what he is, as God, that nobody else is. It is his quality of perfection that can't be improved upon, that can't be imitated, that is incomparable, that determines all that he is and is determined by nothing from outside him."[8]

Once again, we can turn to A. W. Tozer for a hard-hitting declaration of the holiness of God: "Holy is the way God is. To be holy He does not conform to a standard. He is that standard. He is absolutely holy with an infinite, incomprehensible fullness of purity that is incapable of being other than it is... God is holy and He has made holiness the moral condition necessary to the health of His universe."[9]

Dwelling upon the incomprehensible holiness of God, I start to see that God is, therefore, *Righteous, Just* and all his ways are the ways of *Truth*. How could he be anything but? The concepts of righteousness and being just are virtually synonymous in the Hebrew scriptures. Merrill F. Unger relates them to God's holiness in that he sees both righteousness or justice as "divine holiness applied." When speaking of the Justice of God, and that it is theologically the same as the righteousness of God, Unger writes, "The justice of God is both an essential and relative attribute of the divine existence. It is a necessary outflow from the holiness of God."[10]

---

7. Sproul, *Holiness of God*, 40.

8. Piper, "What is God's Glory?" 2.

9. Tozer, *Knowledge of the Holy*, 112-113.

10. Unger, *Bible Dictionary*, 624.

Before the children of Israel, Moses reminds them that God is, "The Rock! His work is perfect, or all His ways are just; A God of faithfulness and without injustice, Righteous and upright is He" (Deut 32:4 NASB). Similarly, the Psalmist declares of God, "Righteousness and justice are the foundation of your throne; love and faithfulness go before you" (Ps 89:14 NIV). And again, in Psalm 119:142, "Your righteousness is an everlasting righteousness, and your law is truth." And then the prophet Zephaniah reminds us that God "…will do no unrighteousness and every morning He brings His justice to light" (Zeph 3:5).

Accordingly, if God is a God of holiness, then he will always be and can only be a God of truth. Isaiah calls him "the God of truth" (65:16) and uses the well-known adverb *amen*. The word "Amen" is related to the Hebrew word for truth, *emet,* and both come from the root which means to support something—to make something firm. When you say "Amen" to something, you are declaring that what has been said is the truth and therefore you support it. We see this in the gospels when Jesus begins a statement by saying "Truly, truly . . . " What Jesus was saying was, "Amen, amen!" The personification of this is when Jesus affirms his description in the seventh letter to the churches of Asia Minor as recorded by John in Revelation 3:14, He declares, "These things says the Amen, the Faithful and True Witness."

We should notice how truth and faithfulness are linked together. God is the God of truth, as Isaiah writes, and he is the faithful God, as Moses declared. The key Hebrew word often translated as "faithful" is *emunah,* which like Amen, comes from the root word for truth. In both Testaments, faithfulness and truth are linked and achieve their highest expression in the person of God. David declares, "For the word of the Lord is right and true; he is faithful in all he does" (Ps 33:4 NIV). And Paul writes, "If we are faithless, he remains faithful, for he cannot deny himself" (2 Tim 2:13 ESV). God would have to lie and be untruthful about himself to become unfaithful. That he will not do. That is something he cannot do!

God is right(eous) and can never do wrong. He is a God of justice and will never be unjust. He is a God of truth and never will he embrace falsehood. And he is the faithful God and will never prove untrustworthy. And all of this is true of God because he is holy! And he is holy unlike anything or anyone to which or to whom we can compare.

Am I Godly?

As stated above, these are all *Inclusive* attributes. What does that mean? It means that not only is God holy, righteous, just, truthful, and faithful but we are called to be the same. Not the same in terms of degree and dimension but the same in concept and application.

Know this, we do not act righteously and justly the same way that God does. When we say that God is Righteous and Just, we are *not* implying that he is acting in a way that conforms to some standard of rightness and justice. God *is* the standard. God is not defined by righteousness, rather righteousness is defined in God. He does not meet the standard of righteousness; he is the standard. That God is righteous, just, truthful, and faithful is affirming his attributes. Each of those attributes is consistent with his character.

When, through the power of his Holy Spirit, we strive to live a life of righteousness, justice, truth, and faithfulness, we are to measure up to that standard, a standard which is God himself. That is why we refer to it as living "godly." This should be rather evident to us. When we pursue living righteously and justly, we can say that we are attempting to live a godly life.

I will never be holy as is God, but I am called upon to live a holy life. I will never be sinless, but I am to sin less! I will hardly be as just and truthful as is God, but I am called upon, nonetheless, to be just in all my actions and to love mercy and truthfulness in all my dealings with my fellow man.

The statements in Scripture declaring these truths are explicit and cannot be evaded. Because God is holy, he would have us live lives of holiness: "But like the Holy One who called you, be holy yourselves also in all your behavior, because it is written, 'You shall be holy, for I am holy'" (1 Pet 1:15–16 NASB).

Because God is righteous, he empowers us to "live righteously, soberly and godly in this present world" (Tit 2:12). John adds, "He who practices righteousness is righteous, just as He is righteous" (1 John 3:7).

Because God is just, he instills in us a sense of justice and therefore calls us to "do justly, love mercy and walk humbly before our God" (Mic 6:8).

Because God is truth, he demands truth in our inmost being so that we will put away falsehood, and always speak the truth with our neighbors (Eph 4:25). We are told, "These are the things you shall do:

Speak each man the truth to his neighbor; Give judgment in your gates for truth, justice, and peace." (Zech 8:16).

Because God is faithful in all his actions, Paul reminds us, "Now it is required that those who have been given a trust must prove faithful" (1 Cor 4:2 NIV).

A godly life will be so because of the application of these inclusive attributes of God, manifested in us through the power and presence of the Holy Spirit as He controls our lives.

The *Love* of God

God also reveals inclusive attributes that are based on his love—*Goodness, Grace, Mercy, Kindness, Faithfulness.*

That God is Love is embedded and embellished on just about every page of Scripture. Powerful words are used in both Testaments to express the Love of God. In the Old Testament, a key Hebrew word is *chesed,* which expresses the loyal love of God. In the New Testament, the Greek word is *agape,* which expresses the unconditional love of God. God's love is enormous and eternal. His love is enduring and encouraging. His love is steadfast and supportive.

Some understand the "agape" of God believing that it is a New Testament invention. This is usually based upon the notion that the Old Testament portrays God, so they think, as rather angry and judgmental most of the time, and hardly "loving."

It is true that in Ancient Near Eastern polytheistic cultures none of the local deities loved their subjects. They were warlike and wrathful. They were vicious and vengeful. And they were always mad and rarely merciful. Years ago, Alexander MacClaren described the gods of ancient polytheism as being lustful gods, and beautiful gods, and idle gods, and fighting gods, and peaceful gods: but not one of whom worshippers said, a loving god. No one said of their god, "He loves me." But it is erroneous to think that the Old Testament does not depict the God of Israel as a God of Love. MacClaren believed that saying God loves is the greatest thing that can be said by lips.

Moreover, it is certainly not correct to say that the Old Testament fails to depict God as a God of love. Immediately what comes to mind is David's great lyric in Psalm 63:3 "Thy lovingkindness is better than life!" Numerous other Old Testament texts attest to his love:

The Lord did not set His love on you or choose you because you were more numerous than any other people, but because the LORD loves you and He would keep the oath He swore to your fathers (Deut 7:7-8).

I have loved you, my people, with an everlasting love. With unfailing love, I have drawn you to myself (Jere 31:3 NLT).

Though the mountains be shaken and the hills be removed, yet my unfailing love for you will not be shaken nor my covenant of peace be removed (Isa 54:10 NIV).

The theme of the love of God is carried into the New Testament, especially revealed through Jesus Christ who is the personification of God's love—the incarnation of Love. It is Jesus who declares that the purpose of his coming was because "God so loved the world" (John 3:16).

The Apostle John's statement is clear, precise, and powerful: "Whoever does not love does not know God, because God is love" (1 John 4:8 NIV). There is an important truth to notice about the final three words of this verse. This is a statement about God—God *is* love (agape). God just does not *do* love, he *is* love. John is not just saying God is loving, he is saying love is who God is, it is his character.

God is Love, and his love is quite different from human love. God's love, *agape,* is based on the divine will and not based on feelings or emotions. God's love is not fickle or capricious. You will never have to worry whether "he loves you or loves you not!" God does not love us because we are lovable or because we make him feel good; he loves us because he *is* love.

He does not love us more when we do good, any more than he loves us less when we do bad. His love is constant, unconditional, and sacrificial. So, John would go on to say: "This is how God showed his love among us: He sent his one and only Son into the world that we might live through him. This is love: not that we loved God, but that he loved us and sent his Son as an atoning sacrifice for our sins" (1 John 4:9–10).

Who can understand such love? Who can fathom the enormity of the Love of God? God's love is indescribable, incomprehensible, incomparable! Perhaps Frederick Lehman comes the closest to comparing the incomparable when he wrote those amazing lyrics for his hymn *The Love of God.* Many believe them to be the greatest lyrical lines in any hymn ever written:

Could we with ink the ocean fill and were the skies of parchment made;

Were every stalk on earth a quill, And every man a scribe by trade.
To write the love of God above, would drain the ocean dry;
Nor could the scroll contain the whole, though stretched from sky to sky.[11]

The enormity of God's love equates to the universality of it (as presented in John 3:16). But never forget God's love is also highly personal. He Loves the world. He loves you. We should be reminded, as Augustine stated, that God loves each of us as if there was only one of us to love.

There is another important truth to unpack from First John 4:8 which is that it also reveals an application—if we do not love others that will prove we do not know God at all. Does God's Love change you? This gets practical right away because we are called upon, not only to love God but also to love our neighbor. God expects us to show love, as well as demonstrate the other inclusive attributes that are born out of that love. So then:

The God who is Good would have us also live lives of goodness.

The God who is Grace would have us be gracious to others.

The God who is Mercy would have us be merciful to others.

The God who is Kind would have us show kindness to others.

For the child of God, the holiness of God is unavoidable, and the love of God is undeniable. And while it is true that his holiness can be difficult and his love demanding, both are needed to ensure that our life in Christ is authentic. And neither are fully possible unless God is at the Center of our lives.

The Great All

We are confronted by the attributes of God moment by moment. His divine character is before us continually, whether we realize it or not. Our lives are affected by him, whether we believe in him or not. He knows us because he is omniscient and knows every one of us. He sees us because he is omnipresent and there is nowhere for anyone to be where he is not. He governs us because he is omnipotent and is Sovereign over all his creation. There can be no one or nothing that lies beyond his accountability. If there were, then he would cease to be God.

11. Lehman, *The Love of God*, 1917.

We stand every day accountable to God in holiness. His righteousness is our standard. His justice is our objective. His truth is our goal. His faithfulness is our hope. We benefit every day from God's love. We are saved by his grace. We are shielded by his goodness. We are sheltered by his mercy. We are sustained by his kindness.

We come, then, to the conclusion of this section on knowing God, and the challenge to do exactly what the Scripture tells us to do—"Love the Lord your God with all your heart and with all your soul and with all your mind and with all your strength" (Mark 12:30 NIV).

At every juncture of life, the whole point is to stretch us and expand our knowledge of God. This is vitally important, for as J. Grant Howard warned, "Christians who don't have an expanding, deepening knowledge of God are like players who have no coach, no rule book, no game schedule, no playing field, no training program. They are depending on one thing—uniforms."[12]

In *The Pursuit of God*, Tozer lays out what happens to us when we have that deeper knowledge of God: "A new God-consciousness will seize upon us and we shall begin to taste and hear and inwardly feel the God who is our life and our all. More and more, as our faculties grow sharper and more sure, God will become to us the great All, and His Presence the glory and wonder of our lives.[13]

Is God for you the "great All" as Tozer puts it? Is God your great Everything? We cannot possibly know everything there is to know about him, but everything he wants us to know about himself he has revealed to us in his word. So that should be our life's goal and our grand pursuit, which is to know God, to pursue the knowledge of the Holy, and to follow hard after God (Ps 63:8, Hos 6:3, Phil 3:8–10).

Does it matter? Will that knowledge change us? It will. It must. And the result will be, as we read in Daniel, "But the people who know their God shall be strong and do great things" (Dan 11:32b TLB). That is a promise in God's word. But the knowledge of whom you are pursuing must be the God of the Bible. Do not settle for a God who is too small.

Patrick Morley reminds us that there is a cultural Christianity that seeks only to pursue after the God we want rather than the God who is. He states, "It is the tendency to be shallow in our understanding of God, wanting Him to be more of a gentle grandfather type who spoils us and

---

12. Howard, *Balancing Life's Demands*, 79.
13. Tozer, *Pursuit of God*, 58-59.

lets us have our way. It is sensing a need for God, but on our own terms. It is wanting the God we have underlined in our Bibles without wanting the rest of Him, too. It is God relative instead of God absolute."[14]

He is correct, and perhaps inspired by the memorable statement by C. S. Lewis, who suggested, "We want, in fact, not so much a Father in Heaven as a grandfather in heaven—a senile benevolence who, as they say, 'liked to see young people enjoying themselves,' and whose plan for the universe was simply that it might be truly said at the end of each day, 'a good time was had by all.'"[15]

If God is to be "Center," if he is going to be your Great All, then be sure you seek him only. The One God who is beyond us, yet always before us. Follow hard after this God of holiness and pursue with passion this God of love.

To that end, the Apostle Paul left us this challenge and prayer in Ephesians 3:16–21. Having referred to the Father, the Creator of everything in heaven and on earth, Paul prays this great prayer for us:

> I pray that from his glorious, unlimited resources he will empower you with inner strength through his Spirit. Then Christ will make his home in your hearts as you trust in him. Your roots will grow down into God's love and keep you strong.
>
> And may you have the power to understand, as all God's people should, how wide, how long, how high, and how deep his love is. May you experience the love of Christ, though it is too great to understand fully. Then you will be made complete with all the fullness of life and power that comes from God.
>
> Now all glory to God, who is able, through his mighty power at work within us, to accomplish infinitely more than we might ask or think.
>
> Glory to him in the church and in Christ Jesus through all generations forever and ever! Amen.

14. Morley, *Man in the Mirror*, 33.

15. Lewis, *Problem of Pain*, 21.

Part Three

What Is Man?

Men go abroad to wonder at the height of mountains, at the huge waves of the sea, at the long courses of the rivers, at the vast compass of the ocean, at the circular motion of the stars; and they pass by themselves without wondering.

AUGUSTINE

What is Man that You are mindful of him,

And the son of man that You visit him?

For You have made him a little lower than the angels,

And You have crowned him with glory and honor.

DAVID

PSALM 8:4-5

This section aims to explore the Bible's revelation about the make-up, mystery, and miracle of man. Who are we, really? Why are we? Do we fully understand the strategic position in which God has placed us so that He can touch the world around us?

Nine | Who Am I?

"There are depths in man that go to the lowest hell, and heights that reach the highest heaven, for are not both heaven and hell made out of him, everlasting miracle and mystery that he is."

THESE ARE THE WORDS OF Thomas Carlyle, the nineteenth-century Scottish-born historian, and philosopher. At the time, Carlyle was considered one of the most influential social commentators during the Victorian era, and his writings had a significant impact on other great thinkers and writers, such as Charles Dickins in England and Ralph Waldo Emerson in America.

However, Carlyle's writings betrayed a sort of literary schizophrenia between his "everlasting no" and his "everlasting yes" (both terms he created in his novel *Sartor Resartus).* The terms seem to reveal his wavering between a life of faith and belief in God (the *Everlasting Yes*) and then also his rejection of and disbelief in God (the *Everlasting No).* That struggle which he projects to all men is seen in the above quote—the lowest hell versus the highest heaven.

I have a suspicion that Carlyle himself may have been influenced by something Blaise Pascal wrote two centuries earlier: "What is man? Oh, the grandeur and littleness, the excellence and the corruption, the majesty and meanness of man!"

The similarities are apparent. Both refer to the *miracle and mystery* and the *majesty and meanness* of man. That is who we are. That is what we are. At the same time, we are "miracle and mystery." Within the one body, we are both "majesty and meanness."

As a result, both Carlyle and Pascal, as well as countless other philosophers and writers, would agree, with the famous observation offered by Augustine, that men go abroad to wonder at the height of mountains, at the huge waves of the sea, at the long courses of the rivers, at the vast compass of the ocean, at the circular motion of the stars; and they pass by themselves without wondering. So, do you ever wonder about who you are, why you are, and what you are made of?

Do we know who we are—really? Are we made up of both heaven and hell? Is our story one of miracle and mystery as Carlyle believed? Are we really great and little, as well as excellent and corrupt, and both at the same time, as Pascal suggested? Are both majesty and meanness part of our DNA? Have you ever asked, "Who Am I?" It may be one of the most important questions you ever ask yourself. Who are you? Why are you? Mark Twain once summarized that quest when he said that the two most important days in your life are the day you were born and then the day you find out why.

David seemed to be on such a quest. The majesty and mystery of his life seemed to grip him. "What is man that You are mindful of him, And the son of man that You visit him? For You have made him a little lower than the angels, And You have crowned him with glory and honor" (Ps 8:4–5). And again, in Psalm 144:3, he would muse, "Lord, what is man, that You take knowledge of him? Or the son of man, that You are mindful of him?"

Comments like this can only be understood in the sense that, for David, it was a recognition that God, so enormous and beyond one's comprehension should condescend to even acknowledge, much less love, mere human beings. Ancient Job certainly pondered this question. "What is man, that you make so much of him, and that you set your heart on him?" (Job 7:17 ESV). Eugene Peterson, in The Message, paraphrases Job by having him say, "What are mortals anyway, that you bother with them, that you even give them the time of day?"

How are You?

If we do not know ourselves, God most certainly does. And know this— God does not know us casually, He knows us completely. He knows who we are. He knows why we are. He knows how we are. God will never come up to you and say, "Hello, how are you?" Rather, he will come up to you and say, "Hello, let me tell you how you are."

He knows where you have been—and why you were there.

He knows what you have done—and why you did it.

He knows who you are—and for how long you will be that way.

And that is not to say he orchestrates any of that, it is just to acknowledge that his foreknowledge demands such knowledge. God knows us, all about us, everything there is to know about us, all the time and at any time. If this is true and we understand that God knows us, and therefore his Word knows us, then if we are going to find out anything about us, we need to go to his Word.

In the previous section, we aimed to expand our knowledge about who God is. As we begin this next section, our goal is to explore the miracle and mystery of who we are and to see how and why we are strategically located where we are in the biblical paradigm of priorities.

That biblical paradigm is based upon Matthew 22:37–40. It is comprised of three essential entities—God, your neighbor, and yourself. We have already mapped that out with a series of three concentric circles, each circle representing one of the essential entities. Most significantly, the center circle is God. God must be our center. But then who is next? Should it be our neighbors, or should it be our self? As we will see, strategically the only logical and theological placement that makes any sense is that the next circle is our "Self."

Even though well-intentioned theologians and deep-thinking philosophers have formulated opinions of who man is, to start with, we are not so much interested in what man says about man, but in what God says about man. What does the Word of God teach us about us? What are some of the things we need to know about ourselves?

Created!

The first thing we should know is that we are *Created* beings. It does not take the first chapter of Genesis very long for it to get around to us. "Then God said, 'Let Us make man in Our image, according to Our likeness.' So, God created man in His own image; in the image of God He created him male and female He created them. Then God blessed them, and God said to them, 'Be fruitful and multiply; fill the earth and subdue it; have dominion over the fish of the sea, over the birds of the air, and over every living thing that moves on the earth'" (Gen 1:26–28).

And we should note that we are not just "created" beings but created in the image of God. The word in the Hebrew text refers to something *cut out*, and therefore an image, a likeness, a resemblance. In the New Testament, the word that is used becomes remarkably familiar to us in our day of images and icons, for the Greek word gives us our word *icon*. Paul refers to Jesus as "the image of the invisible God" (Col 1:15). In Second Corinthians 11:7, Paul refers to man as "God's image and glory." The Greek word *eikon* meant a mirror-like representation or a reflection of something. Jesus used the word when he held up a coin and he asked, "Whose image is this? And whose inscription?" (Matt 22:20 NIV).

So, the question is, in what way do we *resemble* God? In what way are we a *likeness* of him? How do we *reflect* him? Jesus tells us in John 4:24 that God is Spirit, which means therefore that he has no physical form. So, the image cannot be a physical one. Considering this, the debate then usually comes down to, should "image of God" be interpreted in terms of rationality or terms of relationship?

The rational argument relates to *intellect, emotion,* and *will.* It means that the image of God is substantive in that we possess that which separates us from all of God's other creatures. As humans, uniquely created in God's image, we can reason, develop an affective consciousness to feelings, and exercise freedom of will along with a sense of morality. The relational argument, simply put, relates to the belief that the image of God is not something resident in human nature, but is the ability to experience a relationship with God.

While there are proponents of both views, I am not convinced that it has to be understood as an either/or. We are told that being created in the image of God is either a "rational quality" given to us or a "relational ability" for us. I do not see why it would be a problem if both are correct.

Unique!

One thing is for sure, being created in the image of God leads to the next important truth we need to know about ourselves—we are *Unique* beings. The "Image of God" dynamic is what sets man apart from the rest of the animal world, indeed from the rest of the entire creation. Only humans possess the will and self-consciousness that distinguish us so sharply from even the most advanced and intelligent animals.

The evolutionary hypothesis is a theory that assumes humans, as animals, originated from lower primates. But one thing the evolutionist cannot explain is the vast difference between the animal brain, equipped with instinct, and the human mind, with its creative reasoning powers of intellect. Some animals have physical brains as large or larger than man's brain, and with similar cerebral cortex complexity, but none have the powers of intellect, logic, self-consciousness, and creativity as does man.

Kingsley Mortimer discusses that difference: "To the scientist, man is an animal, graciously self-designated as homo sapiens. If he is, at least, he is still the only one discussing what kind of animal he is. Few, however, would deny that man, animal or not has features without parallel in any other member of that kingdom."[1]

The late Dr. Kingsley E Mortimer was Associate Professor in Anatomy in the School of Medicine at the University of Auckland in New Zealand, from 1969 to 1975. He continued to summarize what separates man from all other created beings: "What puts man in the luxury class among all forms of life is his unique capacity for thought and his possession of free will. He can do as he likes; he can go it alone. By his own choice, he can know the mystery of loneliness and solitary rebellion. Indeed, the very capacity to be rebellious or miserable is the property of man alone. For whoever hears of a miserable rose or a rebellious kangaroo?"[2]

Think of it. Man is in a luxury class all by himself. Creation is full of amazing creatures, but none are quite like a man. Man is unique in all of

1. Blaiklock, (Kingsley), *Why I Am Still a Christian*, 138.
2. Blaiklock, (Kingsley), *Why I Am Still a Christian*, 139.

God's creation. The Talmud declares that one man is equal to the whole of creation! Gerald Flurry reminds us that, "Man alone can wonder, 'Why was I born? What is life? What is death? Is there a purpose in human existence?' Man, unlike the animals, not only "knows" how to do certain things, but he also knows that he knows—that is, he is aware that he has "knowledge." He is self-conscious, aware of his own existence as a unique being."[3]

This is why David wrote one of the most memorable statements in all the Psalms, "I will praise You, for I am fearfully and wonderfully made; Marvelous are Your works, And, that my soul knows very well" (Ps 139:14). The Hebrew adverbs in this verse are rich in meaning— "fearfully" (to be in awe of) and "wonderfully" (to be distinct from). The NET Bible restates them simply as "Awesome and Amazing." I like how Kenneth Taylor paraphrases David in The Living Bible, "Thank you for making me so wonderfully complex! It is amazing to think about. Your workmanship is marvelous—and how well I know it."

Physical!

Next, the obvious must be stated—we are *Physical* beings. With creation begins the essential corporeality of human existence. Have we forgotten that God first formed the physical body and then breathed into it his breath of life, and man became a living *being* (Gen 2:7)? The Hebrew word is *nephesh* and has been translated *soul, self, person,* living *being,* etc. Nephesh appears in the Bible over 700 times and attesting to its complexity has been translated by over twenty different English words alone. Suffice to say, the perceived nuances of any meaning of nephesh demand that we take very seriously our physical bodies as that which God created to adorn the human soul.

David's acknowledgment of God's genius in creating him in such a magnificent way certainly gives weight to the importance of the human body. "You shaped me first inside, then out; you formed me in my mother's womb. I thank you, High God—you are breathtaking! Body and soul, I am marvelously made! I worship in adoration—what a creation! You know me inside and out, you know every bone in my body; You know exactly how I was made, bit by bit, how I was sculpted from nothing into something" (Ps 139:13–16 MSG).

3. Flurry, "What Makes Man Unique?" (2013).

The Scripture refers to these wonderfully crafted bodies of ours in at least two significant ways. One way is simply as it relates to the natural and normative references to the human body. So, we read of people walking and talking, sitting and standing, running and jumping, sleeping and eating. The physical body is described, in part, as head, eyes, nose, mouth, ears, arms, hands, legs, and feet.

The Bible also uses the physical components of the body metaphorically. We can taste and see that the Lord is good. We can have ears to hear and eyes to see spiritual truth. We can have a heart to hear and bowels of mercy but be careful because Isaiah identifies being obstinate as having a neck of iron and a brow of bronze.

Moreover, any of these physical members can be seen assisting a connection to the One true God. The voice is lifted in prayer and hands in worship. Eyes are closed in meditation or looking up to heaven. Heads bow in humble adoration and bodies lie prostrate in abject submission. We read in the very first Psalm that if you are going to commit to a life of righteousness, you do not *walk* with the ungodly, nor *stand* with sinners, nor pull up a chair and *sit* with the profane.

Ah, but sometimes we do. And therein lies the problem of the flesh. We know there is something more going on with our fleshly existence besides just complex physiology so that we can sit around, and debate how cleverly designed is our grasping thumb. Here we simply need to acknowledge both a blessing and a curse about our flesh.

As noted, the blessing comes as a result of Creation. The cursing, however, is a result of the Fall. That we have bodies means, inevitably, that we must talk about the *Flesh*, and in Scripture, that is rarely a good thing. The Apostle Paul speaks for all of us:

> For we know that the Law is spiritual, but I am of flesh, sold into bondage to sin. For what I am doing, I do not understand; for I am not practicing what I would like to do, but I am doing the very thing I hate (Rom 7:14–15).

> For I know that nothing good dwells in me, that is, in my flesh; for the willing is present in me, but the doing of the good is not. For the good that I want, I do not do, but I practice the very evil that I do not want. But if I am doing the very thing I do not want, I am no longer the one doing it, but sin which dwells in me (Rom 7:18–20).

> I find then the principle that evil is present in me, the one who
> wants to do good. For I joyfully concur with the law of God in
> the inner man, but I see a different law in the members of my
> body, waging war against the law of my mind and making me a
> prisoner of the law of sin which is in my members. O Wretched
> man that I am! Who will set me free from the body of this death?
> (Rom 7:21–24).

Do you see? "Blessing" and "cursing," with the necessary emphasis usually on the cursing. However, there is hope. The natural progression of life is Birth, Living, Growing, Dying. But there can be a *New Birth*. What is seen to be the last verse of Romans 7 needs to be read in context with Romans 8:1. (This is an instance where a chapter division is not helpful.) Paul writes, "I thank God—through Jesus Christ our Lord! So then, with the mind, I myself serve the law of God, but with the flesh the law of sin." But he immediately follows that up with this glorious truth, "There is therefore now no condemnation to those who are in Christ Jesus, who do not walk according to the flesh, but according to the Spirit."

So, we are physical beings. We have a body—a body of flesh, that can lead to fleshly desires and lusts and all kinds of problems. Yet that body was not created to be a brothel but a temple. "Do you not know that your body is a temple of the Holy Spirit within you, whom you have from God? You are not your own, for you were bought with a price. So, glorify God in your body" (1 Cor 6:19–20 ESV).

Spiritual!

With the acknowledgment that we are physical beings, there must come an understanding that we are *spiritual* beings as well. And now, with the "Who am I?" things get more complex (and that may be an understatement). The complexity is not so much in the reality that we have a spiritual nature, it is in trying to fully comprehend what that nature is. While the Bible sets forth man as a unified being, this unity is seen to be divisible into two dimensions—the material and immaterial, the mortal and immortal, the corruptible and the incorruptible, the flesh and the spirit, the physical and the spiritual.

So, the very first question that confronts us when discussing the spiritual nature of man is, do we focus on our spirit only, and what that is, or do we include our soul and what that is? In other words, should soul and spirit be understood interchangeably, or should we understand them as being uniquely distinct and separate? I agree with Wayne Jackson, editor of the Christian Courier, who reminds us that "There is no simple answer to this question because the words soul and spirit are employed in varying senses within the different biblical contexts in which they may be found."[4]

Theologians have continually debated this issue with sides being drawn up along two camps—that man is a dichotomy; having a body and soul/spirit (which are the same), or that man is a trichotomy; being body, soul, and spirit (in which soul and spirit are distinct from each other).

While I have tended to track along trichotomist thinking, my intention is not to be an apologist for either view, but rather simply celebrate the reality that there is much more to us than just our physical bodies. There is no getting away from the fact that we have physical bodies, but the New Testament reveals that our bodies are supposed to function as a temple of the Holy Spirit. That can only be possible due to our spiritual dimension.

The Hebrew concept surrounding the soul (*nephesh*) pertains to the inner nature and entire personality of man. Nephesh has been described as the life *principle*, the living *being*, the *self* with appetite, emotion, and volitional will. Similarly, in Greek thought, the soul (*psuche*) was understood as the seat of emotions, feelings, desire, and affections.

An important idea in Hebrew thought is that it would not be possible for nephesh to exist without a form or manifestation; that is a *body*. The Hebrew concept would never allow for a disembodied nephesh. In Talmudic teaching, the body was thought to be the "scabbard of the soul." An intriguing analogy was set forth that "As the Holy One, blessed be He, fills the whole world, so also the soul fills the whole body, As the Holy One, blessed be He, sees but cannot be seen, so also the soul sees but cannot be seen."[5]

Franz Delitzsch, the famed German theologian, and acclaimed Hebraist referred to the soul as the spirit-embodied nature of man. In his masterful study, *A System of Biblical Psychology,* released in the late nineteenth century, he wrote: "The soul is the mediator in man, having two aspects, bearing upon the spirit and the body respectfully. Ru'ach (Spirit) would only very unintelligently indicate man since he is not pure

---

4. Jackson, "Soul and Spirit: What's the Difference?" (2020).

5. Cohen, *Everyman's Talmud,* 6.

spirit; and sarx (flesh) indicates him only in reference to the sensuous, perishable side of his nature."[6]

If I understand the great theologian correctly, it would seem that it is man's soul that is the unifying bridge between his spiritual nature and his physical nature. Perhaps another way to approach this is as Elmer Towns relates it. He acknowledges that the terms "soul" and "spirit" appear to be used interchangeably at times in Scripture, but that is because they both can refer to the "life-principle" in man. Dr. Towns writes, "We do not say man is a spirit, but that he has a spirit. On the other hand, we say man is a soul. The soul seems to be related to man's earthly life while the spirit relates to man's heavenly life."[7]

Trying to think through this, I have come to formulate this idea: The soul is clothed by the body, and the spirit is at home in the soul. I realize of course that we are not bodies that have souls, but we are souls that have bodies. The German theologian Ludwig Köhler, in discussing Genesis 2:7 and the nature of man wrote, "It says first of all that man became a living soul and now is a living soul. It does not say man has a living soul. Soul is the nature of man, not his possession."[8]

I am intrigued by the way Martin Luther processed this complex subject. He saw man as a trichotomy, but also as divided into two portions. His description lobbies to be at home in both camps. Luther writes: "Scripture divides man into three parts, as says St Paul (1 Thess v. 23). And every one of these three, together with the entire man, is also divided in another way into two portions, which are there called Spirit and Flesh. Which division is not natural, but attributive; i.e. nature has three portions spirit, soul, and body."[9]

And then, creatively, Luther proceeds to offer a stunning analogy of the makeup of man:

> In the tabernacle fashioned by Moses there were three separate compartments. The first was called the holy of holies: here was God's dwelling place, and in it there was no light. The second was called the holy place; here stood a candlestick with seven arms and seven lamps. The third was called the outer court; this lay under the open sky and in the full light of the sun. In this tabernacle we have a figure of the Christian man. His spirit is

6. Delitzsch, *System of Biblical Psychology*, 181.

7. Towns, *Liberty Bible Commentary*, Vol. I, 1235–1236.

8. Köhler, *Old Testament Theology*, 142.

9. Delitzsch, *Biblical Psychology*, 460–462.

the holy of holies, where God dwells in the darkness of faith, where no light is; for he believes that which he neither sees nor feels nor comprehends. His soul is the holy place, with its seven lamps, that is, all manner of reason, discrimination, knowledge, and understanding of visible and bodily things. His body is the forecourt, open to all, so that men may see his works and manner of life.[10]

Perhaps the best attempt to synchronize any distinction between "spirit" and "soul" is offered by H. D. MacDonald. He believed that both terms refer to man's inner nature in contrast to his flesh or body, which he understood as referring to the outer aspect of man as existing in space and time. In this regard, then, he spoke of man's "psychical" nature, the spirit denoting life which originates in God, and soul which expresses that same life as constituted in man. MacDonald writes, "Spirit is the inner depth of man's being, the higher aspect of his personality. Soul expresses man's own special and distinctive individuality. The pneuma is man's nonmaterial nature looking Godward; the psyche is that same nature of man looking earthward and touching the things of sense."[11]

So, even though unseen, our soul is just as real as our body. Our soul, the *psuche*, is the psychological gateway to the world around us. Watchman Nee provided a summary of the soul in which he believed it was composed of our mind, which enables us to do things like think, reason, consider, remember, and wonder; as well as our emotions, which enable us to have feelings like happiness, sorrow, anger, relief, and compassion; and finally our will, which enables us to choose and make decisions. These three—our mind, emotion, and will make up our personality.

More than that, we have our spirit, that "holy of holies" as Luther saw it, in which and from which we can connect with the spiritual realm and with God. It is in and by our spirit that we can know God, receive his new birth, grow and abide in him and worship and praise him. It is where God will be Center. It is why David would exclaim in Psalm 103:1, "Bless the Lord, O my soul; And all that is within me, bless His holy name!"

10. Pelikan, *Luther's Works*, 21:304.

11. MacDonald, *Evangelical Dictionary of Theology*, 678.

Everlasting!

Because we are spiritual beings, it follows that we are *Everlasting* beings. This life is not all there is, and your physical body is not all you are. Scripture affirms that we are *forever* beings, which is not a statement about our physical bodies. John writes, "The world and its desires pass away, but whoever does the will of God lives forever" (1 John 2:17 NIV). It is our inner being, our "soul" which can live on forever.

It is interesting to note, given the previous discussion, that an argument could be made for man as a trichotomy (body, soul, and spirit), especially when you consider the destiny of each. We know the body goes to the grave. "All your life you will sweat to master it, until your dying day. Then you will return to the ground from which you came. For you were made from the ground, and to the ground, you will return" (Gen 3:19 TLB). We understand that the soul goes to heaven (or hell), for "To be absent from the body is to be present with the Lord" (2 Cor 5:8). And then we see that the spirit goes back to God: "Then the dust returns to the ground it came from, and the spirit returns to God who gave it (Eccl 12:7 NIV).

Now, that is interesting. Our bodies return to dust. Our souls will live on, but where they live on is determined by whether we have been born again and have received the gift of everlasting life in Jesus Christ. The Bible sets forth two places for the soul—either heaven with all its rewards, or hell and its abject separation from the manifest presence of God. We need to be careful here, as I have heard some say that what makes hell so awful is the total absence of God. This cannot be possible unless you reject the Omnipresence of God. Read Psalm 139:7–8 and you will understand what I am talking about.

But what about the spirit? While the soul may go to hell, I do not believe the spirit can. And the reason why is that the spirit belongs to God. He gave it. He "breathed" it into man, and we became a living soul once he did. Solomon's statement makes perfect sense when you see that our spirits return to God upon death because our spirits are his. He gave them, he owns them.

The idea of everlasting life is not easy for us to fully understand. How can it be? It is hard to wrap our minds around the concept of life that is not constrained by time nor limited by space. All we know about eternity is that it is a very long time! Buttrick described eternity as a clock that says tick in one century and tock in the next! But even that imaginative description betrays the fact that you cannot describe with time-oriented words that which is timeless.

The Scripture acknowledges our shortcomings in fully comprehending eternity. "He has also set eternity in the hearts of men, yet they cannot fathom what God has done from beginning to end" (Eccl 3:11). There was an old saying, aimed at making Christians feel a little guilty if they were too preoccupied with thoughts of eternity, the hereafter, and heaven. It went like this—you can be so heavenly-minded that you are no earthly good. Catchy? Clever? It sounds good and seemed convincing enough. But then, when you stop to think about it, is it accurate? Perhaps we should seek to redefine it with a greater truth, which is that we are not going to do this world any good until we become heavenly-minded!

C. S. Lewis believed that and thought that a continual obsession with looking forward to the eternal world was something a Christian was supposed to do. He wrote, "It is since Christians have largely ceased to think of the other world that they have become so ineffective in this (one)." And then he offered this insightful challenge, "Aim at Heaven and you will get earth thrown in; aim at earth and you will get neither."[12]

The key to this topic on being everlasting beings is the *life* with which it is associated. We need to appreciate everlasting life and what it means. I believe that at least two especially important concepts need to be stressed. The first may be the most obvious but may not be the most important (nor practical). It is that, at the very least, everlasting life must mean a *quantity of life.*

In the New Testament, the Greek word is *aionios.* This is the adjective based on the noun *aion,* which most scholars agree on means an *age.* There is significant disagreement when it comes to understanding *aionios,* especially given the grammatical reality that an adjective cannot mean something greater than the noun from which it derives.

Having said that, it is also clear that in many contexts in which this word appears it certainly implies that which is perpetual and, as some old lexicons suggest, that which has no horizon. Mostly, we understand it to mean that which is never-ending. This idea can be clearly understood from verses like First John 5:13 and John 3:16 in which everlasting must mean lasting forever. The promise of everlasting life is the promise of God for a never-ending existence with him.

12. Lewis, *Mere Christianity*, 134.

Admittedly, the term *quantity* cannot adequately describe the reality of eternal life. We simply cannot calculate eternity. The great nineteenth-century Methodist preacher, William Munsey, described it this way:

> Eternity cannot be defined. Beginningless and endless it cannot be measured. Its past cannot be increased, and its future cannot be diminished. It has no past, it has no future, it has no ends, it has no middle, it has no parts—it is an unanalyzable, tremendous unity. It began when God began, and He had no beginning; it will end when He will end, and He will have no ending. It is unoriginated, beginningless, endless, measureless, imperishable, indescribable, undefinable thing. Itself is its only definition. It is older than the world, older than the sun, older than the stars, older than the angels, as old as God; yet no older now than when world, suns, stars and angels were made, and never will be any older, yet never any younger.[13]

So, while we think of eternal life in the concept of time and duration, the reality is, it is beyond our human understanding to do so. It is the quantity of life, but that quantity is beyond defining, incalculable, and virtually indescribable. And yet, it is probably accurate to say that most Christians think of eternal life in this most basic way. That it is an indescribable long time which we will receive (realize) once our time on earth has ended and we are ready to begin a life that then becomes timeless.

But eternal life is also something else, something even more than that, in terms of what it is and when you get it. Besides being a quantity of life, it is also a *quality of life*. Eternal Life is not just a quantitative statement, it is a qualitative statement. It is not just a life highlighted by its duration it is a life that should also be marked by its donation. It is not just a life that has no end (an indeterminate quantity of time) that affects only our future, it is also a life that has an unmistakable impact and influence on who we are and what we do right now in the present.

Eternal life is not just a life of future promise, it is a life of present possession. The reality is that God offers us, in this life, another life, which is to be lived right now, as the old preachers used to say, in "the nasty now–and–now, before you ever get to experience it in the sweet bye–and–bye." Therefore, there is an unmistakable dimension in the Bible where we are to understand eternal life as a higher quality of life.

This is an enormous truth—that everlasting life is a present possession. We often think of eternal life as a future possession. It is something

13. Munsey, *Eternal Retribution*, 62.

we will appropriate after death; an inheritance awaiting us in heaven. But when you understand the two-fold nature of eternal life, you will realize that it is not only a life to come, but it is a life to live now.

To Timothy, Paul refers to "having the promise of Life that now is, and of that which is to come" (1 Tim 4:8). In John 5:24, Jesus tells us, "he who hears My word and believes in Him who sent Me has everlasting life, and shall not come into judgment, but has passed from death into life." The two verbs are significant. The first one "*has* everlasting life," is present tense, and therefore means action occurring right now, and the second verb, "*has passed* from death into life," is perfect tense and means completed action that continues to occur. Either one of them proves, and both together is conclusive evidence, that eternal life is a present possession.

It is not hard to see why God would want it this way. The life we receive from him, which affects the quality of our living for him demonstrates its effectiveness in our lives by giving us power over sin (1 John 5:18–20), the capacity to love (1 John 3:14–15), and the willingness to serve God and man.

Perhaps what Jesus says in John 10:10 helps us understand this dynamic. Remember in the context of Jesus identifying himself as the good shepherd, he says regarding his sheep, "The thief does not come except to steal, and to kill, and to destroy. I have come that they may have life and that they may have it more abundantly." The word translated "abundant" is the Greek word *perissos* and can be translated by several related adjectives and adverbs, such as *more, greater, excessive, abundant, exceedingly.* The question we need to ask is, are any of those words intended to describe the life Jesus is talking about quantitatively? The answer is no.

Jesus is not talking about a life that is abundant in years, greater in time, excessive in duration. He is talking about a life that is abundant in living. Abundant life cannot mean quantity, it must be quality. Jesus is talking about a quality of life and not a quantity of life.

Various New Testament versions capture this meaning, for instance, the New Living Translation has it, "My purpose is to give them a rich and satisfying life." The New International Version translates it, "I have come that they may have life, and have it to the full." And we read in the Good News Translation, "I have come in order that you might have life—life in all its fullness."

Interestingly, as a noun, this word can mean *preeminence* or *advantage.* Think of that. Having eternal life is life with an advantage. Albert Barnes, in his *Bible Notes* (1834), suggests what those advantages might be, as he parses the word *perissos,* he wrote: "The word denotes that which is superadded to make life happy. They shall not merely have life—simple, bare existence—but they shall have all those superadded things which are needful to make that life eminently blessed and happy."[14]

Eternal life is not an ordinary life, it is an extraordinary life. It is not just a natural life; it is a life that traffics in the supernatural. It is not a mundane life; it is a remarkable life. I think what Jesus meant is that we can have a never-ceasing, always abounding, over-flowing life in him. It was Benjamin Disraeli who said that life is too short to be too little. The life that Jesus offers us is not too little (and neither is it too short for that matter). It is everlasting life! "And this is the testimony: God has given us eternal life, and this life is in his Son. He who has the Son has life; he who does not have the Son of God does not have life. I write these things to you who believe in the name of the Son of God so that you may know that you have eternal life" (1 John 5:11–13).

Years ago, I wrote a book that was based on this compelling statement that we could have an abundant life. I entitled the book *If I Should Die Before I Live,* the premise being that so many will go through this life without ever experiencing that abundant life that God has for us in Christ. That is beyond sad. It is incredibly tragic. Toward my conclusion, I quoted Franky Schaeffer who wrote in his book *Addicted to Mediocrity* that, "It is time that we Christians who claim to have such an interest in life after death begin to show some interest in a little life before death."[15]

Amen to that!

But it's not easy and we all know it. Perhaps that is why so many give up. It is like the gravestone marker that said *Here Lies John Doe, Died At 45, Buried At 68.* Perhaps too true to be really funny. Similarly, I remember hearing about two friends who were talking and one asked "Do you believe in life after death?" And his friend said, "Heck no, believing in life *before* death is hard enough!" Life is tough, and "real life," abundant life, is constant accountability to the one who gives it. There is a cost that comes with that accountability, but it is so worth it.

The Apostle John concludes his great gospel account with these majestic words informing us why he wrote his life of Christ: "But these are written that you might believe that Jesus is the Christ, the Son of God, and that believing, you might have life through His name" (John 20:31).

---

14. Barnes, *Bible Notes,* John 10:10.
15. Schaeffer, *Addicted to Mediocrity,* 66.

Life with Jesus is endless hope and without him, it is a hopeless end. And this leads to a final observation of what we are to know about ourselves as human beings.

Fallen!

We are *Fallen* beings. The reason we need life is that we are dead; "dead in our trespasses and sins," as Paul says in Ephesian 2:1. We need a Savior and need to be saved because of our sin. We need to be found because we are lost.

I remember reading somewhere that Daniel Boone, the historic American pioneer, and frontiersman, was once asked if he had ever been lost. He responded, no, but he was bewildered a lot! Well, man is not only bewildered—he is also lost.

"Lost" is a biblical word and carries heavy Scriptural and spiritual weight. It signifies the condition of unregenerate man—man separated from God. The word cannot, and must not, be trivialized or marginalized. It is essentially and ultimately tied to the mission of Christ, "for the Son of Man has come to seek and to save that which was lost" (Luke 19:10).

The Greek text gives us the word *apollumi* which means to destroy or to perish. It pictures permanent destruction, the implication of which is total ruin. The Hebrew equivalent (for instance, as seen in Ps 119:176 or Jer 50:6) is *abad*, which also means to perish, destroy, to annihilate. To experience "apollumi" / "abad" is to utterly perish by experiencing the most miserable end imaginable.

The famed mid-nineteenth-century southern preacher William Elbert Munsey (known for his oratorical skills) tried to imagine it. He kept his audiences spellbound as he described the lost soul "plunging into an ocean of darkness interminable, where no sight or sound will ever greet its aching sense and doomed to wander in the pathless void while cycles roll, and ages go grinding on." "Lost!" he would bellow, and then continue, "where no echoes will ever mock thy misery. Lost in boundless, bottomless, infinite darkness where thou shalt never find company till the ghost of eternity will greet you over the grave of God, and thou shalt never find rest till thou art able to fold thy wings on the gravestone of thy Maker!"[16]

16. Munsey, *Eternal Retribution*, 103–104.

Wow, hard to miss his point isn't it?

If you go out into eternity lost, you are never coming back! This is a frightening prospect and one that should give us great pause. There is much debate as to whether traditional views of "hell" as a place of never-ending punishment are biblical. I will admit that my understanding has shifted somewhat as I continue to process the possible distinction between eternal punish*ment* and eternal punish*ing*, which makes God an eternal punish*er*. We can save that argument for another time because none of those distinctions change any facts relating to being lost.

Getting back to the fiery oratory of Munsey, is this just some southern fire and brimstone sermonizing? Are people really lost? Are your neighbors and friends lost? Are your coworkers and colleagues lost? Are there some in your family, immediate or extended, that are lost? Are people lost today and if they die and go out into a Christless eternity, will they be forever doomed to wander that way only until "God dies and is buried" (which of course means never!)?

Some want to say that people are misguided, but not really "lost." They are misinformed, but not lost. Surely, they are just somehow misplaced, but that doesn't mean that they are lost. But what does the Bible say? "For all have sinned and fall short of the glory of God" (Rom 3:23).

We know that the root of the fall of mankind is traced to the account in Genesis 3, in which Adam and Eve disobey God's word and will. As a result of Adam's intentional disobedience, all of Adam's "helpless" race is plunged into sin, and lostness, and death. Paul is succinct in his description of this in Romans 5:12: "Sin came into the world because of what one man did, and with sin came death. This is why everyone must die—because everyone sinned" (NCV).

When most theologians speak of the total depravity of man, they refer to the reality that as a result of the Fall, man is corrupt in the totality of his being. No part of man's being is spared from this corruption, untouched by this defilement. There is no area within man that remains unspoiled and uncorrupt. Man is depraved and morally bankrupt in his body, soul, and spirit.

That what occurred in the antiquity of Genesis chapter Three spans into the New Testament era of the apostle Paul, and indeed, beyond to our very day, is proof-positive of the seriousness of the Fall. That what befell mankind because of the transgression in the garden ultimately led Jesus Christ to a garden tomb is all you need to know about the Fall.

I remember my Old Testament professor in Bible College saying that he thought Genesis Three was the most important chapter in the entire Bible. And why? Because without it, you would not understand or know what Genesis chapter Four through Revelation chapter Twenty-two was all about. I think he was correct. Genesis 3 is the reason for John 3:16.

This leads to an important observation about lostness and God's perfect plan to *find* us. As we talk about who we are and the complexities of being human beings; created, unique, physical, spiritual, everlasting beings, it comes down to this—there are only two types of people on earth. There are those who are "lost," and those of us who have been "found." Which one are you?

At the end of the day, after all the posturing and positioning, after all the labeling and libeling, after all the defining and defaming, it comes down to this: There are only two types of people on earth—just two! The distinction has nothing to do with race, color, or creed. It has nothing to do with nationality, commonality, or ethnicity. It has nothing to do with country, citizenship, or political parties. It has nothing to do with liberalism, conservatism, or progressivism. It has nothing to do with alternate lifestyles, gender identity, or sexual preference. It has nothing to do with social status, tax brackets, or financial portfolios. It has nothing to do with sectarianism, denominations, or religious affiliations.

It has only to do with how many births you have and how many deaths you're going to have. Therefore, we can state it this way: there are those who have been born once but will die twice, and there are those who have been born twice and will die once.

We all have our one physical birth, and we will all experience our one physical death. But God offers us a second birth, a new birth (John 3:3–8), and when we are born again, we are therefore spared from a second death, which awaits all those who are lost.

That second death is referred to in Revelation 20:14, "And death and hell were cast into the lake of fire. This is the second death." Compare that to John 11:26, where Jesus said, "Whoever lives and believes in Me shall never die." He was not talking about physical death, but rather the far worse spiritual death that awaits all who do not believe in Him.

So, that is all there is. There are those born twice and who only die once (the natural physical death), and those born once but who will, therefore, due to never receiving God's gift of eternal life through the new birth, die twice. It remains every man's choice.

Through You

You have been created by God—do you appreciate your uniqueness? You are called upon to love the Lord with all your heart, mind, soul, and strength. We are challenged to bring into submission our entire Body, Soul, and Spirit to the will of God. Our privilege is to commit our inner man and outward nature into service for Christ.

This has been a whirlwind tour of who we are "warts and all." It is the *miracle and mystery* and the *majesty and meanness* of man. We have to know both sides. We have to see ourselves completely. In *Pensées,* a collection of his random thoughts, Pascal was thinking clearly on this subject. He wrote: "It is dangerous to make man see too clearly his equality with the brutes without showing him his greatness. It is also dangerous to make him see his greatness too clearly apart from his vileness. It is still more dangerous to leave him in ignorance of both. But it is very advantageous to show him both."[17]

If Pascal is right, then the greatest advantage is that we come to realize that we are, after all, very important in the biblical scheme of things. We are significantly and strategically positioned in the paradigm outlined in Matthew 22:37–39. We are one of the three entities that make up this Scriptural equation – God, Neighbor, Self.

We are not an unnecessary evil thrust into the mix. We are an essential ingredient in the recipe of redemption and the proliferation of the gospel. As God is our center, he can touch those around us, through us, and he can be seen by those around us, through us. That is how special he has made us.

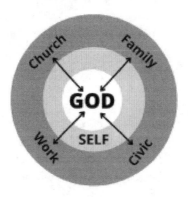

---

17. Pascal, "Pensées," No. 418.

Ten | How To Love Self And Not Sin!

IT IS SURPRISING HOW MUCH of our modern life is affected by the residue of ancient mythological concepts (for instance, every day of our week has a name linked to ancient mythology, as well as every month of the year, except for the four numbered months). I am fascinated with Greek mythology, as well as how ancient Greek culture and language impact us to this day.

Hardly Scriptural revelation and truth, the reality is ancient Near Eastern mythological beliefs occur frequently on the pages of the Bible. The word of God accurately records stories and events in their historical and cultural context. Effective Biblical interpretative methods understand the value that such cultural context brings in the process of unpacking a Bible text accurately. In the New Testament, both Greek and Roman mythology lend historical coloring and provide valuable context in interpreting numerous passages, such as Acts 12:21–24, Acts 14:11–18, Acts 17:16–33, and Acts 19:23–41, just to name a few.

An imperfect and fanciful spin on reality as it was, I am convinced that the Greeks developed their elaborate mythology to help them understand the complexities of their world and to somehow lessen the pain of their human predicament. It was a way they could give expression to the natural phenomena all around them. Accordingly, they became quite proficient at crafting an allegorical worldview that impacted everything they did and provided an epic explanation for everything they were.

Beware the Reflection

For instance, consider this intriguing story originating in Greek mythology that sets the stage for a dramatic anecdote that may tell us a little something about ourselves. It is the story of a young man, the son of the river god *Kephissos* who was told by a seer that his son would live a long and prosperous life as long as he never got to know himself. And so, some years went by and the boy grew up into a young man, and he was very handsome to look upon.

One day while he was out hunting in the woods, he was followed by the nymph *Echo*, who loved him but was too afraid to approach him. Knowing he was being followed, he turned and yelled out, "Who is there?" and Echo replied, "Who is there?" (Of course, what else?) Being discovered, she approached him and confessed her love, but was immediately rejected by him. Pushing her away, *Echo* fled brokenhearted and, as a result, eventually withered away leaving only her voice to be heard.

The young man continued his journey and came upon a clear pool and bending over to drink he was captivated by the reflection of himself in the water. Immediately he was spellbound by his own beauty! Enthralled by his elegant face, he attempted to kiss the image in the water, but every time he did so, the ripples disturbed the image. He found himself transfixed, starring into the water at his image, and was so enraptured with it, he refused to move or even to look away. Unwilling to take his eyes off himself, eventually as a result of hunger and thirst, he expired where he lay.

From that time on, to mark the tragedy on the spot where he died, a flower emerged and blossomed every spring. Whereupon the Greeks then named the flower after the name of the young man who fell in love with himself. For you see, the name of *Kephissos'* son was *Narcissus*, and so then is the name of the flower. You may know it by its more modern name, which is a Daffodil. (And I am sorry, but it's hard not to think that the more modern name came about because let's face it, is it not "daffy" for you to love yourself that much!)

Today, those overcome with their own reflection, who are so totally absorbed with their own person, so in love with themselves while rejecting all others, are referred to as being narcissistic. (And now you know why.) Narcissus is alive and well in our modern world.

Lovers of Ourselves

Today, psychologists and sociologists are increasingly alarmed by the epidemic proportions of narcissism and how much of it is being fueled by an addiction to social media. In an article entitled *Humility and Haughtiness,* Dr. Ryan Fraser, who is an associate professor of clinical mental health counseling at Freed-Hardeman University and a licensed clinical pastoral therapist wrote, "Without a doubt, we live in a narcissistic world. Self-promotion and self-aggrandizement are seemingly part-and-parcel of our society. Social media sites like Facebook, Twitter, Tumblr, Instagram, Snap Chat, Pinterest, and YouTube tend to exacerbate this cultural epidemic."[1]

Recent statistics show that almost half of the entire world population will be Online, and that two-thirds of all Internet users will visit social media sites. The prediction is that one in every three people in the world will use one or more of the social media platforms. Social media is changing the world as we know it.

Narcissism is on the rise in our culture, a direct result of the increasing social-networking platforms that become, among other things, narcissistic playgrounds. Perhaps some of this was inevitable and predictable. The Apostle Paul saw it coming and wrote that in the last days, "People will be lovers of themselves" (2 Tim 3:1 NIV). J. B. Phillips renders it: "Men will become utterly self-centered." There seems to be little disagreement that social media platforms tend to encourage self-promotion and it is self-promotion that drives narcissism.

Narcissism is an unhealthy preoccupation with *Self.* It is egocentrism when we should be acknowledging God as Center. The narcissist is focused upon self-interests, self-promotion, and self-dependency. And this flies in the face of numerous Scriptures which admonish us to do just the opposite: "Do nothing out of selfish ambition or vain conceit. Rather, in humility value others above yourselves" (Phil 2:3 NIV). "Do not think of yourself more highly than you ought, but rather think of yourself with sober judgment"(Rom 12:3 NIV). "Turn my heart toward your statutes and not toward selfish gain" (Ps 119:36 NIV).

In his book, *What is Man?* German theologian Wolfhart Pannenberg observed that "men repeatedly interrupt their course through the world toward God, (and instead) they establish themselves in the world and forget their quest for God." Explaining further, he writes, "Men do

1. Fraser, "Humility and Haughtiness," (2018).

not forget God simply because they are lazy. This forgetfulness has a deeper root, namely, man's ego-centricity."[2]

Elaborating on this premise, he suggests that too often "man remains imprisoned in his selfhood," and that this closes man off from the God who summons him to his destiny. Pannenberg's verdict is that this "selfhood" that closes us up within itself is sin and that this sin "asserts itself on the one hand in unbelief by denying God the reverence and grateful trust due Him, and on the other hand in the greed by which man makes himself a slave of the things for which he strives."[3]

So, how are we to avoid this sinful selfhood with its imprisonment and slavery? We must think of ourselves the way Scripture exhorts. We know we are to follow the example of Jesus Christ, as Paul challenges us in Philippians 2:5–8. Eugene Peterson's paraphrase in *The Message* is compelling reading:

> Think of yourselves the way Christ Jesus thought of himself. He had equal status with God but didn't think so much of himself that he had to cling to the advantages of that status no matter what. Not at all. When the time came, he set aside the privileges of deity and took on the status of a slave, became human! Having become human, he stayed human. It was an incredibly humbling process. He didn't claim special privileges. Instead, he lived a selfless, obedient life and then died a selfless, obedient death—and the worst kind of death at that—a crucifixion.

Peterson's insertion of the idea of *special privileges* is important to point out given that our day is also marked by an increasing sense of entitlement. It seems clear that narcissism and entitlement are consorts. Scott Barry Kaufman wrote a thought-provoking blog entitled *Do Narcissists Ever Grow Up?* In the article he wrote, "Entitlement is the narcissism facet most toxic for maintaining satisfying relationships and is associated with expecting special treatment, devaluing others, and being disagreeable."[4]

The relationship between narcissism and a sense of entitlement is underscored in an important book co-authored by psychiatrists Jean M. Twenge and W. Keith Campbell. The title of their book is *The Narcissism Epidemic (Living in the Age of Entitlement)*. In the first chapter, *The Many Wonders of Admiring Yourself*, the good doctors label narcissistic

2. Pannenberg, *What is Man?* 55.

3. Pannenberg, *What is Man?* 63.

4. Kaufman, "Do Narcissists Ever Grow Up?" (2019).

personality disorder (NPD) as being traits that "include grandiosity, a lack of empathy and a need to be admired."[5]

Narcissists demand respect they have not earned, expect rewards they have not achieved, crave recognition that is not warranted, and believe they deserve admiration without accomplishment. It has been said that entitlement is the attitude that the world owes you something in exchange for nothing. There are those today who feel they are entitled to things they have not earned, enjoy things they have not paid for, and experience benefits they do not have any valid claim to.

In reality, the only ones who actually should be allowed to act entitled are infants. And if we acknowledge that, doesn't it tell us something about the attitude of entitlement? Kaufman was right to question whether narcissists ever grow up. As a personality disorder, it is a character flaw that fluctuates between being infantile and insane.

One thing seems clear, narcissism and immaturity go hand in hand. Many psychologists recognize that narcissism is the opposite of maturity. John Townsend is a life coach and psychologist and has written that a sense of entitlement is based upon two beliefs – a belief that you are exempt from responsibility and the belief that you are owed special treatment. He warns that both lead to alienation, frustration and are ultimately destructive to the person's future.

Not Who We Think We Are

Why are we so obsessed with the idea that people are always thinking about us? And because we think they are, we allow it to shape who we are. I remember a quote I read somewhere some time ago and I have never forgotten it. It provides a stimulating philosophical challenge. It went something like this: "We are not who we think we are. We are not even who people think we are. We are who we think people think we are!"

Now think about that for a moment. Ask yourself honestly, do you fashion who you are based on who people *think* you are? It may be unavoidable at times, but we become (intentionally or not) the very person that has been projected upon us by those around us. There is certain inauthenticity about the whole thing.

More than that, there is an unhealthy ramification to that type of living my life based on what I think someone thinks I am. One of the

5. Twenge and Campbell, *The Narcissism Epidemic*, 22.

ramifications is that it fuels a narcissism that is driven by low self-esteem. The truth is, we need to get over ourselves. You will be liberated once you come to terms with the fact that not everyone on Facebook is thinking about you. Wise Winston Churchill once observed that when you're twenty you care what everybody is thinking about you, and when you're forty you stop caring what everybody is thinking about you, and when you're sixty you realize that no one was ever thinking about you in the first place!

Of course, the key thing here is not so much what people are thinking about you (or, whether they are even thinking about you, or not), it is how much you are thinking about yourself. As has been suggested by some—we should not think less of ourselves, just think of ourselves less. One betrays low self-esteem, which is not humility, while the other would portray true humility. In any case, the real battle is against pride. Jason Meyer is correct in saying, "The problem of pride does not boil down to whether we think high thoughts or low thoughts about ourselves but that we think lots of thoughts about ourselves."[6]

The Deal-Killer

Pride is certainly a preoccupation with self. Pride is a sinister fixation on me, myself, and mine. It is an obsession with an obeisance of myself. I pay homage to who I am. It is self-exaltation, self-promotion, and self-service. And for those reasons, pride is a deal-killer in our relationship with God.

The Scriptures lining up against pride keep coming and could not be any clearer. "When pride comes, then comes shame" (Prov 11:2). "A man's pride will bring him low" (Prov 29:23). "The haughtiness of men shall be brought low" (Isa 11:17). "The proud shall stumble and fall" (Jer 50:32). "Pride goes before destruction and a haughty spirit before a fall" (Prov 16:18). "God resists the proud but gives grace to the humble" (Jas 4:6, 1 Pet 5:5). "Whoever shall exalt himself shall be abased; and he that shall humble himself, shall be exalted" (Matt 23:12).

Jesus offered an interesting story which serves as a parable about pride. It is a comparison of two men, both of whom approach God as they enter the Temple to pray:

6. Meyer, "Think of Yourself Less," (2015).

He also told this parable to some who trusted in themselves that they were righteous, and treated others with contempt: "Two men went up into the temple to pray, one a Pharisee and the other a tax collector. The Pharisee, standing by himself, prayed thus: 'God, I thank you that I am not like other men, extortioners, unjust, adulterers, or even like this tax collector. I fast twice a week; I give tithes of all that I get.' But the tax collector, standing far off, would not even lift up his eyes to heaven, but beat his breast, saying, 'God, be merciful to me, a sinner!' I tell you; this man went down to his house justified, rather than the other. For everyone who exalts himself will be humbled, but the one who humbles himself will be exalted" Luke 18:9–14 (ESV).

While we should keep an eye on the humble publican, it is hard not to see the pride of the pharisee. And when you look at him, you will notice that he had a *Good Eye* on himself. He had "I" trouble (vss 11–12). What links sin and pride together? The "I" in the middle. If this self-righteous Pharisee had favorite hymns, undoubtedly, they were "How Great I art" and "Joyful, joyful, I adore me."

This Pharisee also had a *Bad Eye* on others. He treated others with contempt. He despised others. No doubt in typical pharisaical fashion, he prayed every morning thanking God that he was not created a Gentile, a dog, or a woman. What hubris! what arrogance!

And then, ultimately, this Pharisee had *No Eye* on God. He seems to "address" God rather than pray to Him. It seems like he is going to pray, but notice in verse11 Jesus says, "He prayed thus with himself" (one version has it, "The Pharisee stood and prayed *to* himself," WEB) The Lord said he trusted in himself, believed in his own righteousness, and wound up praying to himself.

The statement in verse 11, that "The Pharisee stood and prayed thus" is especially compelling. The word can be translated as "to take a stand" and even to "strike a stance" (as in strike a pose). It seems that what is implied is an attitude of defiance. The Amplified Version renders it, "The Pharisee stood [ostentatiously] and began praying to himself [in a self-righteous way]." To be ostentatious is to be showy, designed to impress. Compare this then with the Publican, who would not even lift his head. The proud Pharisee had no eye on God, and the humble publican, without even looking up, saw God more clearly. Seventeenth-century Anglican cleric Richard Crashaw also saw what was happening rather clearly, as he penned his compelling epigram, "Steps to the Temple."

> Two men went up to pray, or rather say,
> One went to brag, the other to pray.
> One stands so close and treads on high,
> Where the other dare not lift his eye!
> One, nearer to the altar trod—
> The other, to the altar's God.

Sadly, this stiff-necked attitude can be woven into the DNA of the religious. It was with Israel. The prophet Hosea decried the attitude that was evident in Israel of his day. He wrote about those who, "do not direct their deeds toward turning to their God, for the spirit of harlotry is in their midst, and they do not know the Lord. The pride of Israel testifies to his face; Therefore, Israel and Ephraim stumble in their iniquity; Judah also stumbles with them" (Hos 5:4–5).

An interesting interpretation hinges on who is the antecedent for the pronoun "his" in verse 5? Some suggest that the pride of Israel testifies back on them. The "his face" is, therefore, a reference to Israel. I find that to be a curious interpretation. I believe, rather, that the pronoun is a reference to the God of Israel, and that their pride testifies to *His* face. The context can support both views, but I think this one is the correct one and has a more powerful application.

When we are proud, when we are striking a pose, when we are taking that defiant stance (like the Pharisee in Luke 18), then we are shouting in the face of God! We are saying "Look at me!" "Look what I've done!" "I'm so important!" But never forget, when you want to get into God's Face, be careful what you ask for because God resists the proud! Uniquely, especially in light of the above, the Greek word is *antitasso* which means to be *set* or *stationed against*. Remember, when you want to take your stance—God has a bigger stance!

Let me illustrate with an old story I heard once. A ship was making its way through a thick fog when the captain on the bridge noticed a light beacon dead ahead. He transmitted a light signal: *We are on a collision course, turn five degrees south.* He was surprised to receive a response which signaled: *You must turn five degrees north.* The ship's captain decided to pull rank by ordering: *This is Admiral Cloudman, you must turn five degrees south.* He was further irritated by the response, *This is Seaman First Class Wesley, you turn five degrees north.* Outraged by the apparent insubordination, the Admiral was ready for a fight, signaling, *This is a battleship turn five degrees south immediately!* Flashing out the last message, Seaman Wesley replied: *This is a lighthouse. you better turn five degrees north!*

God hates pride. God resists pride. The forces of heaven are marshaled to bring down the proud. And why? Because, as Augustine said, pride is the sin of sins. It is not just the first sin it is the root cause of all sin. Saying that pride is the worst of all sins may challenge some conventional thinking, especially when we want to believe that all sin is sinful in God's sight. Of course, it is, but not all sin is equal in God's sight.

Then we hear someone say, "Well, all sin is the same in God's eyes." Well, no, actually it is not. That statement is only true insofar as it relates to the effect of sin, which is missing the mark of God's holy standards and the subsequent separation from God that can result. Jesus believed that some sins were greater than others. His statement to Pilate in John 19:11 that those delivering him to be crucified had the "greater sin" proves it. If there are greater sins, then there are lesser sins. Is your teenager who just lied to you about doing his homework sinning at the same level as a mass murderer? They are both sins to be sure, but they are not morally nor dynamically equivalent.

The Most Sinister Sin

When it comes to pride, God knows that it is more sinister than any other sin. Pride is the worst because it is the first! Pride is the "taproot" of sin. It leads to all other sins, greater or lesser. Pride is the underlying cause of all sin. Excavate your sin and beneath it all, you'll discover the rotting debris of pride and arrogance. Legion are the sins that are the direct fallout of pride: envy, bitterness, strife, deceit, hypocrisy, slander, greed, just to name some, and all find their root in pride.

C. S. Lewis was once asked what is the great sin, what sin is worse than any other? And his answer was, "The essential vice, the utmost evil, IS PRIDE. Unchastity, anger, greed, drunkenness, and all that, are mere fleabites in comparison. It was through pride that the Devil became the Devil: Pride leads to every other vice. It is the complete anti-God state of mind."[7]

Pride is also a direct assault on God himself. No other sin is as a direct assault on Him! Pride defies God and deifies self. As has been said by many, God resists the proud because the proud resist God. Pride is

7. Lewis, *Mere Christianity*, 109.

spiritual rebellion; it is treason against the King and his kingdom. Pride supplants the rule of God over your life with the rule of your own will. That is why Psalm 10:4 declares that pride is practical atheism: "In the pride of his face the wicked does not seek him; all his thoughts are, 'There is no God.'" C. S. Lewis is right. Pride is the *complete anti-God state of mind*. He would write, "It is a terrible thing that the worst of all the vices can smuggle itself into the very center of our religious life."[8]

As a result, pride puts us into direct conflict with God. We need to understand that some crises are thrust upon us, but some we bring on ourselves. Pride in our lives is an invitation to have a throw-down with God, and we started it. And God will finish it. We cannot win this fight (nor should we). The psalmist gives us God's word on the matter, "The one who has a haughty look and a proud heart. Him I will not endure" (Ps 101:5). One translation has God saying, "I will not tolerate" the proud and another has it, "I will not allow the proud to prevail."

When the Scriptures say that God resists the proud, that does not mean that he simply ignores the proud or avoids the proud or keeps his distance from the proud. The word means He actively resists them. He works in opposition to them. He wages war against them! And the resistance is personal. The Word does not say that he stands against pride, it says that he stands against the proud! More than opposing the concept of pride, God opposes the proud person. When you display a proud heart, God is against you. Wow!

You are *not* going to win that confrontation. There is no other cause and effect that affects us more quickly than pride. First comes pride then comes destruction. First comes pride then comes calamity. First comes pride then comes a fall. (Prov 16:18)

And here is yet another reason God hates pride so much—pride presents a distortion of who we are. Pride declares our self-sufficiency when, really, we are not sufficient of ourselves (2 Cor 3:5). Pride announces our self-dependency when what we desperately need is to lean upon the Lord (Prov 3:5). Pride is always telling you to do something you should not and be someone you are not. It messes with your head as well as your heart. It creates in us what I call the "Babylonian heart" (after a study of the Book of Daniel). The Babylonian heart loves to boast in itself. We learn this from Nebuchadnezzar. And it has been true of all those like him, from Haman to Herod, to Hitler to Hussein.

---

8. Lewis, *Mere Christianity*, 111.

Proverbs 26:12 says appropriately, "Do you see a person wise in their own eyes? There is more hope for a fool than for them." Why? Because at least a fool knows that he does not know anything. But the proud person thinks he knows it all and is responsible for it all.

If our analysis is correct, then pride is at the core of narcissism and the sense of entitlement so prevalent in our society today. One thing about the proud and that is they share the same three tell-tale traits. First, they seek *Recognition*. They thrive on publicity and must be noticed. Secondly, they crave *Respect*, even if they haven't earned it. And a third trait is that they will always demand their *Rights*. Currently, our culture is obsessed with "rights-mania." We live in a time when an emphasis on personal autonomy is being severed from personal accountability. I heard it said once that God created *right* and Satan came along and added the "*s.*"

What about Loving Myself?

Okay, so let us get back to Paul's statement that "People will be lovers of themselves." Now we have a little bit of a problem—a seeming contradiction in Scripture. We have Paul saying that people will love themselves and his meaning is that it is not a good thing that we do. But then in Matthew 22:37–38, Jesus says we are to love ourselves! So, which is it? Adding to our dilemma, doesn't the Bible teach that we should deny ourselves as well? Doesn't the Bible teach that we should prefer others over ourselves? And is not self-love a pride of self, which we know brings us into opposition with God? Therefore, considering everything presented up to this point, would not "loving yourself" equal classic and clinical narcissism?

This seeming contradiction must be tackled head-on. Is Jesus teaching self-love and if so, how can we do that and not be narcissistic? How can we love ourselves and not be guilty of pride? How can we love ourselves and not sin? Being confident that Jesus is not going to contradict the clear teachings of Scripture, there is one thing we can be sure of and that is when Jesus said we are to love ourselves he was not talking about the love of self that is driven by narcissism and motivated by pride.

I have always employed a hermeneutical principle that when two verses of Scripture appear to be in contradiction with each other, the resolution of the problem lies elsewhere. That is to say, another passage of Scripture will provide a solution to the seeming contradiction and in doing so, bring clarity. That hermeneutical principle can now be applied to this problem. The passage that I think provides the solution is where Jesus says, "So in everything, do to others what you would have them do to you, for this sums up the Law and the Prophets" (Matt 7:12 NIV).

Consider this statement, related as it is both to Leviticus 19:18 and what Jesus says in Matthew 22:39, and see how it provides an understanding of what Jesus meant by saying we should love ourselves. In Matthew 22:39 we are told to love our neighbors as we love ourselves. In Matthew 7:12 the word love is not used, but the verb *do* is used. Combining the two ideas we understand that we are to treat our neighbor the way we would want our neighbor to treat us, and in so doing, we are showing God's love to them.

In the statement "love your neighbor as yourself," the command is aimed at how you will extend God's love to your neighbor. Notice that Jesus is not commanding us to love ourselves. Self-love is assumed in the text, but not commanded. Why? Because self-love is our default position. The command assumes the reality of our natural and normal love and cares for ourselves. The apostle Paul verifies that when he writes, "After all, nobody ever hates his own flesh: he feeds it and takes care of it" (Ephesians 5:29 NTE).

The reason Scripture never says to love yourself is that it is normal to love yourself (and therefore, it would be abnormal not to love yourself). No one has to tell you to love yourself because it ought to come naturally. We love ourselves and so it makes perfect sense for Scripture to tell us to love our neighbors as we love ourselves. The command is to love our neighbor, the comparison is as we love ourselves. What Scripture does warn us about is the self-love that is an inordinate preoccupation with self. Our focus should not be on ourselves but others. We must trade any self-centered love for agape love because agape love is the love that serves and sacrifices for others.

Therefore, the command to "love your neighbor as yourself" is essentially telling us to treat other people as well as we treat ourselves. Self-love is not an introspective prioritization of self. Various biblical injunctions on self-denial warn us about making a priority of ourselves. There is no doubt that we must be careful when dealing with "self." Calvin Miller wrote that "self" is the original four-letter word!

It is also clear that most Christians do not understand what a "denying of self" means. Miller reminds us that "Scripture never encourages us to *negate* ourselves (become nonexistent). Scripture teaches us to *deny* ourselves, to abdicate our passions and get rid of those things that claim our lives with petty self-interest."[9]

In his excellent book, *Into the Depths of God*, Miller has a chapter on *Arriving at Self-Understanding* in which he identifies the two choices before us; either choose to deny ourselves and live in a relationship with Christ or pursue that which he refers to as a meaningless pursuit on the wide road. Describing that prioritization of self, he writes: "The body beautiful is the ultimate value on that road. Ego is the small Baal of the surface generation, who choose in favor of themselves. Their values are all chalk and plaster. On that road, Mr. Dow and Mr. Jones direct the traffic. Life is generally conceived to exist at the corner of Wall Street and Sunset Boulevard. There Calvin Klein has an obsession and Victoria a secret."[10]

In the Book of Proverbs, Solomon said "To acquire wisdom is to love yourself" (Prov 19:8 NLT), so to love yourself and to accomplish it with biblical wisdom requires some understanding. We need to know how to do it. So, we come to a "how-to" moment. Allow me to suggest that the *how* and the *way* we are to love ourselves can be understood with three proactive mindsets. I say mindset because we need to think clearly and biblically about who we are and what we are supposed to be. Scripture promises us a sound mind (2 Tim 1:7) and a renewed mind (Rom 12:2) and ultimately the mind of Christ (Phil 2:5) so that we can think upon all things surrounding us with honesty, purity, and virtue (Phil 4:8). The three mindsets that I have in mind are these:

- We need to *sustain* healthy self-esteem,
- We need to *refrain* from feelings of inferiority, and,
- We need to *maintain* biblical humility.

Sustaining Self-Esteem

Self-esteem is usually described as how we view and think about ourselves. As a result of the way we think about ourselves, we then arrive at varying degrees of how we value (or devalue) and approve (or disapprove) of ourselves. Simply put, self-esteem is the set of feelings you have

9. Miller, *Into the Depths of God*, 107.
10. Miller, *Into the Depths of God*, 164–165.

about yourself. The core of self-esteem is formed around whether you like yourself or not.

The idea, then, of self-esteem and particularly low self-esteem, is crucial to our day. Years ago, when he was one of the leading, nationally known ministers in America, Robert Schuller published a book entitled *Self Esteem, The New Reformation*. It was a Schullerized exposition of the Lord's prayer and fell short of achieving a "new reformation," but he did leave us with an outstanding definition of self-esteem: "Self-esteem is the human hunger for the divine dignity that God intended to be our emotional birthright as children created in his image."[11]

In defining self-esteem, Schuller pointed out that he had struggled over the years with just what term to use. Earlier he would have referred to *self-love*, at another time it was *self-dignity*, then, *self-value*. Others have struggled similarly; Norm Wright referred to *self-image*. Peter Wagner used *self-concept*. Still, others have suggested *self-worth*. I would like to offer the term *self-significance*.

I am convinced that at the heart of this issue is discovering significance to life. Professional counselor and founder of Rapha, Robert S. Mcgee is the author of the much-heralded book *The Search for Significance: Seeing Your True Worth Through God's Eyes*. He addresses the various terms, but as his title suggests, he too sees the significance in self-significance. He writes, "Whether labeled 'self-esteem' or 'self-worth,' the feeling of significance is crucial to the emotional, spiritual, and social stability of people. The need to believe we are significant is the driving element within the human spirit."[12]

What happens when this self-esteem dips too low, and a person is running on empty? We refer then to *low self-esteem*. We are overcome with a sense of little or no worth. We believe that life has no or little value. A feeling of insignificance overwhelms us, and life starts to stagnate. Any further development stalls and our growth is stunted.

In ancient times prison cells were purposely constructed with slightly lowered ceilings. They were just low enough so that the average man occupying the cell would never be able to stand up straight to his full height. Cruelly, it was believed that this was an effective means by which to torture and demoralize a victim. Psychologically, low self-esteem accomplishes the same damaging distortion. Oppressed by such inadequate

---

11. Schuller, *Self Esteem, The New Reformation*, 15.

12. McGee, *Search for Significance*, 13.

views of self-significance, people are never able to stand up straight and attain a full stature emotionally, socially, and spiritually.

Do not forget that Paul spent time in those undersized prisons such as Mamertine in Rome. I remember visiting Mamertine prison and I could not stand up straight in the cell. It gave me a graphic perspective on why Paul wrote often of expanding and growing and reaching fullness in Christ. You can see why Paul, from that prison cell, exhorts Christians to grow "to the measure of the stature of the fullness of Christ" (Eph 4:13). We can have a better understanding of why Paul prayed for us that we might be able to know "the breadth and length and height and depth" of the love of Christ (Eph 4:18).

So, we need to know how to stand up to our full height. There is certainly enough of life that depresses us and squashes us. Essentially, then, what we are dealing with is a dynamic that robs a life of fullness, that threatens you with a sense of being a nobody, even though you would like to be a somebody. It is a preoccupation with meaninglessness. It betrays potential. It enslaves its victim in a prison of inadequacy and inability.

It is one of Satan's chief devices and is at the center of what the fall of humanity is all about. Satan's taunt is that we are nothing. We are a zero with the rim rubbed out. We are useless, miserable, sorry excuses for the once noble creation of God. We are rejected and wretched and, on top of that, worthless. We will never amount to anything, so don't even try.

I can recall, during a family devotion time when my two daughters were little, I was reading from Luke chapter four concerning the temptation of Christ. To make it meaningful, I decided to delegate the reading parts among the family. My wife took the narration lines, and I gave my older daughter the lines where Jesus was speaking, and not feeling comfortable in giving Satan's part to anyone else, I was going to read those verses.

Well, my younger daughter, seeing that mom was going to be somebody, and her sister was going to be somebody, and dad was going to be somebody, immediately felt left out. She had no part. She had no lines to read. She had no identity. And so, with a sad look in her eyes she objected and said, "Oh daddy, I'm nothing!" It occurs to me that so many people feel just like that. They are not narrators, they are not saviors, they are not even devils, they are just "nothings."

We live in a complex world that is becoming ever-increasingly an impersonal one. We are constantly bombarded by propaganda informing us that this project or that program is significant; that some group's issues or someone's ideas are significant; that owning more things is significant, or attaining more wealth is crucial. But the truth of the matter is that only people are significant. You are what matters. You are significant. You are important. You are not "nothing." That is the devil's idea, it is not God's.

Jesus died for people, not programs. He invested His life to purchase back human dignity, not home mortgages. His goal is to undo that which the Fall occasioned; that is, to infuse back into men and women their significance and their worth.

Unworthy but not Worthless

A sense of inferiority is a by-product of unhealthy self-esteem. Our word inferior comes from the Latin word that means *below* or *beneath*. But it is more than just feeling "low." We talk about an inferiority *complex* because the issue itself can be quite complicated. Most describe low self-esteem as being "a burden" or "a failure" and a feeling that life seems "pointless" and that this is due to the belief that we are "worthless."

But the Bible never says you are worthless. Unworthy, yes, but not worthless. Do not confuse "unworthiness" with worthlessness. In God's eyes, you are not (nor have you ever been) worthless. I think it is unfortunate that some of our theology, as well as hymnology, have suggested the worthlessness of man. Again, the problem is mostly a result of confusing worthlessness with unworthiness.

This transposition of concepts can be seen in several areas in our theological-speak. For instance, we say "humility," and we think it means "inferiority." We say "meekness," and right away think of "weakness." And so, it follows that when we say we are "unworthy," it must mean that we are "worthless."

But meekness is *not* weakness. And humility *does not* imply inferiority. And while it *is* biblical to identify the fact that we are unworthy, the Bible nowhere states that man is worthless. One has only to read Psalm 8 or Psalm 139 to have an appreciation for the Lord's view of the crowning achievement of his creation. Man, although tainted by the Fall and tottering on the brink of perdition, nevertheless is still worth something to God. And once and for all time he proves that at Calvary.

Robert McGee identifies in his book, *The Search for Significance*, the equation that reveals much of our problem in this area. He notes that Satan has enslaved most of mankind by convincing us that self-worth *equals* performance *plus* other's opinions. So, the sum of that equation is that we are always comparing ourselves to others in both performance and what opinions others have thrust upon us. More times than not, this can result in feelings of failure, inferiority, and insecurity. We realize that we do not like who we are and therefore, we wish we could be someone else. But listen, it is a waste of time trying to be someone else because that is a waste of the person you are. And somebody has to be you!

Do not allow yourself to be duped into believing that you must compare yourself to others to find fulfillment. Do not pine over someone's opinion. There is only one opinion that counts. I delighted in hearing college quarterback Trevor Lawrence respond to questions in an interview about his performance following one of Clemson's games. He said, "It really does not matter what people think of me or how good they think I play. That does not really matter. I put my identity in what Christ says, who He thinks I am and who I know that He says I am."[13] Now that is a young man displaying stability of life that evades many people much older than he is. Such solid wisdom at such a young age. Good for him.

We have worth because God says we do! God says in Isaiah 43:4, "You are precious in my sight and you have been honored." Our worth will always be in what God has said about us and not in what others have said about us. To paraphrase a popular lyric, "We are who God says we are!"

Less than the Least

Perhaps there is nothing which has been written about and referred to more and practiced less than the subject of humility. There is a great story that the legendary actor Kirk Douglas told about himself. Late in his life, Douglas returned to his Jewish roots and became quite involved in numerous philanthropic endeavors on behalf of the state of Israel. As a result, he was invited to visit Israel and receive an award. On the night of his arrival and after checking into his hotel in Jerusalem, he was delighted to see that the bathrobes in his suite had the initials KD embroidered on them. He gushed to his wife Anne how honored he felt that they would put his initials on his bathrobe. Imagine how he felt when she reminded him, "Kirk, the KD stands for King David." Sufficiently humbled, he realized that they were staying in the famed King David Hotel in Jerusalem.

13. Lindsay, "Trevor Lawrence Talks Faith," (2018).

A question we should always ask ourselves is are we less than the least or do we consider ourselves more than the most? Paul would answer that this way, "Although I am less than the least of all the Lord's people, this grace was given me: to preach to the Gentiles the boundless riches of Christ" (Eph 3:8 NIV). The godly French monk Bernard of Clairvaux taught that there are four Christian virtues: "The first is humility. The second is humility. The third is humility. And the fourth is humility."

There is nothing that incurs the condemnation of God more than a spirit of pride, and I don't know of anything that God blesses and rewards more than a spirit of humility. Both James and Peter quote Solomon (Prov 3:34) that, "God resists the proud, but gives grace to the humble." The benefits of humility are astounding. The concepts associated with humility are those which present themselves as the most desirable for a holy and healthy life:

> Grace (Jas 4:6)
> Honor (Prov 22:4)
> Victory (Ps 149:4)
> Favor (Prov 3:34)
> Wisdom (Prov 11:2)
> Guidance (Ps 149:4)
> Support (Ps 147:6)

No wonder the prophet Micah announced those memorable lines, "He has shown you, O mortal, what is good. And what does the Lord require of you? To act justly and to love mercy and to walk humbly with your God" (Mic 6:8 NIV).

As it relates to our ongoing discussion of self, humility is having an accurate view of self and that would include our willingness to recognize both our weaknesses and our strengths. It means looking to God for our identity rather than judging our self-worth through comparisons.

I like how Tyron Edwards (the great-grandson of the great Jonathan Edwards) described humility. He said, "True humility is not an abject groveling, self-despising spirit, it is but a right estimate of ourselves as God sees us."[14] Somehow we've adopted the view that thinking less of ourselves is the solution to humility. But low self-esteem is just as much a distortion of who we are as is pride. Both are extremes and both are not healthy. Tozer was certainly correct when he said that "self," whether swaggering or groveling, can never be anything but hateful to God!

14. Edwards, *A Dictionary of Thoughts*, (1908).

Philips Brooks (the nineteenth-century Episcopalian pastor, best known for writing *O Little Town of Bethlehem*) offers this insightful perspective on humility: "The true way to be humble is not to stoop until you are smaller than yourself, but to stand at your real height against some higher nature that will show you what the real smallness of your greatness is."[15]

The late Archbishop of Canterbury William Temple, when he was the Bishop of Manchester defined humility this way: "Humility does not mean thinking less of yourself than of other people, nor does it mean having a low opinion of your own gifts. It means freedom from thinking about yourself one way or the other at all."[16]

I think that what all three of these quotes have in common is that these great servants of Christ shared a view of humility that is based upon honesty and integrity. In their perception of humility, they understood that to belittle ourselves would be to belittle God's Creation. For them humility was not an abnormal oddity, it was the normal adjustment of attitude and action. And, as William Temple offered, it resulted in unmistakable freedom.

Think of it. Humility is freedom *of* self. It is freedom *from* self. You are not trying to *be* free you *are* free. You are not trying to *be* humble you simply *are* humble. And still, having said that, we must acknowledge that humility is an odd and elusive commodity. The moment you think you have it—you have lost it. The point being, if you are seeking it, you are probably thinking too much of yourself, which in turn means you will not find it. I know that sounds strange and maybe even a little contradictory, but that's how precariously fluid this whole biblical humility thing is. So, how do we love ourselves? We do it by sustaining healthy self-esteem, refraining from feelings of inferiority, and by maintaining biblical humility.

Affirming Your Value

There is a certain value attached to a proper view of oneself. Seeing yourself as God sees you and therefore submitting to his will and authority will produce a biblical humility that he favors. You are then free to value yourself as you ought to. And when you value yourself, you will value

---

15. Skoglund, *Burning Out for God*, 11.
16. William, "Christ in His church," (1924).

others. And when you value others, you will be empowered to serve them. M. Scott Peck said that until you value yourself, you won't value your time and until you value your time, you won't do anything with it.[17] We must not forget the reason Jesus injected us into the Great Commandment equation was so that we could do something with our lives. We are to love God *and* love our neighbors. The Lord knows that if we do not value ourselves, it is unlikely that we will value others.

If we do not see a significance in who we are, it is doubtful that we will think anyone else is significant. A balance is needed. If we esteem ourselves too much, we will esteem others too little. And if we under-esteem ourselves, we will underachieve in life's performances and goals. Your life matters. How you view yourself matters. Your time matters. How you choose to spend your life matters.

We are living in a day when there are volatile debates about whose life matters, and aside from the minefield of political and social sensibilities about this topic, the only thing that matters is what God says about it. If we would assume that in God's view, all lives matter, then we must acknowledge, as does Isaiah, that "All we like sheep have gone astray, we have turned, everyone, to his own way; and the Lord has laid on Him (Christ), the iniquity of us all (Isa 53:6). What matters is that all of us are lost until we are found and in finding us and reclaiming us, God gives to us that sense of value and worth that can never be taken away for us.

A healthy self-image is God's will for your life. It frees you to serve, without reservations and restrictions, and it properly positions you to reach others. Loving myself the way Jesus meant it is to affirm my value as having been bought with a price which means, therefore, that I am not my own but I belong to Christ (1 Cor 6:19–20). Once I know my life is his I can actively live a life that shuns egocentrism, seeking and acknowledging instead God as Center.

Narcissism has no place to hide in the powerful presence and searing light of the Holy Spirit. Pride is vanquished as a result of the Spirit-filled life. And the Spirit-filled life will be a life of humility. The child of God controlled by the Spirit of God does not seek to be humble, that Christian will simply be humble. You will have an abiding sense of value, a worth associated with and affirmed by the sacrifice of Christ at Calvary.

Think of the value God has placed upon you. You are not worthless; unworthy yes, but not without worth. You are God's treasured possession,

17. Peck, *Road Less Traveled*, 4.

sealed with and by his Holy Spirit. In the next chapter, we need to see just what it means to live a Spirit-controlled life before God. For now, it is enough to know that you will never love yourself the way Jesus meant without the presence of God's Spirit in your life.

Eleven | Coram Deo

IN THE RELIGIOUSLY TURBULENT TIMES of sixteenth-century Europe, there were two men, contemporaries but who never met, who demonstrated what living a life before God meant and what it cost. One man you know of rather well, and the other perhaps not so much. Both were learned Catholic priests, one in Germany and the other in England, and eventually, both broke away from the grip of the Roman Papacy and championed faith and conduct driven by the dictates of the Word of God alone. The one you know is Martin Luther and the one you probably have not heard much about was a contemporary in England, Hugh Latimer.

In 1517. at thirty-four years of age and disgusted with the excesses and abuses of the Roman Catholic church, Luther nailed his famous Ninety-five Theses to the church door in Wittenberg, an act which became the *de facto* beginning of the Protestant Reformation. At that time Latimer was thirty years old, having been ordained two years early and soon would become the chaplain of the University of Cambridge. On his admission, he was an obstinate papist, but eventually, Latimer embraced the teachings of the Reformation that was sweeping Europe and called for the Bible to be translated into English.

Luther was excommunicated by Pope Leo X in January of 1521 and his Ninety-five Theses were banned and any of his books that were found were to be burned. In April of 1521, he was also ordered to appear before German Emperor Charles V and other state officials and religious leaders at a convocation called a *Diet* in the town of Worms. It is at the *Diet of Worms* that Luther stood firm and gave his defense for his beliefs. He is reported to have said: "Unless I am convinced by the testimony of the Scriptures or by clear reason, for I do not trust either in the pope or in councils alone, since it is well known that they have often erred and contradicted themselves, I am bound by the Scriptures I have quoted, and my conscience is captive to the Word of God. I cannot and will not recant anything since it is neither safe nor right to go against conscience. May God help me. Amen."[1]

Standing Before God

For Luther, it was a moment where, although standing before an earthly tribunal he knew he was standing before the heavenly Throne. Luther refused to recant his writings and deny his faith. He is also reported to have declared rather defiantly yet respectfully that this was his stand, and he could do no other.

In England, some years later, Hugh Latimer also faced his defining moment. Luther died in 1546 with Pope Leo X's ex-communication still in effect, but the flames of the Reformation were still burning brightly. The Church of England solidified its separation from Rome under Henry VIII (even though for less than noble reasons) and continued under his young son and successor Edward VI, who with his advisors embraced Protestantism for more Scriptural reasons. During this time the popular preaching of Dr. Hugh Latimer was well known and protected by the English monarchy.

Unfortunately for the reformers, with the death of Edward in 1553 at the tender age of 15, England came under the rule of his older half-sister, Mary. The daughter of Henry VIII and his first wife, the Spanish Catholic Catherine of Aragon, Mary passionately embraced the Catholic faith of her mother. Now, under Queen Mary I, England was again brought under the authority of the papacy, and many subjects who refused to renounce their reformed faith had their heads chopped off or were burned at the stake. It was not without reason that this horrific time in the history of England earned the queen her nickname, "Bloody Mary."

Latimer had served as chaplain to King Edward VI, but this did not protect him from the Protestant purge being conducted by the queen and her inquisitors. Arrested, his trial began in April of 1554 at which he gave reasoned and powerful explanations as to his adherence to the Protestant understanding of the Gospels. He was convinced the stance he

---

1. Brecht, *Oxford Encyclopedia of the Reformation*, 1:460

took directly affected the souls of the many common people who needed to believe the simple teachings of the Word of God. Such was the heavy burden and responsibility he placed upon himself.

Fearless in his resolve and unwilling to recant his beliefs, Latimer was denounced by the Council and sentenced to die. Along with fellow reformer Nicholas Ridley, he was burned at the stake in Oxford on October 16, 1555. As the flames erupted, it is part of his legend and legacy that he yelled courageously to his fellow martyr, "Play the man, Master Ridley; we shall this day light such a candle, by God's grace, in England, as I trust shall never be put out!"

But there is another powerful moment displayed in the life of Hugh Latimer that we need to hear. It came back in the spring of 1530 when he was summoned to appear before King Henry VIII and the royal court at Windsor to preach a Sunday sermon. This was during a volatile time when Henry was seeking to have his marriage to Catherine of Aragon annulled so that he could marry his mistress, Anne Boleyn.

Knowing that he must always preach the truth, it is reported that Latimer spoke this admonition audibly to himself as he approached the pulpit: "Latimer! Latimer! do you remember that you are speaking before the high and mighty King Henry VIII; who has the power to command you to be sent to prison, and who can have your head cut off if it pleases him? Will you not take care to say nothing that will offend royal ears?"

Then he paused as if to think about what he just said, and then continued his self-admonition: "Latimer! Latimer! do you not remember that you are speaking before the King of kings and Lord of lords; before Him, at whose throne Henry VIII will stand; before Him, to whom one day you will have to give account yourself? Latimer! Latimer! be faithful to your Master and declare all of God's Word."

Both Luther and Latimer committed themselves to a similar belief, that regardless of who they had to stand before and no matter who they had to give a defense of their faith, they knew that ultimately, they were standing before God and would have to give an account of themselves to Him. Both knew that accountability to the Lord of lords and the King of kings was far greater and could never be compromised, not even at the risk of their own lives.

Coram Deo

Among the things that Martin Luther and Hugh Latimer had in common was a knowledge of Latin. Both had to give their defense twice, the second time by speaking in Latin (the official language of the Church). That being the case, they would have known that the early church had embraced a phrase in Latin that became a powerful and purposeful catchphrase for Christians. The phrase was *Coram Deo.*

What did it mean? It is a simple phrase that has a dynamic meaning. Appearing as it does in Psalm 55:13 of the Vulgate (Jerome's fourth-century Latin translation of the Bible) the context seems to be clear enough. Turning to modern English versions, where the verse is Psalm 56:13, we read, "For you have delivered me from death and my feet from stumbling, that I may walk *before God* (coram Deo) in the light of life" (NIV).

Jerome of course was translating into Latin the original Hebrew phrase, which is *lifney Elohim.* The Hebrew word *lifney* (which appears many times in the Old Testament) can be translated as either "before" or in the "presence of." In Psalm 56:13, coupled with the word "Elohim," it should therefore be rendered "before God" or in the "presence of God." This explains Jerome translating the phrase into Latin as "Coram Deo." Furthermore, the root of *lifney* is the Hebrew word for face (*panim*), and so conveys the stunning metaphor of doing something before the very face of God.

Quite literally then, "Coram Deo" means "before God" and is intended to express the idea that we are living our lives out in the very presence of God. Nothing can be hidden from him as he sees us, watches us, and watches over us. The KJV and Douay-Rheims version translates the phrase in Psalm 56:13 as "in the sight of God." This is yet another dynamic translation and makes good sense given that many believe that *coram* comes from the Latin noun *cora* signifying the pupil of the eye.

R. C. Sproul captured the spirit and depth of the phrase when he wrote that Coram Deo "literally refers to something that takes place in the presence of, or before the face of, God. To live Coram Deo is to live one's entire life in the presence of God, under the authority of God, to the glory of God."[2]

That we should conduct our lives in such a way that is pleasing to God and glorifies him in all that we do is a recurring theme throughout Scripture:

2. Sproul, *"What does 'coram Deo' Mean?"* Ligonier Ministries (2017).

"Whatever you do, do all to the glory of God" (1 Cor 10:31).

"And whatever you do, in word or deed, do everything in the name of the Lord Jesus, giving thanks to God the Father through Him" (Col 3:17).

"For you were bought with a price. So glorify God in your body" (1 Cor 6:20).

"Let your light shine before others, so that they may see your good works and give glory to your Father who is in heaven" (Matt 5:16).

"I give thanks to you, O Lord my God, with my whole heart, and I will glorify your name forever" (Ps 86:12).

The Great Motivator

Coram Deo is based upon the unshakeable reality that God loves me, and that the basis of that love is rooted in the nature of God and not in the performance of anything I can do. I cannot *do* anything to make God love me more than he already does. God's love is not conditioned on what we do, when we do it, or how we do it. He loves us because God is love (1 John 4:8).

Many Christians assume the mistaken idea that there are things we can do that will move God to love us more and, inversely, by failing to do certain things, God will love us less. But be careful. Do not reduce God's love to the way we love. What we do and how we act towards each other may indeed affect how we love (or don't love) one another. But God and his application of love are not altered by us, it is firmly set in him. What you do or not do does not affect God's love for you.

This truth can be demonstrated with the familiar story of Jesus' baptism. In each of the Gospel records of Jesus being baptized by John the Baptist, there is the testimony that the heavens open, the Spirit like a dove descends upon Jesus, and God's voice from heaven is heard to say, "This is My beloved Son, in whom I am well pleased" (Matt 3:16–17, Mark 1:10–11, Luke 3:21–22, John 1:32–34).

Certainly, Jesus is going to *do* many things that will be pleasing to God and following His will. He will *do* three-plus years of amazing and miraculous things; heal the sick, raise the dead, cast out demons, calm the sea, walk on water, preach the word, teach the parables, perform signs and wonders, and so much more, that if they were all written about one by one the world would not have enough books to contain them all (John

20:30, 21:25). But—and here is the point—at the time of his baptism he had not *done* any of those things yet.

God said that he loved his son and was well-pleased in him and none of that love or pleasure was based on anything that Jesus had done (yet). All that Jesus was going to do was still in the future, yet God's love for him was not based on anything that had to do with the future, or the past, or even the present. And why? Because God loves with eternal, steadfast love and it is not limited to nor conditioned by time. The prophet Jeremiah tells us this, "Long ago the Lord said to Israel: 'I have loved you, my people, with an everlasting love. With unfailing love I have drawn you to myself'" (Jer 31:3 NLT). Some translations state it as a *constant* love.

God's love is not capricious. He does not love me today because I am good and loves me less tomorrow when I am not so good. He loves me today and tomorrow the same. God's love is unconditional. There are no conditions to be met to *earn* God's love. God's love is not cheap, and it is not up for sale. It cannot be bargained for or bartered against. We are not competing for God's love. He loves us all equally and irrevocably and thank God for that! Unlike us, God does not *do* love, God *is* love.

When you realize that God loves you and that his love for you and pleasure in you is not based on what you have done, or are going to do, or will do, then you will be free to serve God motivated by that love rather than by your guilt or fear of not earning his love. Brennan Manning wrote that God loves us unconditionally, as we are and not as we should be because nobody is as they should be. In an interview in the Wittenburg Door magazine some years ago, Manning captured the essence of the Love of God and what it should mean to us and do for us:

> The only way to survive is to know that God loves me as I am and not as I should be; that He loves me beyond worthiness and unworthiness, beyond fidelity and infidelity; that He loves me in the morning sun and in the evening rain, without caution, regret, boundary, limit or breaking point; that no matter what I do, He can't stop loving me. When I am really in conscious communion with the reality of the wild, passionate, relentless, stubborn, pursuing, tender love of Christ for me, then it's not that I have to, or I've got to or I must or I should or I ought. Suddenly, I want to change because I know how deeply I'm loved.[3]

3. Manning, Wittenburg Door Interview, (1986), 13.

Practicing the Presence

Nicolas Herman grew up poor in eastern France and as a young man fought in the Thirty Years War that ravaged Europe in the first half of the seventeenth century. Seeking solitude and sanity, he later joined the Order of Discalced Carmelites in Paris. As a lay brother, he took the religious name, "Lawrence of the Resurrection," and would spend the rest of his life with the Parisian community.

His primary task in the monastery was working in the kitchen and, in his later years, repairing sandals. Though maintaining a lowly position in the priory, his godly and humble character attracted many, and his reputation for experiencing profound peace resulted in many coming to seek spiritual guidance from *Brother Lawrence*. The wisdom and insights he shared in many conversations and letters would later become the basis for the book, *The Practice of the Presence of God*, which was published posthumously in 1692.

Lawrence believed that the practice of the presence of God involved the realization that we are constantly under God's gaze. The oft-quoted summary of Brother Lawrence's Coram Deo is that it includes a daily determination to be sensitized to God all around us. And that meant to be aware of God's sovereignty and to be submitted to God's will and authority. Furthermore, it involves the realization that God loves us and delights in us, and that He desires a close, personal relationship with us.

Living in the presence of God demands that we are constantly aware of God's saving actions on our behalf and that all our actions and everything we do each day become nothing less than acts of service to God. Brother Lawrence proved that in his life. (We will revisit more of his wisdom in the chapter on Work.)

Practicing the presence of God is something we see lived out in several celebrated lives in the Bible. One of the most celebrated is Abraham, and it should be noted that God let him know in no uncertain terms that that is what He expected of the patriarch. "I am the Almighty God; walk before me, and be thou perfect" (Genesis 17:1 KJV).

The Hebrew word translated "before me" is *lifney* which, as we noted earlier, comes from the root word *panim*, meaning the "face." God is telling Abraham that he is to walk before the very face of God. How can we understand this? I think it means something like, "I am watching you," or "I see your every move," or "There is nothing hidden from my eyes!"

This constant gaze of God would therefore explain what follows in the verse—the challenge to be "perfect." The Hebrew adjective means "blameless," as well as that which is sound, wholesome and refers to someone who is unimpaired. It is often understood as one having integrity (as in the life of Job, who, we are told was "blameless—a man of complete integrity. He feared God and stayed away from evil" (Job 1:1 NLT).

Some have suggested that this phrase in Genesis 17:1 could well be translated as "walk, looking at my face." Similarly, the First Commandment, in which God states we must have no other gods before him, could also be translated as "Do not let any other god get between your face and my face."

In the New Testament, the Apostle Paul understood Coram Deo when he wrote: "I appeal to you, therefore, brothers, by the mercies of God, to present your bodies as a living sacrifice, holy and acceptable to God, which is your spiritual worship. Do not be conformed to this world, but be transformed by the renewal of your mind, that by testing you may discern what is the will of God, what is good and acceptable and perfect" (Rom 12:1–2 ESV).

Secularizing the Sacred

In a blog entitled *What Does It Mean to Live "Coram Deo?"*, pastor Nick Cady wrote, "The principle of Coram Deo is important because it reminds us that our lives as the people of God are to be integrated, not compartmentalized. In other words: it isn't that our lives are compartmentalized into different areas: work, family, faith, etc.—but that our faith is integrated into every aspect of our lives: we do our work before the face of God, and unto God's glory! Our family life is lived before the face of God, and unto His glory!"[4]

Cady is certainly correct. The tendency to compartmentalize our lives, especially into the two monolithic categories of that which we declare secular and that which we deem sacred, is not only counterproductive to the specific idea of *Coram Deo* but the Christian life in general. It fosters and perpetuates the idea that our secular life is kind of our everyday, work-a-day world, and that which we identify as religious activity is that part of our life which is sacred (and therefore it is the only part of our life for which we are accountable to God).

4. Cady, *What Does It Mean To Live "Coram Deo?"* (2019).

I will address this attitude more fully in the chapter on how we view our commitment to work (our employment) but suffice to say here, if we buy into the idea that our lives can be divided between secular and sacred, we have virtually no chance to live *Coram Deo* and intentionally practice the Presence of God.

While the tendency to distinguish between things secular and sacred is commonplace in our culture, it is not biblical and will prove counterproductive for Christians. Some years ago, social critic and Christian author Os Guinness wrote the book *The Gravedigger File: Papers on the Subversion of the Modern Church*. A significant subversion of the church, perpetrated by the enemies of the church, that Guinness artfully discusses is this move towards secularization. It is described this way: "Secularization is the acid rain of the spirit, the atmospheric cancer of the mind and the imagination. Vented into the air not only by industrial chimneys but by computer terminals, marketing techniques, and management insights, it is washed down shower by shower, the deadliest destroyer of religious life the world has ever seen."[5]

What Coram Deo Demands

To live Coram Deo demands recognition of and commitment to several spiritual concepts that are constantly showcased in Scripture. Here are four that come to mind: Faith, Obedience, Courage, and Perseverance.

The writer of Hebrews reminds us that without faith it is impossible to please God (Heb 11:6), so surely, exercising faith in our lives is something God is watching for. The consistent challenge of Scripture, first declared by an Old Testament prophet and then repeated three times in the New Testament (in Romans, Galatians, and Hebrews), is that "The Just shall live by Faith." It is a radical faith, this belief system of the Christian. True faith will revolutionize and upset our whole life and make us into another person altogether (to paraphrase Tozer).

It is power in paradox. The world cannot understand it and the Christian cannot thrive without it. One of the most amazing passages in Scripture which spells out the paradox of the Christian faith is seen in Second Corinthians 4:8–9 in which the apostle Paul gives us a series of statements that demonstrate just how paradoxical our faith should be. I

5. Guinness, *Gravedigger File*, 60.

have summarized his four couplets, seeking to capture the amazing paradox and power of faith:

> We are *crowded* but never *crushed*,
> We are *cornered* but never *confined*,
> We are *chased* but never *caught*,
> We are *cast down* but never *carried out*!

Along with faith, there must be obedience, which is the necessary proof of a life lived by faith. It is the doing of what you are trusting. It is the behaving of what you are believing. It is James 2:22 to Paul's Romans 4:5. It is the performance of my practicing the presence of God in my life. The Hebrew Scriptures understand this perfectly in that the same word translated "to hear," *shema*, is also translated "obey." The Jewish believer understood that when you heard the word of God the necessary outcome of that hearing was the doing. To hear meant to obey, and that attitude must be cultivated if we are to live Coram Deo.

When Solomon was facing the prospects of becoming king of Israel, the Lord appeared to him in Gibeon and offered to give to him anything that he requested. To his credit, Solomon did not ask for temporal things but rather for an "understanding heart" (NLT), or a "discerning heart" (NIV), and, given what he became known for, a heart of wisdom (1 Kgs 3:5–15).

But what Solomon asked for was a *lev shome'a*, which meant a "heart to hear." What does that mean? It means that Solomon was asking for a heart to obey God, knowing that was the only way he could effectively govern God's people! I like the Holman Christian Study Bible's version of First Kings 3:9, Solomon says, "So give Your servant an obedient heart to judge Your people and to discern between good and evil. For who is able to judge this great people of Yours?"

The commitment to wanting not only to hear the word of God but to obey the word of God will demand a fair degree of courage. The charge to be courageous, like a baton, is passed down from one Bible great to the next. Moses, as well as God, charges Joshua to be strong and to be very courageous (Deut 31:23 and Josh 1:6–9).

David tells Solomon his son, "Be strong and courageous and do the work. Do not be afraid or discouraged, for the Lord God, my God is with you" (1 Chr 28:20). He also encourages all believers, "Oh, love the Lord, all you saints! For the Lord preserves the faithful. Be of good courage, And He shall strengthen your heart, all you who hope in the

Lord" (Psalm 31:23–24). Good king Hezekiah rallied Jerusalem to "Be strong and courageous" as they faced Sennacherib and the Assyrians (2 Chr 32:7).

Paul challenged the Corinthians to stand firm in the faith; be courageous, and be strong (1 Cor 6:13). And Jesus often encouraged his disciples and therefore all of us, "Do not let your heart be troubled, nor let it be fearful" (John 14:27). Former mayor of New York City, Rudy Giuliani, reminds us that courage is not the absence of fear, but rather courage is feeling fear and being able to overcome it. Courage, he believes, is managing fear to accomplish what you need to accomplish.

Lastly, consider how perseverance would be another important discipline that contributes to living our lives before God. Perseverance is defined as continuing your effort despite difficulties, obstacles, opposition, or even failure. You can see that in the origin of the Latin which comes from the preposition *through* and the word *severe*, i.e., keep going "through the severe."

Perseverance is the characteristic of steadfastness and stability, both of which are essential especially in our culture of continually shifting attitudes and alliances. One of my favorite challenges from Paul is found in Second Corinthians 15:58, "Therefore, my beloved brethren, be steadfast, immovable, always abounding in the work of the Lord, knowing that your labor is not in vain in the Lord."

Winston Churchill is an example of this type of courage and perseverance. After the Second World War, he was asked to give a commencement speech at his boyhood alma mater. Upon being introduced with all the accolades that might be expected for the bulldog of British resolve, the weary but victorious statesman approached the podium, looked out over the student body, and then delivered his speech. It was only nine words long! "Never give up. Never give up. Never, never, never!" He then slowly returned to his seat, with the stunned audience pondering the power of his words.

So, be a person of faith, like Abraham. And like Solomon seek an obedient heart. Be a person of courage, like Joshua. And inspired by Paul, be a person of perseverance.

A Church in Checkmate

These characteristics, and more, shape us and mold us and are essential to living an authentic, intentional life before God as a disciple of Jesus Christ. None of what has just been described is for living a marginal Christian life maintaining a certain safety on the sidelines. Living Coram Deo is life on the offensive and not a life always on the defensive. This is a critical distinction in our culture which continually attempts to put the Church in checkmate. It seems we are always reacting instead of enacting. It appears we are always circling the wagons and bracing for the attack rather than unfurling the flag and sounding "charge!"

Recently, for a class I was teaching, I was reading our textbook, *Jesus the Messiah*, by New Testament scholar Robert H. Stein. In the chapter on the temptation of Jesus, Stein offers an observation that was revelatory for me. He noted that after his baptism, the text says that Jesus was *led* by the Spirit into the wilderness. We often miss that important bit of information. Stein writes, "Because the Holy Spirit initiated the temptations, they should be understood not as a defensive struggle but as an offensive attack on the rule of Satan."[6]

What an important distinction to make. Jesus was not stumbling around the Judean wilderness fending off attacks by the evil one. He was out there looking for a fight! He invaded Satan's wilderness domain and, as it were, coaxed him out of his lair so that he could get a heavy dose of God's word and truth fired at him. Stein concluded, "The kingdom of God had come, and the ruler of this evil age was now challenged."[7]

Amen! Time for the church to sound the attack. We have retreated enough.

Living your life Coram Deo is living a life on full display before God and in front of a world that often despises God. It is a life of faith, a commitment to hearing God's voice, courage to obey God in all circumstances, and the perseverance to never quit.

Judah Cofer offers a bit of practical insight in his article on *The Spiritual Benefits of Practicing the Presence of God*. He writes, "The natural human bent is thoughtlessness and disregard toward God, and it must be renounced and put off so that the beautiful practice of thoughtfulness

6. Stein, *Jesus the Messiah*, 105.
7. Stein, *Jesus the Messiah*, 105.

and regard for God in all things may be adopted into our lives. This is the practice of living Coram Deo."[8]

I am also inspired by the way Eric Smith describes the concept of Coram Deo. For him, it is "the delightful, thrilling, awe-inspiring, beautiful, Biblical vision of the Christian life."[9] Reading that description, I was immediately drawn to the beautiful and equally inspiring statement by the psalmist, "Blessed are the people who know the festal shout, who walk, O Lord, in the light of your face, who exult in your name all the day" (Ps 89:15–16).

What will I Become?

We began this section on "What is man?" by asking the question, "Who am I?" From there it was important to fully understand what Jesus meant by loving ourselves (and will next move into our final section on loving our neighbors). Then, in this chapter, the concept of *Coram Deo* has been explored and explained.

Again, we must recognize that we are strategically positioned between God and our neighbors and therefore on full display by both. One controls who we are and the others are affected by who we are and how we react to the One who seeks to lead us. I must live my life understanding that I have an obligation to both. I live my life before God, in his presence, and by his power, and that life is on display like a book, a living letter viewed and read by all men, as Paul declared to the Corinthian Christians (2 Cor 3:2–3).

Many years ago, Annie Johnson Flint reminded us of the stakes involved. She wrote, "We are the only Bible, The careless world will read; We are the sinner's Gospel, We are the scoffer's creed; We are the Lord's last message, Given in deed and word; What if the type is crooked? What if the print is blurred?"

Living Coram Deo is not only an issue of how you live before God, but it is also how you live before men and whether they will see God in you. It is living a life of faith, obedience, courage, and perseverance so that who you are and what you are may rub off on others. As has been said, the true test of Christianity is whether you have enough of it to get across to someone else.

---

8. Cofer, "*Spiritual Benefits of Practicing the Presence of God*," 3.

9. Smith, "*What Does 'Coram Deo' Mean?*" (2010), 1.

We talk about being a Christian witness, but too often that amounts to the verb and those times when we are verbally witnessing. We need to understand witness as a noun as well. We are a witness for Christ whether we open our mouths and declare the gospel or not. Thought of that way, we acknowledge that witness is not so much what we say, but who we are and how we live.

There is a lot of truth in the adage, "I'd rather see a sermon than hear one!" Perhaps whoever said that first was inspired by Frances of Assisi who said that we should preach the gospel at all times, and when necessary, use words.

There was a Christian businessman who was walking on a busy street in his city. As he stopped at a corner, he was confronted by a street preacher who handed him a gospel tract and asked him, "Are you a Christian?" The man took out his pen and started writing on the gospel tract and then handed it back to the street preacher. He said, "I have written the name of my wife and my children and my home phone number. I have also written the name of my secretary and her number, as well as my business partner and his number. Please call them and ask them if I am a Christian or not."

Exactly.

Who I am is what God has made me, and what I become is what I make of my life with the gifts God entrusted to me. The *who* is God's, the *what* is yours for God's sake (see Second Corinthians 4:5). I am therefore reminded of something I read once about dancer and actress turned author and minister, Eleanor Powell. She believed that what we are is God's gift to us and what we become is our gift to God. To that I would only add this extended truth: *And what we become is also our gift to our neighbors.* In the next section, we will learn how.

To bring this chapter and this section to a close, let me say that the key to Coram Deo (living before God) will always be *Centrum Deo* (God at center). And what makes Centrum Deo a possibility is *Amorem Deo* (love God). To love God with all my heart and soul and strength, to have a "love affair" with God (which is literally what the Latin means), makes it possible and desirable for me to allow God to be at the center of my life. And when God is at the center, I am now positioned to live my life before Him.

Amorem Deo
Coram Deo
Centrum Deo

Part Four

Where Is My Neighbor?

There are no ordinary people. You have never talked to a mere mortal. Nations, cultures, arts, civilizations - these are mortal, and their life is to ours as the life of a gnat. But it is immortals whom we joke with, work with, marry, snub, and exploit—immortal horrors or everlasting splendors.

C. S. LEWIS

The commandments, "Do not commit adultery; do not commit murder;

do not steal; do not desire what belongs to someone else"—all these,

and any others besides, are summed up in the one command,

"Love your neighbor as you love yourself."

PAUL

ROMANS 13:9 (GNT)

This section aims to gain insight, inspiration, and encouragement to minister to all those who are around us – from our spouses and families to our relationships at work and community. We are to fulfill the commandment to love our neighbor, whoever they are, wherever they are.

Twelve | Who Then Is My Neighbor?

TOWARDS THE END OF THE nineteenth century, a self-educated Appalachian preacher named Sam, came down from the Smokey Mountains in Tennessee to the city to be questioned by a group of ministers on his fitness to be ordained into the ministry. This is how the examination proceeded:

Can you read, Sam? *Of course, I can read... some.* Can you write? *Yes, suh, I can write... a little.* Well, do you know your Bible Sam? *Yes, of course, I do. I'm pretty smart in them there Scriptures. I know my Bible from lid to lid.* Well tell us Sam, which part of the Bible do you like the best?" *I like the Book of Mark the best.* And what do you especially like about the Gospel of Mark, Sam? *Ah likes the parables best.*

And which one of the parables is your favorite? *Well, suh, the parable of the Good Ol' Samaritan is my specialty! Ah certainly likes that one the best.* Well, that's good Sam, tell us everything you know of the Parable of the Good Samaritan? *Yes suh, I will.*

Once there was this man a-travelin' from Jerusalem to Jericho, and he fell among thorns, and the thorns sprung up and choke him. An' as he went on, he didn't have no money, and he met the Queen of Sheba, and she give him one thousand talents of gold and one hundred changes of raiment. An' he got into a chariot and drove furiously, and when he was a drivin' under a big juniper tree, his hair got caught on the limb of that tree, and he hung there many days, and the ravens brought him food to eat and water to drink, and he ate five thousand loaves of bread and two fishes.

One night when he was a hangin' there asleep, his wife Delilah come along and cut off his hair, and he dropped, an' he fell on stony ground. But he got his self up and went on, and it began to rain, an' it rained forty days an' forty nights, an' he hid hisself in a cave, and he lived on locusts and wil' honey.

Then he went on 'til he met a servant who say, "Come, take supper at my house. An' he made excuse and said, "No, I won't. I have married a wife, an' I can't go! An' the servant went out into the highways and in the hedges an' compelled him to come in. After supper, he went on and come on down to Jericho. An' when he got there, he look up an' saw that ol' wicked Queen Jezebel a sittin' away up high in a window. An' she was a laughin' at him, an' so he say, Throw her down out o' there! An' they throw her down. An' he say, Throw her down again! An' they throwed her down seventy times seven, and of the fragments there remained, they picked up twelve baskets full, besides wimin' and chillin', and they said, Blessed are the piece-makers.

And the conclusion of the parable is, Now, whose wife do ya think she'll be in the Judgment Day?"

Well, I'm not sure if ol' Sam passed his ordination exam, but at least he's got us a–thinkin' 'bout the Parable of the Good Samaritan. And that parable just may be the most famous story Jesus ever told. It is certainly one of the clearest teachings by Jesus on answering the question: "Who Then Is My Neighbor?"

We are now ready to move into the final phase of our study. The third Circle of our Responsibilities chart should comprise all our relationships outside of God and Self. This third circle is classified as "Neighbor." Remember Jesus said, "You shall love the Lord your God with all your heart, with all your soul, and with all your mind. This is the first and great commandment. And the second is like it: You shall love your neighbor as yourself" Matthew 22:37–39).

A Neighbor, Who's That?

First and foremost, we must understand the word *neighbor*. What does it mean? I offer a broad, yet simple definition: "A neighbor is someone nearby wherever you are." While the Old Saxon origin means "near dweller," this short definition is important because, by employing the word "wherever," it stretches our understanding beyond our neighbor being someone who just lives in close proximity to where we live.

That is how we often think of "neighbor" is it not? Our neighbors are those people across the fence or across the street from us. As such, they are those with whom we have a good relationship and some with whom we do not. That is why Benjamin Franklin once said that you should love your neighbors but do not pull your fence down. Similarly, G. K. Chesterton quipped that the Bible commands us to love our neighbors as well as our enemies and that is probably because generally, they are the same people.

In Scripture, we are called upon, no less than eight times, to love our neighbor:

- You shall not take vengeance, nor bear any grudge against the children of your people, but you shall love your neighbor as yourself: I am the Lord (Lev 19:18).

- "Honor your father and your mother," and, "You shall love your neighbor as yourself" (Matt 19:19).

- And the second is like it: "You shall love your neighbor as yourself" (Matt 22:39).

- And the second, like it, is this: "You shall love your neighbor as yourself." There is no other commandment greater than these (Mark 12:31).

- So he answered and said, "You shall love the Lord your God with all your heart, with all your soul, with all your strength, and with all your mind, and your neighbor as yourself" (Luke 10:27).

- For the commandments, "You shall not commit adultery, You shall not murder, You shall not steal, You shall not bear false witness, You shall not covet," and if there is any other commandment, are all summed up in this saying, namely, "You shall love your neighbor as yourself" (Rom 13:9).

- For all the law is fulfilled in one word, even in this: "You shall love your neighbor as yourself" (Gal 5:14).

- If you really fulfill the royal law according to the Scripture, "You shall love your neighbor as yourself," you do well (Jas 2:8).

Interestingly, however, there is only one time when anyone actually asked the question—Who is my neighbor? And that question comes amid a very fluid time of ministry as Jesus is determined to go to Jerusalem and face that which awaits him there. We are told that one Samaritan village is less than hospitable to Jesus and the disciples (Luke 9:51–26), followed by the Lord sending out seventy disciples to cities throughout the region (Luke 10:1–12). This is followed by a stern denunciation of other cities (Chorazin and Capernaum) that proved to be especially closed-off to light and life. Soon after the seventy return with their reports of signs and wonders, there was understandably genuine excitement, joy, and rejoicing (Luke 10:17-24).

But in the crowd of onlookers, there was also doubt and skepticism, as well as self-righteousness and sarcasm. That becomes evident as one man decides to take Jesus to task: "A man stood up who knew the Law and tried to trap Jesus. He said, 'Teacher, what must I do to have life that lasts forever?' Jesus said to him, 'What is written in the Law? What does the Law say?' The man said, 'You must love the Lord your God with all your heart. You must love Him with all your soul. You must love Him with all your strength. You must love Him with all your mind. You must love your neighbor as you love yourself.' Jesus said to him, 'You have said the right thing. Do this and you will have life.' The man tried to make himself look good. He asked Jesus, 'Who is my neighbor?'" (Luke 10:25–29 NLV).

And there it is. Who is my neighbor? Where is he? It actually is a loaded question, and we must understand it as such. Do not forget, we are told that this religious Jewish "scholar" had some hidden motives. He was attempting to trick Jesus somehow. I am willing to suggest that perhaps he was hoping this trouble-making teacher would suggest that Jews should look favorably upon the goyim (Gentiles) and worse, women! The orthodox Jew of Jesus' day would wake up every morning and say a prayer something like this: "Lord, I thank you that I am not a dog, a Gentile, or a woman." Hard to get someone like that to agree to be neighborly to any of those three!

Of course, we know that he asked the right person because Jesus will provide the right answer. In response to this important (and again, loaded) question, Jesus gives an absolutely brilliant answer. He proceeds to tell an amazing story, one that remains today perhaps the best known "parable" in the New Testament:

> Then Jesus answered and said: "A certain man went down from Jerusalem to Jericho, and fell among thieves, who stripped him of his clothing, wounded him, and departed, leaving him half dead. Now by chance a certain priest came down that road. And when he saw him, he passed by on the other side. Likewise, a Levite, when he arrived at the place, came and looked, and passed by on the other side. But a certain Samaritan, as he journeyed, came where he was. And when he saw him, he had compassion. So, he went to him and bandaged his wounds, pouring on oil and wine; and he set him on his own animal, brought him to an inn, and took care of him. On the next day, when he departed, he took out two denarii, gave them to the innkeeper, and said to him, 'Take care of him; and whatever more you spend, when I come again, I will repay you.' So, which of these three do you think was neighbor to him who fell among the thieves?" And he said, "He who showed mercy on him." Then Jesus said to him, "Go and do likewise" (Luke 10:30–37).

The backdrop to this famous story is essential in helping us envision what Jesus was describing. The potential dangers when traveling in the ancient world are well known. Lawlessness prevailed, and that would be true of one road, in particular, that was notoriously dangerous. It was the road from Jerusalem and Jericho, and although it was less than twenty miles, physically it was treacherous due to the switchbacks and drop in elevation. Jerusalem is some 2000 feet above sea level and Jericho is close to 1000 feet below sea level. That 3000 feet difference was navigated along mountainous terrain, along with limestone caves which offered shelter and ambush for thieves.

A traveler would not know who or what might spring out before him just around the bend. It was a journey watched by jackals. It was a thoroughfare for thievery. It was a "toll" road and thugs were collecting the tolls. For that reason, it was known as "The Way (or Ascent) of Blood."

That is where Jesus takes us in response to the lawyer's question. Everyone would have understood that which he was describing. An unidentified man (presumably Jewish) "went down" from Jerusalem To Jericho. As he traveled the treacherous path, he fell among thieves. The word Jesus uses means to fall into something that results in being encompassed or surrounded. There is little doubt as to what happens next; he is assaulted, stripped, robbed, beaten, and left for dead.

At this point, it would seem clear that Jesus intended for his hearers to understand that this poor man lying at the side of the road requires assistance. He is fallen humanity in need of help. His dilemma demands deliverance. His condition cries out for comfort and compassion.

So, Jesus continues by saying that a priest is the first to come upon him, but incredibly the priest ignores the wounded man and hurries on his way. Then a Levite is next to arrive at the scene, but quickly switches to the other side of the road and likewise scurries past the scene. Both of these men, who could have helped, chose rather to avoid any contact with the stricken stranger. The late Keith Green, in his song *On the Road to Jericho,* crafted, as he usually did, a compelling retelling of the parable. He has the beaten man lying wounded, almost slain, by the side of the road. He is crying out in pain and notices the priest walking by him. Then he notices a second man, but he too walks on by, avoiding involvement. You get a sense that in dismay, he realizes with heartbreak, that although both were of his kind, they were just "strangers on the road to Jericho." Witnessing the scene, as it were, we are left feeling utterly sorry for this man.

But then, Jesus continues, a Samaritan (yes, a despised Samaritan!) comes upon the scene. He is not named, only identified by his ethnicity. He too is journeying the dangerous road, and no doubt, he too is just as occupied with thoughts of his safety as were the others. But unlike the others, he is cannot ignore the unavoidable circumstance he happens upon. Where the passing priest and lazy Levite would not take action, this man springs into action.

Jesus details what the Samaritan does; he treats and then bandages the man's wounds, lifts him up and onto his animal, and personally leads him to an Inn where he then stays with him for the rest of that day. And that is not all he does. He is not done. Having to continue his own journey, he then pays for the wounded man's room and board, along with the promise to the innkeeper that upon returning that way he will pay for any other expenses that might occur.

With everyone listening intently to Jesus' graphic story, the Lord then drops the inescapable question, "So which of these three do you think was neighbor to him who fell among the thieves?" In Luke, the word Jesus uses is *plésion,* and means neighbor, as virtually every English version of the New Testament renders it and is from the root to be near or nearby. (Recall, if you will, my definition at the beginning of this chapter: "A neighbor is someone nearby wherever you are.")

I Will Take It

One of the important side stories of this great parable is that in telling it, Jesus reveals three clear philosophies of life, each of which have been observed by many down through the years. There is first of all the philosophy of the thief which is, "What is yours is mine and I will take it."

This is the lifestyle of the conman, the scam artist, the one who wants to rip you off. It is the way of life for the burglar, the rapist, the murderer. Those committed to this philosophy ply their trade in back allies and board rooms, on street corners, or in cyberspace. This philosophy, no doubt, is what drives most crime.

Statistics prove how all-to-common this philosophy is. A burglar strikes every ten seconds; someone's car is stolen every thirty seconds; robberies occur every seventy seconds; a rape is committed every eight minutes; and a murder every twenty-seven minutes. This philosophy makes for a dangerous world indeed. It is why Vance Havner once wrote that we are smart enough to walk on the moon, but not safe enough to walk in the park.

I Will Keep It

The second lifestyle philosophy and that which is demonstrated by the Priest and Levite is, "What is mine is mine and I will keep it." We might say that this is the lifestyle of rich and selfish. It is the credo to get what you can, save as much as you can, and give away none of it.

This philosophy is damaging to society in general and deadly to the spiritual life in specific. It is the blindness of the religionist to the real need around him. It is walking around in piety but not showing much pity. This philosophy is best summarized by Bob Rowland in *Listen Christian:* "I was hungry and you formed a humanities club and discussed my hunger. I was naked and you debated the morality of my appearance. I was homeless and you preached to me of the shelter of God's love. I was lonely and you left me alone to go pray for me. You seem so holy and so close to God—and yet, I am still hungry and lonely and cold."[1]

1. Rowland, "Listen Christian." (1969).

I Will Give It

Thankfully, there is yet another philosophy of life that can be embraced and that which is demonstrated by the Samaritan. This is the philosophy of life that believes, "What is mine is yours and I will give it."

In presenting this story, this philosophy of life is certainly the one that Jesus would challenge all of us to follow. It will become the spirit of Christianity. It will be a radical and revelatory lifestyle. It will prove to be the only philosophy of life that is suitable for Kingdom culture and conduct. Amid greed, it speaks of grace. Amid stealing, it demonstrates giving. Amid selfishness, it demands serving others. Amid the darkness, it shines the light, and in the midst of death, it offers life.

It is what Paul writes about in Philippians 2:4: "Let each of you look out not only for his own interests but also for the interests of others." And also in Romans 13:10: "Love does no wrong to a neighbor [it never hurts anyone]. Therefore, unselfish love is the fulfillment of the Law" (AMP).

Willing to Get Involved

There is another corollary truth from the story of the Good Samaritan, and it is one of involvement. And I should point out, this can mean non-involvement as well. It is obvious from the parable that three different people could have gotten involved, but only one did. Focusing then on the one who did get involved, it would be beneficial to discover what that involvement entailed.

The first thing we must notice is that the Samaritan got involved *Emotionally*. Jesus tells us that when he saw the man, "he had compassion" on him (Luke 10:33). It should be obvious that the others saw the beaten man but had truly little compassion on him if any. To be like the Samaritan is to be like Christ, who, as an old hymn states, *Saw our poor fallen world, pitied our sorrows, poured out His life for us, wonderful love!*

But just being empathetic is not enough, the Samaritan also got involved *Personally*. This is important to note in that we can get emotional about something but still without personal involvement. You may be moved by a need but not allow that need to move you to the point of action. Like the Priest or the Levite, we may have all the excuses for not getting involved; we are too busy, or it is not our concern, or we believe someone else will help. Opportunities of service will often present themselves in an inconvenient manner, and in an opposite way from the direction you are headed.

But compassion, to be real, must result in action. The church my wife and I attend has a weekly ministry of feeding those in need in our community. The name of this ministry is *Love Active*. That is as it should be. Not just love but love in action. Jesus tells us what action the Samaritan takes, "So he went to him and bandaged his wounds, pouring on oil and wine; and he set him on his own animal, brought him to an inn, and took care of him" (Luke 10:34).

Perhaps James was thinking of this when he wrote, "Suppose a brother or a sister is without clothes and daily food. If one of you says to them, 'Go in peace; keep warm and well fed,' but does nothing about their physical needs, what good is it?" (Jas 2:15–16 NIV). John as well remembers the story, "If anyone has material possessions and sees a brother or sister in need but has no pity on them, how can the love of God be in that person? Dear children, let us not love with words or speech but with actions and in truth" (1 John 3:17–18 NIV).

Real involvement will almost always cost us something, and so it follows that the Samaritan also got involved *Financially*. "On the next day, when he departed, he took out two denarii, gave them to the innkeeper, and said to him, 'Take care of him; and whatever more you spend, when I come again, I will repay you'"(Luke 10:35).

A denarius was the equivalent of a day's wages, and the average cost of room and board was usually around a tenth of a denarius. By those calculations, the Samaritan paid enough money to take care of the man for three weeks! The Samaritan got involved and it cost him, and he paid it gladly and became the centerpiece of Jesus' sermon on service.

Involvement has its own set of economics and in this great story, they are the economics of grace and mercy. And that is God's way. God got involved, and it cost Him (John 3:16). Jesus got involved, and it cost Him (John 13:35). Paul got involved, and it cost him (2 Cor 11:24–28). David understood this and so declared, "I will not offer to God that which costs me nothing" (2 Sam 24:24). John Henry Jowett warned that a ministry that costs nothing usually accomplishes nothing.

The cost of ministry is great, for both the one ministering and the one who may be receiving the ministry. The day before he was assassinated Martin Luther King Jr. spoke about the dangers of the Jericho Road. He said because the road was so dangerous, the first question that the self-serving Levite asked was, "If I stop to help this man, what will happen to me?" But Dr. King knew that was not the more important question. And so, he said that when the Good Samaritan came by, he reversed the question and asked, "If I do not stop to help this man, what will happen to him?"

For this reason, Jesus wants us to know that we owe others our service. In Romans 1:14, Paul says he was a debtor, and make a note he does not say we are debtors to the Lord (which we are) but he says we are debtors to men. You may be familiar with the *I Am's* of Jesus and how each one affirms his messiahship, but did you know Paul presented some *I Am's* for the follower of Jesus? He said, "I am a debtor both to Greeks and barbarians," and "I am ready to preach the gospel," and "I am not ashamed of the gospel" (Rom 1:14–16). We must be impressed with Paul's level of commitment and his sense of obligation to communicate the gospel to those who so desperately need to hear it. That aside, are we willing to own the same obligation in our own lives? Will we be compliant or just complacent?

Just what do we owe the world? I would suggest we owe the world truth. I would suggest that we owe other men and women hope. And I would suggest we owe those who are walking around in darkness and death, life. Sometimes you hear someone say, "The world owes me a living!" But the world does not owe us a living, rather we owe the world a life.

If we are to love our neighbor as ourselves, then we cannot avoid the economics of involvement. Loving our neighbor, whoever and wherever they are, will challenge us to give of our *Heart* emotionally, give our *Hand* personally, and give our *Help* financially. Nothing costs as much as getting involved, except not getting involved.

My Neighbor, or Me?

A closer look at the dialogue of the story of the good Samaritan is enlightening. We know it begins with the Lawyer who asks a question which Jesus then answers with a question. We also know that the Lawyer answers Jesus' question and that Jesus replies with an affirmation. But then it gets interesting.

The Lawyer, not wanting to disengage, continues with a second question. Now we have to ask, why this question? The Law, to which both he and Jesus referred, mentions both God and neighbor. Would not issues relating to God be more obvious to ask the one claiming to represent God? But he wants to talk about people and so he says (and perhaps almost flippantly), *who is my neighbor?* It seems he did not think his relationship with God needed any scrutiny. He had his religious "act" together.

Note that Luke says he wanted to justify himself. What does that mean? Ellicott, in his commentary on this section, describes exactly what is going on: "The question implied a conscience half-awakened and uneasy. It is characteristic that no doubt seems to cross his mind as to his love of God. There he felt that he was safe. But there were misgivings as to the second commandment, and, as if feeling that there had been a tone of rebuke in our Lord's answer, he vindicates himself by asking the question, 'Who is my neighbor?' No one, he thinks, could accuse him of neglecting his duties to those who lived in the same village, attended the same synagogue, who were Pharisees like himself, or even Israelites."[2]

Knowing what is in the heart of every man, it is this question that solicits from Jesus the famous parable. The bottom line is that Jesus shows him that if he thought he was loving God (and that needed little scrutiny), but he was not loving his fellow man, then he was sadly mistaken. The Lawyer asked, "Who is my neighbor?" and Jesus' answer took it to the next level. In effect, Jesus would be asking in return, a soul-searching question—Who are you?

The brilliance of this parable then is that it shifts the discussion and moves it from one about who qualifies to be treated as a neighbor into one about how a good neighbor treats others. Loving our neighbor is not a matter of trying to figure out who he is. It is coming to terms with who we are. It is a matter of knowing that whenever we see someone in need, they are our neighbor, and we are to respond to them as did the Samaritan. Hence Jesus concludes with the unmistakable application, "Go and do likewise."

I am convinced that confronted with this story, I need to see that Jesus wants me to ask myself, not so much, "Who is my neighbor?" but "Who am I?" The issue is not what is he like, but what am I like. When you do that, it makes no difference if that person is white, black, Hispanic, or Asian, or if they are Catholic, Protestant, Jew or Muslim, or whether they are Republic, Democrat or Independent, or whether they are conservative, liberal or progressive.

2. Ellicott, *Commentary for English Readers*, Luke 10:29.

The question is, who are you? What are you like? And the necessary corollary question is, "Are you like Christ?" Because if you are like Christ, then you will be like the good Samaritan. And, if you are not; if you are more like the priest or the Levite who ignored the need, then you are denying the very Christ you claim to follow.

John Piper is certainly correct when he explains, "When we are done trying to establish, 'Is this my neighbor?'—the decisive issue of love remains: What kind of person am I?"[3] So, the question is not "who is my neighbor?" The real question is—"How can I be a good neighbor, to anyone, no matter their rank, race, or religion?"

Go and Do!

Getting the lawyer to admit that it was the Samaritan (although he could not bring himself to refer to him as such) was the one who was neighbor to the man in need, Jesus' challenge to him, and by extension, to all of us today, is "Go and do likewise" (Luke 10:37). The New Century Version has it, "Then go and do what he did." The New Living Translation renders it, "Now go and do the same."

So, who is our neighbor? To whom do we commit such involvement? At this point, it will help to come to some agreement as to how we can understand the general term "neighbor." We must parse this term out so that we appreciate we are not just talking about some total stranger (as was the case in the parable).

For our Circle of Responsibilities, I have chosen to divide the outer circle into four entities, knowing that there will be necessary overlapping from each to the others at times. Accordingly, our Neighbor Circle is divided into these four entities: *Family, Church, Work,* and *Civic (Society).*

3. Piper, *"What Jesus Demands from the World,"* 264.

What will this circle teach us about these four?

- Any one of these and all of these can demand our time and attention.

- Any one of these can become our priority at any given time.

- How we react to any one of these, at any given time, will determine whether we are fulfilling Jesus' command to "love our neighbor as our self."

- How you manage your priorities concerning your Family, Church, Work, and Civic responsibilities will be driven by God at the center of your life.

Furthermore, this Circle of Responsibilities reveals another important spiritual truth, and it is powerful and unavoidable. You may be the only one through whom your neighbor will ever see God! You are positioned between those around you and the God who is in you. Will your spouse and children see God because of you? Will the people with whom you work know there is a God because they know you? Will those in your fellowship at church, as well as your fellow citizens down the block, be impacted for good and for God because He is at the center of your life?

Human Wreckage Everywhere

One afternoon when I was crossing one of the commons areas on the campus of California State University in Fullerton. I came upon the broken form of a large statue of David lying in the grass. It was a marble replica of Michelangelo's famous statue of David which was set up at Forest Lawn Memorial Park in Cypress, and which had toppled to the ground during the Whittier Narrows earthquake in 1987. Fallen, it had broken into eight pieces and would have been discarded, but a professor at CSUF arranged to have it donated and transferred to the campus in 1989. It quickly became an icon on the campus, as students began a tradition of walking by the toppled artifact and rubbing David's bare bottom to invoke the hope of scoring a passing grade on upcoming exams.

I remember thinking what a tragic image this presented. There he was, David, sprawled out in dismembered anguish; immobile, broken, eyes open staring up as if in shock, and worse, reduced to the laughs and snickers and handprints of those passing by. Perhaps that is our world today. Not just ignoring the fallen, but the trivialization of those who lie stricken by the roadside.

The parable of the good Samaritan is Jesus' reminder to us that our neighbor just may, in reality, be the fallen victim we come upon on the roadside. G. K. Chesterton observed that we make our friends, and we make our enemies, but God makes our neighbors.

Do we understand what he meant? God has put someone in your path. They may be on the other side of the fence, or across the street, or in the next cubicle at work. They might even be someone that you pass by on the way to work and they are crying out in need. They are out there, all around us, waiting for us to show up. They are on their Jericho Road, bruised and bloodied and broken.

And we need to know this: nobody cares if we have piety if we do not show pity. No one will care how much we know until they know how much we care. Nobody cares about our talk until they see our walk. People are not interested in our creeds as much as they are in our deeds. And, if they have any interest at all in what we believe, it will only be because they see us behave what we believe.

We may strive to be spiritually minded, but what is effective is when we become servant-hearted. The true test of that will be exposed when we are on "the Jericho road." Someone has well said that you will only know if you are a servant or not by the way you act when you are treated like one. So, every one of us must decide, on today's "Jericho roads," are we going to be a stranger or a servant?

Thirteen | My Family Circle

A FEW YEARS AGO, A man sent in the following comment to the *Family Q&A* page of Focus on the Family, and this is what he said:

> Is there really any scriptural basis for "focusing on the family"? "Family first" has always been my motto. I spend every weekend with my wife and kids, and I'm committed to putting their needs ahead of my own. But at times I find it hard to reconcile these personal values with the Gospel message. Jesus actually tells me to hate my family. His words seem to say that the church trumps the family system. I'm confused.[1]

Without trying to decipher his comments or his theology, I would simply point out that he speaks for a lot of people in our society today who are equally confused about family. They may not be as confused as he is from a religious perspective, as their uneasiness about today's family life is more the result of a culture that struggles to even define what the family is.

It is rather surprising just how divisive the task of defining "family" is in our modern society. Try to define the family as the traditional nuclear family (two married parents of opposite gender along with their biological and/or adopted children) and you are bound to offend someone, and the political correctness police will be banging on your door at midnight.

Nevertheless, to avoid any confusion, allow me at least to offer a rather short but working definition: "Family is a relationship, initially

---

1. "What the Bible Says About Family," *Focusonthefamily.com* (2017).

begun by a husband and wife and then children, in which personal growth and responsibility are nurtured."

This definition works for me because it involves a husband and wife (a biological male and a biological female) in a relationship, then (most normally) children, the addition of which adds another important level of relationship. And then the goal of those relationships is the interactive experiencing of growth and maturity whereby each member of the family benefits from being nurtured and protected.

The United Nations Human Rights Council passed a resolution in June of 2015 entitled *Protection of the family*, in which, rather surprisingly, they upheld a more traditional family portrait by declaring: "The family, while respect for the rights of its members is ensured, is a strong force for social cohesion and integration, intergenerational solidarity and social development, and that the family plays a crucial role in the preservation of cultural identity, traditions, morals, heritage, and value system of the society."[2]

G. K. Chesterton said that the natural family, the father, mother, and child, has been the success of every society. It is what he referred to as the "Triangle of Truism," which, he warned, cannot be destroyed but would only destroy the civilization that disregards it.[3]

Nothing Like Family

There is nothing quite like family. We think we know all about families. After all, we know about the First Family, The Addams Family, the Partridge Family, All in the Family, Family Ties, the Family Affair, and the Modern Family, and any number of other family-based programs and presentations, all of which should remind us that almost none of them represent the family as does the Bible.

The Scripture gives the family supreme status. The Bible gives the family a preeminent position throughout history. The Family is the most basic and essential component of society. The creation of "Family" predates all other earthly institutions. The family is first, before human government, before the priesthood, before the church. The family is society's foundation.

---

2. Human Rights Council Twenty-ninth session, Agenda item 3.

3. Chesterton, *Superstition of Divorce*, 13.

According to the apostle Paul, there certainly was a mystery surrounding the creation of the church (Ephesians 3:9). And we would all agree that there always has been a certain mystery as to who and what politicians are supposed to be doing in terms of human government. But there is NO mystery as to what the family is supposed to be.

Former Secretary of Education William J. Bennett has proven to be a strong advocate for the traditional family, claiming that the family is the nucleus of civilization and the basic social unit of society. In his book *The Broken Hearth: Reversing the Moral Collapse of the American Family*, he writes that "the family is and always has been the first and most important incubator of those habits of trust, altruism, responsibility, and mutual obligation on which civil society depends." He then quotes Michael Novak's well-known statement, that the family is the first, best, and original Department of Health, Education and Welfare.[4]

I like that. Our homes should be a place of "health," a place for "education," and a place where the "welfare" of each family member is of utmost concern. Civilization can continue if governments and states fall. Society will suffer but still, go on if churches falter. But society will begin to crumble and disintegrate when the family fails!

Focus on the Family

There must be no confusion about this one thing, which is we ought to *focus on the family*. The family is worth our attention. Each of our families merits our obsession. And why? Because God has made the family a priority. It does not take long in the Bible to hear what God thought about family: "The Lord God said, 'It is not good for the man to be alone. I will make a helper suitable for him'" (Gen 2:18 NIV). "Then the LORD God made a woman from the rib he had taken out of the man, and he brought her to the man. The man said, "This is now bone of my bones and flesh of my flesh; she shall be called 'woman,' for she was taken out of man." That is why a man leaves his father and mother and is united to his wife, and they become one flesh" (Gen 2:22–24 NIV).

Consider that in creating family, God addresses the prospect of human loneliness and therefore the need for human companionship, which also touches on the need for unity and oneness. Furthermore, and rather

---

4. Bennett, *Broken Hearth*, 178.

obvious, the relationship provides for the successful and biological formula for procreation.

If there is a theology of the family, it seems obvious that focus is put on the levels of relationships within the family unit. Accordingly, Scripture has something to say about them, often and in both Testaments. Simply stated, these primary relationships can be set forth as Husband to Wife and Wife to Husband relationships (Eph 5:25–33), and Parent to Child and Child to Parent relationships (Eph 6:1–4).

Paul also summarizes basic family relationships in his Epistle to the Colossians: "Wives, submit yourselves to your husbands, as is fitting in the Lord. Husbands, love your wives and do not be harsh with them. Children, obey your parents in everything, for this pleases the Lord" (Col 3:18–20 NIV). The ideal is harmonious relationships, but it is not always so, and we all know that. Given that we are all distinct personalities, whenever we are thrust together that distinctiveness may be on full display. Disharmony and dysfunction quickly follow. It has been said that a dysfunctional family is defined as any family with more than one member. There is some truth to that!

Still, the Scriptural norm for the family is that there should be more calm than chaos, more serenity than hysteria, and more bottom floor of Heaven and less top floor of Hell. Yet, as is too often the case in many families today, there is plenty of chaos and hysteria to go around. Tragically, for some, family life is a living hell.

I have an idea that most of us know where the tension and dysfunction are coming from. The inability to resolve interpersonal and relational conflicts is ongoing. The Scriptural plea to prefer the other over oneself is going unheeded. The Biblical mandate to love one another is too often ignored. And yet, it is only the application of God's love that will heal our relationships. We have to apply *agape* love, which is a love of the will more than just a love of the emotion. We must decide, and quickly, that we are going to love our family no matter what.

No one said it was going to be easy. There are going to be husband and wife issues. There are going to be difficulties with childrearing. We have kids and they do not come with instructions. It can be extremely frustrating and exasperating, taxing a parent to the breaking point. Yet, those family relationships are God's gift to you. Desmond Tutu saw it that way, saying that we do not choose our family but that they are God's gift to us as we are to them.

So, especially as it relates to childrearing, God's grace and wisdom are essential to be an effective parent. They may tire us but train them we must. They may exasperate us but encourage them we must. They may anger us but love them we must. They may hurt us but help them we must.

And one thing is certain, our children are watching us. They are learning from us. They witness the good and the bad. Hopefully, they will export the positive examples, but they also may import the negative ones. A rather lazy and unmotivated dad complained to his equally lazy and unmotivated teenage son, "Why don't you go out and do something! Don't you know what Abraham Lincoln was doing at your age?" To which the boy replied, "No, I don't, but I do know what he was doing at your age."

In *The Message* paraphrase of Colossians 3:21, the apostle Paul writes, "Parents, don't come down too hard on your children or you'll crush their spirits." I remember reading about a college sophomore who spent most of the school year in one kind of trouble or another. Towards the end of the school year, he received a postcard from his parents who were vacationing in Greece: "Dear Son, We are now standing high on a cliff overlooking the Aegean sea from which the ancient Spartan women once hurled their defective children to the rocks below. *WISH YOU WERE HERE.* Love, Mom and Dad."

Nice one! But in all seriousness, don't throw your kids onto the rocks, throw them upon The Rock. Bring them to the Cross. It is at the foot of the Cross where families come to find each other, forever! (John 19:25–27) It is because of Calvary that we can fulfill God's word and will for their lives and our families.

And that is what life is all about. Certainly, that is what the Christian life is all about. It is about life and that life more abundantly. It is about being made alive in Christ and then translating that quality of life to those around us. And who needs to see and experience that life more than our children? I agree with Patrick Morley who said that most fathers would die for their children, but what we need are fathers who will live for their children![5]

Living for the benefit of the children God has allowed us to have is one of the great callings and challenges of life. A serious and heartfelt response to that calling is the only way we can apply the numerous

5. Morley, *Man in the Mirror*, 97.

Scriptural challenges, such as: "Bring up our children in the nurture and admonition of the Lord" (Eph 6:4). The Contemporary English Version translates this: "Raise them properly. Teach them and instruct them about the Lord." Then there is the well-known "Train up a child in the way he should go" in Proverbs 22:6, which the New Century Version has as "Train children to live the right way, and when they are old, they will not stray from it." One of my favorite "family" verses in the Bible is in Genesis where we read, "The Angel of the Lord says of Abraham—I have chosen him to teach his family to obey me forever and to do what is right and fair" (Gen 18:19 CEV).

Our Family Circle

This series is based on the premise that God should be at the center of our lives, and when he is, whoever is around us can be touched by God through us. And so, who is closer to us than our family? This premise (and promise) is no more acute than when it comes to our family. Of those comprising your neighborhood of relationships, none are more important nor closer to you than your family.

The family is needed in our society as never before. Yet, the family has always been needed in society. The family faces difficulties in our society as never before. Yet, it has always faced difficulties. And, you know as well as I do, that the family is under attack in our society as never before. Yet, the family has always been under attack. Why?

The family is under attack, has been under attack, and will remain under attack because it is important to God, and therefore all who hate

God, Satan leading the charge, have always tried to disrupt it, discourage it, destroy it!

Criticism and attacks on the family have increased since the last half of the twentieth century. In 1970 Feminist Kate Millet's book, *Sexual Politics* advocated that the family must go because it is the family that has oppressed and enslaved women.[6] In the same year, British Liberal physician David Cooper released his book, *The Death of the Family*, in which he claimed that the best thing society could do was to abolish the family altogether.[7]

In *Marriage and the Family: An Ideological Battleground*, Wendy McElroy provides this analysis as an excerpt from her book *Sexual Correctness: The Gender-Feminist Attack on Women*. She identifies what she refers to as an ideological brawl between the two opposing voices over the institutions of marriage and the family:

> Conservatives champion the family as indispensable to civilization. Only families can offer the long-term emotional stability and commitment that child-rearing requires. Only families can ensure reproduction and the proper socialization of children . . . families provide a support system for married couples, who need shelter against the buffets of a hostile world. Without the family, conservatives predict the breakdown of moral values and an upsurge of social anarchy. From the opposite end of the political spectrum, gender feminists roundly reject the family for much the same reasons that conservatives embrace it. It is a bastion of traditional values and a training ground for society's institutions. In short, the family is the foundation of patriarchal capitalism, which gender feminists claim is the source of women's oppression.[8]

The ongoing outcome of all this is that, as in all battles, there will be casualties on both sides and usually with devastating consequences. There will also be collateral damage, and in this war, the damage is both physical and spiritual, emotional, and psychological, economic and educational.

A Post-Modern and humanistic society, infatuated with Political Correctness, will continue to advertise to our children alternative lifestyles and a continual redefining of who and what the family is. As

6. Millet, *Sexual Politics*, (1978).

7. Cooper, *Death of the Family*, (1970).

8. McElroy, "Marriage and the Family: An Ideological Battleground," (1996).

a result, one can only imagine how families will be defined and what families may look like in future generations to come. Gene Edward Veith, Jr. correctly observed that "The breakdown of the family has had catastrophic effects at every level. It is difficult for children to develop any sense of continuity and permanence when the most basic institution of their lives has no stability."[9]

While pastoring the National Presbyterian Church in Washington D.C. when President Ronald Reagan attended, Louis H. Evans, Jr. believed that the decay of the home as the national unit was one of the most perilous characteristics of our age. He warned then that when the home is destroyed, God loses one of the greatest theological seminaries in the world.

Miqdash Meyat

What a stirring idea that is, that our homes can be a theological seminary. Have you ever thought of your home that way? Would you be committed to making sure your family receives the spiritual and Scriptural underpinnings it deserves? Is that practical? Is that possible?

As Christians, we know that teaching our children is paramount. We know that loving and nurturing our families is God's will. And, as Christians, we have plenty of encouragement and tools in the New Testament to make this task effective. Certainly, the control and leading of the Holy Spirit are available to us, as Jesus promised. In concert with that let me suggest that there is something else we can learn to do, and it comes to us as we observe our Jewish friends. We can put into practice what Jews in their families have practiced for thousands of years: *Miqdash Meyat*.

Jews believe the family unit is more important than the Temple or synagogue. The Temple was called *miqdash*, from the Hebrew verb *qadash*, which means to be set apart, holy, consecrated. For that reason, the Jewish marriage is called *qiddushin*, a term also is derived from *qadash*, and conveys the sacred and consecrated bond established between the husband and wife.

After the destruction of the Temple in 70AD, rabbis began referring to the Jewish home as a *miqdash meyat* - a small sanctuary, a little temple (the adjective *meyat* means small). Some scholars believe that the rabbis might have taken the phrase from Ezekiel 11:16 where God is

9. Veith, Jr., *Postmodern Times*, 144.

making a promise to the Jews in exile (assuming *meyat* is understood as an adjective and not an adverb): "I shall be a little sanctuary for them in the countries where they have gone." The Jewish Talmud states "God will dwell in the holy spaces we create, for they are the Temple in miniature."[10] Accordingly, a Jewish father never thinks of his home as his "castle," but rather something greater, something far higher! The home is his *Sanctuary*. His home is his *Temple*. And as such, it is holy, sacred, set apart, consecrated. No wonder Satan hates it!

We need to take more seriously the New Testament injunction and instruction that there is a priesthood of the believer. I noticed in Larry Christenson's well-known book, *The Christian Family*, that he has a chapter entitled *The Priesthood of Parents*. Referring to Peter's charge that Christians are a royal priesthood (1 Pet 2:9) and that this extends to our homes as well, Christenson writes, "What a field of service the Christian home affords for this privileged ministry. Parent-priests of the Lord! Called and ordained by God as priests unto their children."[11] As priests, functioning in the conventional sense (presenting God to the people, and then presenting the people to God), Christenson reminds us that the priesthood of parents involves this similar, most basic of tasks; presenting God to our children and then presenting our children to God.[12]

So, there is something incredibly special about this idea of *Miqdash Meyat*. As Martin Luther revived the concept of the priesthood of the believer in the Reformation, perhaps it is time for Christians today to renew our commitment to being priests as parents with our children. We need to realize that we owe a lot more to our *Jewish roots* than just our Savior.

Considering this amazing truth from Jewish life, it stands to reason, then, that such an environment would be given over to teaching the life-changing truths from God's Holy Word. Consider then, that the Hebrew word for a teacher is *Moreh* and the Hebrew word for parent is *Horeh*, and both words come from the Hebrew word *Torah* (the *Law*, but better, the *Teachings*). Jewish parents know that *Horeh* identifies them as those who are "directing and instructing" (their children). Therefore, as teachers themselves, Jewish parents know that they are to teach. But teach what?

> These are the commands, rules, and laws that the LORD your God told me to teach you to obey in the land you are crossing

---

10. Talmud (*Megilah* 29a)

11. Christenson, *Christian Family*, 157.

12. Christenson, *Christian Family*, 158.

the Jordan River to take. You, your children, and your grand-
children must respect the LORD your God as long as you live.
Obey all his rules and commands I give you so that you will live
a long time. Listen, Israel, and carefully obey these laws. Then
all will go well for you, and you will become a great nation in
a fertile land, just as the LORD, the God of your ancestors, has
promised you.

Listen, people of Israel! The LORD our God is the only LORD.
Love the LORD your God with all your heart, all your soul, and
all your strength. Always remember these commands I give you
today. Teach them to your children, and talk about them when
you sit at home and walk along the road, when you lie down and
when you get up. Write them down and tie them to your hands
as a sign. Tie them on your forehead to remind you, and write
them on your doors and gates (Deut 6:1–9 NCV).

It's All About Family

Given that it provides the most significant theme for this book, did
you notice that the Great Commandment is in the context of Family?
Jewish parents assumed the responsibility of loving and serving God and
communicating that to children. Jewish children learned the word and
will of God, and to be obedient to both God and parents.

Certainly, this is the theological backdrop for Paul's exhortation
in Ephesians: "Children, obey your parents because you belong to the
Lord, for this is the right thing to do. 'Honor your father and mother.'
This is the first commandment with a promise: If you honor your father
and mother, 'things will go well for you, and you will have a long life on
the earth.' Fathers, do not provoke your children to anger by the way you
treat them. Rather, bring them up with the discipline and instruction that
comes from the Lord" (Eph 6:1–4 NLT).

Listen, guys. Listen up, dads. The Hebrew term *moreh* is masculine.
The challenge in Deuteronomy 6 is intended initially for fathers. And
Paul affirms that in Ephesians 6:4, starting the verse by saying "Fathers." It
should not surprise us that the attack on the home and the family has always been to marginalize men. The tactic has always been to undermine
the man, the husband, the father. The attacks range from subtle suggestions to outright assaults. I have often cringed at the way men are usually
portrayed in TV commercials. Men (especially husbands and dads) are

usually depicted as bumbling morons, unable to figure anything out on their own. Idiotic dads are "exposed" as being incapable of taking cold medication to shopping in grocery stores to buying cars.

I am convinced that this incessant assault on American manhood has taken its toll. Men are heading for the exits, fed up and no longer interested. And, of course, when this happens the family does indeed suffer. Weldon Hardenbrook wrote an insightful book some years ago entitled, *Missing From Action: Vanishing Manhood in America.* In just one sentence he captures what has happened as a result: "Men have been delegating their spiritual duties to women, walked out of the church, and have lost sight of God as Father."[13]

If he is correct and we have lost generations of men, the impact on the family will continue to be devastating and in a state of decline. Sociologists who have any sense know how damaging it can be to have a family where the father has gone AWOL.

We must own this. Our wives are suffering, our children are suffering, our families are suffering. And the solution, once again, lies in the call to allow God to be the center of your life. Solomon wrote that "reverence for God gives a man deep strength; his children have a place of refuge and security" (Prov 14:26 TLB).

Think of how important this one verse of Scripture is. The man who has not walked out on God or his family, the man who has a reverence and love for God will be a man of deep strength. And not only that, that strength will reinforce the sense of security that his wife and children will feel. His children will flourish in that environment of security and safety.

But do not fail to see the effects of the opposite of this. Once again, as fathers, we are always teaching our children, but it is *what* we are teaching that matters. Our children are listening, watching, waiting. Austin Sorensen is correct when he said that a child is not likely to find a father in God unless he finds something of God in his father.

Abraham is the father of the faithful (Rom 4:16) and therefore it follows that you could even say that he is the father of families (at least, devotionally). What is said of him and to him by God should be of great importance to all men who would lead their families, "For I have known him, in order that he may command his children and his household after him, that they keep the way of the Lord, to do righteousness and justice" (Gen 18:19).

13. Hardenbrook, *Missing From Action*, 62.

Family as a Flock

Psalm 107:4 tells us that God "sets the poor on high, far from afflic-tion, and makes their families like a flock." So, Scripture informs us that our families are like a flock. But a flock of what? A flock of geese? A flock of penguins? A flock of eagles? (That would fit nicely with Isaiah 40:31.) Well, no, the reference would imply a flock of sheep, which would be the most obvious and oft-used Biblical motif.

This designation and alignment with sheep are not without sig-nificance. The family is not likened to a pack of wolves (even though we certainly live in a dog-eat-dog world). The family is not likened to a pride of lions, because, well, everyone knows that God resists the proud. The family is not likened to a lonely bear roaming the forest (even though we are called upon to bear one another's burdens).

The family is likened to a flock of sheep. We should acknowledge that, at first glance, this may not be all that flattering. We often think sheep are dumb, defenseless, and always in danger, and they are. (We are!) For this reason, along with the pastoral environment of much of the landscape of both Testaments, Scripture has tabbed them to be symbolic of the people of God.

But to fully understand this symbolism, we need to appreciate some of the other unique characteristics of a flock of sheep. You might be sur-prised that it is all not just so much dumbness and danger. Haven't you cringed at times when you hear all the negative stereotyping of being sheep? Isn't there anything good that can be said about being sheep? Are there any positive points that we can embrace about the alignment Scrip-ture makes of us as sheep? Well, actually there are.

For instance, did you know that sheep are relatively clean animals? We should be glad that the Scripture does not say that we are pigs or goats, who roll around in the mud and like it, as well as eat anything that they can find, junk or not, and like that too. Translate this into social dy-namics and what is affecting our children today. Years ago, Jesse Jackson nailed it when he said that we allow our kids to eat junk, see junk, listen to junk, own junk, and then we wonder why they grow up to be social junkies!

But Sheep? They will not eat junk. Sheep will only eat fresh grass and drink clean water. That is the reason shepherds find the proper graz-ing pastures. That is the reason we read, "He makes me to lie down in green pastures; He leads me beside the still waters."

Another truth we must know about sheep is that they are intelligent enough to hear and recognize the voice of their shepherd. This can be demonstrated when multiple flocks of sheep are gathered at the same watering hole to drink. Once finished, each shepherd calls out to his sheep, and they will respond and follow their own shepherd.

Notice how Jesus acknowledged this positive trait when he was speaking of the shepherd (and that He was the Good Shepherd) and that, "the sheep recognize his voice and come to him. He calls his own sheep by name and leads them out. After he has gathered his own flock, he walks ahead of them, and they follow him because they know his voice. They won't follow a stranger; they will run from him because they don't know his voice" (John 10:3–5 NLT).

It is certainly true that sheep more than any other animal need protection that only a Shepherd can provide. That is why Psalm 23 is the all-time greatest passage of Scripture highlighting the dependency of sheep on their shepherd.

And along with this, it is also true that sheep more than any other animal depend on the fellowship of the flock. Sheep need to be flocked together because sheep know that the flock provides at least three things. Simply put, those three things would be warmth, support, and strength.

The application to families as a flock should be obvious. Sheep know about "flocking" together—the warmth that their family huddle provides. Sheep know "flocking" time means support—to hold up each other (literally "lean on me"). And sheep know that sheer numbers of the flock can increase the strength of the flock. Perhaps the most amazing analogy about a flock of sheep and the family is this idea of togetherness and community. Sheep are not loners. They are not like lone wolves. It is the wolves that prey upon them. They depend on each other, even to the point of not being fully able to function or even survive without each other.

George Barna, in *The Future of the American Family*, tells us that "successful families are successful largely because they offer safety, trust, and permanence." His surveys show that once a family ceases to offer those protections, the atmosphere for love and intimacy is lost, and opportunities for personal and joint growth are largely forfeited, and, ultimately, the family falters.[14]

---

14. Barna, *Future of the American Family*, 35.

This assessment should alert us to the increasing danger to our families—that of our current culture's penchant for fragmenting the family. Even before mobile phones moved us farther away from interacting with each other, there was the inclination for each family member to pack up their stuff and go their way for whatever activity beckoned them. It is certainly normal and acceptable to each have varied interests and the time and space to pursue them but pushed to the extreme this tendency has not always been healthy, especially if it continually deprives the family of doing things together as a family.

Gene Veith comments on this and sees it as a result of modernism and even post-modernism: "Modernistic values have atomized the family. The exaggerated individualism that characterizes modernism has split families, with each parent seeking his or her own private identity with no regard for the children, who likewise are left on their own. Ironically, such extreme individual autonomy does not allow for the formation of a strong sense of identity, which is generally formed by nurturing solid families." [15] (He goes on to refer to a generation therefore that has been left to fend for itself.)

Legion are the Enemies

While all of this is true, it is also important to point out that the warmth, support, and strength that family provides does not however prevent our family from being attacked. Family interaction should help us cope with threatening times, but it does not ensure that we will not experience threatening times.

Our families need our attention. Enemies of the family are legion. The problems are complex. But the solution to many of the ills of our society is right in front of us. The healing starts in our own homes. It is parents and not politicians that will save the family.

Hillary Clinton wanted to convince us that it takes a village to raise our children, and more or less by that, she meant getting the government and the greater community's involvement in the process. But do we really need the government to raise our kids? We need fathers who have been engaged and challenged by God's Word, and moms who have been established and honored because of God's Word, and children who have been encouraged and trained in God's Word.

15. Veith Jr., *Postmodern Times*, 80.

In June of 1990, then First Lady Barbara Bush delivered the commencement speech at prestigious Wellesley College in Massachusetts. Her well-thought-out words included a challenge that still has relevance to our day. Among the choices facing them, she told the graduating class that one of the choices that must not be missed was to cherish their relationships with family and friends. She said:

> For several years you've had impressed upon you the importance to your career of dedication and hard work, and of course that's true. But as important as your obligations as a doctor, a lawyer, a business leader will be, you are a human being first and those human connections with spouses, with children, with friends are the most important investment you will ever make. At the end of your life, you will never regret not having passed one more test, winning one more verdict, or not closing one more deal. You will regret time not spent with a husband, a child, a friend or a parent.[16]

And then with keen insight and years of experience, she concluded her speech with this challenge: "You must read to your children and you must hug your children and you must love your children. Your success as a family, our success as a society, depends not on what happens in the White House, but on what happens inside your house."[17]

She is right, of course. Her words remain true today. It starts with our house. It is all about the focus on our family. It is all about the shepherding of our flock. It is all about leading and directing our children. As Christians, we need to borrow from and emulate the Jewish concept of *Miqdash Meyat*. Be parent-priests. Consecrate your home to be a special place of holiness, healthiness, and happiness. Set it apart to God.

Consecrate your home to be a place where God is at the center because that is where he is in your life. And then, as that becomes your biblical paradigm, watch how your family takes on the characteristics of the Great Commandment. A place where God is loved and served. A place where each family member is loved and served. A place where your extended family is loved and served. And a place from which your neighbor is loved and served.

As you continue to build into that type of priority relative to your family, with confidence you will be able to say more and more the words

16. Bush, "Believe in Something Larger that Yourself," *Time.com*, (1990).

17. Bush, "Believe in Something Larger that Yourself," *Time.com*, (1990).

of Joshua about his family, "As for me and my house, we will serve the Lord" (Josh 24:15). A home like that; a family embracing those biblical principles, will have the blessing of God upon it. It will be a holy, healthy, and happy place. And as George Bernard Shaw once observed, a happy family is but an earlier heaven.

What can you do to make society safer? It starts with sheltering your family. What can you do to strengthen our country? It starts with strengthening your family. What will increase the effectiveness of outreach by churches? It starts with teaching your family. What will have a lasting impact on your neighbors? When your neighbors see your family endure, even in the face of all the enemies surrounding it.

So, we certainly must focus on our families. We cannot avoid this calling and challenge. We cannot duck the responsibility. We cannot expect someone else or some other entity to do it for us. God has put you into your family. It is your family circle and no one else's. It is your circle of responsibility. Yours! Therefore, it is up to you. It is up to us. We Christians!

Given that the family is the foundation upon which society will survive, it needs the special attention of us all. Mother Teresa when asked what could be done to promote world peace, answered simply, that everyone should go home and love their family. Sound, spiritual advice.

Fourteen | Watch Out For Work

I am in no hurry, I'm on my way to work

THAT IS WHAT THE BUMPER sticker announced on the car in front of me one morning. Hard to tell if it was a warning to not follow too closely because I would also then be late, or not to follow too close because having to get up and go to work obviously irritated this person and they would probably be reckless and maybe even dangerous. In any event, I thought that it probably spoke for a lot of people in our culture who share a similarly dim view of work (they just do not plaster it on the back bumpers of their cars).

All we need to do is listen to the way people refer to their jobs. Mostly it is with a battery of derogatory terms, such as a rat race, or coal mines, or prison, or chains and shackles, and so on. No wonder we see that when someone hits a lottery and comes into more money they could have ever imagined, the first decision they make is to do what? Quit their job!

Our love/hate relationship with our jobs is further illustrated in our culture by how we advertise our dread of Mondays but, of course, delight in the prospect of Fridays. We even give a nod toward God, as we abbreviate that delight and our relief by saying "TGIF!" And so, here is something you will probably never hear—"Thank God it's Monday!"

Surveys routinely show that upwards of 80 percent of those polled dislike their jobs, are dissatisfied with their career choices, and simply hate to go to work. Forbes Magazine reported a Gallup survey showing that over 70 percent of workers are not engaged by their work, and/or are actively disengaged from their work. It was also reported that work is more often a source of frustration than fulfillment for nearly 90 percent of the world's workers. Ninety percent!

This tendency to dislike work is not new, but it is getting worse. A hundred years ago, Arnold Bennett referred to men in his day that lacked a passion for their work, who would reluctantly begin their workday as late as they could and end that day with joy as early as they could![1] Closer to our day, it is the reason comedian Drew Carey quipped, "Oh, you hate your job? Why didn't you say so? There's a support group for that. It's called EVERYBODY, and they meet at the bar." Haha, funny. But, then again, really it isn't.

We spend one-third (or more) of our days at work. Work defines us as people, and sociologists tell us when we are not happy at work, other areas of our life suffer. So, work—having a vocation—holding down a job, is a priority we must allow for in our Circle of Responsibilities.

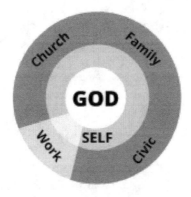

Work's Theology

Because I am going to come at this topic from a Christian mindset and worldview, I believe it is essential that we explore and affirm what we might call a theology of work. That is to say, are there identifiable truths in the Bible that pertain to the concept of work, and by that, I mean work as a job, that which is identified as one's employment?

Most would agree with and understand this basic definition, that "Work is our employment for which we receive compensation in order to provide for ourselves and our family." And that would be the basic Bible idea as well, insofar as it pertains to mankind.

---

1. Bennett, *How to Live on 24 Hours a Day*, 15.

But the Bible does have more to say about work, especially in a general sense, and that which would include God himself. We note early on in Scripture that God worked. Indeed, the very first verse of the Bible tells us that God created the heavens and the earth (Gen 1:1). That is some serious work, as the opening chapters of Genesis attest. Then throughout the pages of Scripture, in both Testaments, we witness the works and working of God. In one succinct statement, Jesus declares, "My Father is always working, and so am I" (John 5:17 NLT).

The next thing we can affirm in our theology of work is that God then challenges us to work. We like the idea of leisure and rest incorporated into the Sabbath instruction, but do not forget the reason for it is the necessity of and instruction to work. "Six days you shall do your work..." (Exod 23:12). In the New Testament, Paul declares, "Let him who stole steal no longer, but rather let him labor, working with his hands what is good, that he may have something to give him who has need" (Eph 4:28). Solomon confesses in Ecclesiastes 2:24, "So I decided there is nothing better than to enjoy food and drink and to find satisfaction in work. Then I realized that these pleasures are from the hand of God."

Coming to terms with a theology of work will also result in an understanding that work glorifies God. As with anything else we do, if we do it as unto the Lord and for his glory, it will receive his blessing. Moses understood this and so prayed in his great Psalm, "Let Your work appear to Your servants and Your glory to their children. And let the beauty of the Lord our God be upon us and establish the work of our hands for us; Yes, establish the work of our hands" (Ps 90:16–17). James Moffatt renders this verse, "Lord, may Thy Loving favor rest on us, and prosper all the work we undertake."

A theology of work carries with it unavoidable accountability to God. Furthermore, for Christians, it is an issue of faith as well as family. This must be the reason why Paul would remind Timothy, "But if anyone does not provide for his own, and especially for those of his household, he has denied the faith and is worse than an unbeliever" (1 Tim 5:8). Why would Paul say that? Why would a believer be *worse* than an unbeliever? It can only be because at least the unbeliever is working and providing for his own. And he is not even doing it to glorify God.

On Your Honor

We must also sense in this accountability equation that working honestly and providing for your family is the honorable thing to do. There is a nobility about work. There is a sense of that in Solomon's statement in Proverbs 22:29, "Do you see a man who excels in his work? He will stand before kings." The Good News Translation fleshes it out this way, "Show me someone who does a good job, and I will show you someone who is better than most and worthy of the company of kings."

A man must live with honor. And one way to live honorably is to work with a sense of integrity and accountability. Pretty much in any job, someone is counting on you. You have been entrusted with a task (whatever that might be, in whatever profession you have chosen). Do it honorably and faithfully. There is a great line in the movie *Rob Roy*, in which the Scottish MacGregor clan leader, Robert Roy MacGregor, is reminded by his wife Mary, that "Honor is the gift a man gives himself." That is such a great statement. You cannot be forced to be dignified. You cannot be coerced to be honorable. You can only decide to live your life that way on your own. And it will be the type of life that God will bless abundantly.

What would be God's perfect will for any man as he should be, is seen in the fact that the Lord has bequeathed honor to man as well. David said that man has been "crowned with glory and honor" (Ps 8:5). Those two Hebrew words could be translated as "weight" and "dignity." I like to think of it as "gravity" and "integrity." You cannot fake these things, nor can you request others to think of you as such. Like respect, these traits are earned. The Apostle Paul knew that and so wrote to the Christians in Thessalonica, "Make it your ambition to lead a quiet life, to mind your own business and to work with your hands, just as we told you, so that your daily life may win the respect of outsiders and so that you will not be dependent on anybody" (1 Thess 4:11–12 NIV). Thomas Carlyle wrote, "There is a perennial nobleness and even sacredness in work. In idleness alone is there perpetual despair. A man perfects himself by working. All work, even cotton spinning is noble. Work alone is noble."[2]

At this point, it might be necessary to mention the calamity of just the opposite trait and that which causes such perpetual despair. The Bible refers to it as "sloth;" a characteristic of idleness and laziness that is soundly rebuked in Scripture. The Proverbs unload a steady barrage

2. Carlyle, *Past and Present,* in *The Great Quotations,* 985.

of warning: "Lazy hands make for poverty" (Prov 10:4); "Life collapses on loafers; lazybones go hungry" (Prov 19:15 MSG); "A nap here, a nap there, a day off here, a day off there, sit back, take it easy—do you know what comes next? Just this: You can look forward to a dirt-poor life, with poverty as your permanent houseguest!" (Prov 24:34 MSG); and "All hard work brings profit, but mere talk leads only to poverty" (Prov14:23 NIV).

Lebanese poet Kahlil Gibran, with a middle-eastern flare, wrote that "Work is love made visible. And if you cannot work with love but only with distaste, it is better that you should leave your work and sit at the gate of the temple and take alms of those who work with joy."[3]

Work: Curse or Blessing?

For so many in our culture, the verdict is still out on whether work is a blessing or a curse. It is at the very least, in the minds of many, a necessary evil. Why is that? Part of the problem, I believe, is that too many people have bought into a false narrative about work. Erroneous ideas surround the concept of work and as such our complaints and dissatisfaction with our employment become a self-fulfilling prophecy.

Let us consider that, in practice, we consistently make three common mistakes in our understanding of work. The first mistake is that we believe that work is a result of the Fall. We read in Genesis 3 that man is now going to have to slave away in sweat and tears and that work will forever be a burden. But we fail to recognize that Adam was given work to do before the Fall. Man was a worker before he was a sinner. Work is not a direct result of the Fall; the concept of work was victimized by the Fall.

The effect of the "Fall" was that the curse would affect our "work." As a result of man's rebellion, man's work would now become toilsome. Work would now be harsh, grievous, unsatisfying, sweaty, dirty. Instead of meaningful, it now had the potential to be just plain mean!

Eugene Peterson paraphrases this important passage thus: "The very ground is cursed because of you; getting food from the ground will be as painful as having babies is for your wife; you'll be working in pain all your life long. The ground will sprout thorns and weeds, you'll get your food the hard way, planting and tilling and harvesting, sweating in the fields from dawn to dusk, until you return to that ground yourself,

3. Gibran, *The Prophet* (1923).

dead and buried; you started out as dirt, you'll end up dirt" (Gen 3:17–19 MSG).

So, it is the corruption of the work ethic that is a result of the Fall, rather than work itself being levied on mankind due to Adam's sin. Initially, work was intended to be a blessing, not a burden. It was supposed to be a gift, not a grief. It was supposed to be satisfying and fulfilling, not unsatisfying and unfulfilling.

The Biblical paradigm was to follow Genesis 1:31, "Then God saw everything that He had made (His work) and indeed it was very good!" But, through Adam's choice and Satan's plan, man now looks upon work as a curse and does not see any good in it at all.

Lawrence Richards summarized the reality of work affected by the Fall. He writes: "Human beings live in a world in which work has meaning. Sin has affected the universe to the extent that work has become a struggle with an unresponsive earth rather than the simple and creative joy intended in the original creation. Work can be productive and satisfying or fruitless and frustrating. Work can exhaust us with its drudgery or exalt us with a sense of accomplishment."[4]

Just a Paycheck?

There is another mistaken notion that most people embrace concerning their job—the belief that the only reason to work is so that we can get a paycheck. Now, I am realistic enough to know that we certainly work to make money, but I am also idealistic enough to believe that there are other reasons why we should work.

Some of those reasons might include seeking your place in society, making a contribution, achieving a sense of fulfillment, enjoying a sense of accomplishment, the thrill of being productive, the necessity to be challenged, our need to tackle tasks and to solve problems, the benefit we gain by having interpersonal relationships, our need to have a sense of responsibility and accountability.

All these things are valid and have very little to do with money or getting a paycheck. We need to be reminded of the theological truth that God would have us work for other reasons than just money. To that impressive and necessary list must be added this—the ultimate satisfaction of having a purpose in life. A recognition of this allows us to experience

4. Richards, *Creative Bible Teaching*, 67.

our employment evolving from a job to a career to a calling. Our work then moves from that which we think is necessary to that which gives us an identity to that which, ultimately, gives life meaning.

Our jobs should add to our lives, not just add to our bank account. David McKenna wrote what I think is one of the best articles on this subject in *Toward a Theology of Work*. In his paper, he expresses what the biblical work ethic should mean to those of us who claim to follow Christ as our Lord and Savior. He writes: "The biblical ethic integrates work with the meaning of life. A sense of 'vocation' is the motive that a Christian brings to work in the context of the totality of life and the rhythm of work, rest, worship, and play. Joy is the immediate by-product of our calling, satisfaction is the intermediate value, and the glory of God is the chief end to which we live and work."[5]

In *To Be A Man* (*Lifestyles for today's Christian—at Work—at Leisure*), author Robert Spike observes, "No man can say he believes that Christ is the sign of God's purposing work in history and then step back and say, 'I'll spend my life sitting this one out,' or worse, frittering his life away with petty embellishments and nonsense. Every man is called to be something by the very act of what God did in Christ. And how a man earns his money and uses his creative capacity is an important part of that calling."[6]

Is It Really Important to God?

This leads us then to yet one more mistake we make when trying to understand our jobs—we believe that our work because it is "secular," is therefore not as important to God as work that is "sacred." This is easily one of our biggest misconceptions, especially amongst Christians, as well as religious people in general. Simply put, it is the belief that there are two categories (or ideals), one that is sacred and holy and the other that is secular and profane.

As it pertains to the subject of work and employment, it identifies certain vocational "professions" as sacred, for instance, the clergy, while all the rest of work is of necessity, secular. While there has always been a certain distinction between these two worlds, it has taken on more compartmentalization over the last hundred years or so. Many believe it can

5. McKenna, *Theology of Work*, 5.

6. Spike, *To be a Man*, 43.

be traced to French sociologist Émile Durkheim, who referred to it as the sacred–profane dichotomy and that it is the central characteristic of religion.

Clearly, the Scriptures do make a distinction between that which has been sanctified, "set apart," and therefore in contrast with that which simply is of this world. However, as it relates to our understanding of work, the Bible does not make a distinction between that which is sacred and that which is secular. As Christians, we know that all that we do, we are to do for the Lord, as unto the Lord, and for His glory. Paul reminds us that whatever we do, do all to the glory of God (1 Cor 10:31).

When we compartmentalize life into the sacred and secular, we set ourselves up for massive frustration and disillusionment. And this is especially true in the area of employment. We have come to devalue our jobs as the necessary evil of having to live in a decidedly secular world. The problem with this, as McKenna correctly identifies, is that "Secular work, like a secular society, is organized as if God does not exist."[7] Malcolm Muggeridge wrote, "Either life is always and in all circumstances sacred, or intrinsically of no account; it is inconceivable that it should be in some cases the one and in some the other."[8]

Currently in our culture, like no time before, we fight the trend of the secularization of the sacred. In what could very well be the end times, this seems to be all but unavoidable. However, as Christians, we can push back on this trend, providing some balance as we seek, at least where it matters, the sanctification of the secular. And by that, I mean this—rather than allow for the compartmentalization of our lives and jobs into that which is sacred (Sunday) and that which is secular (the rest of the week), we need to see a sanctity of all life; every day, any day, and a spiritual calling in work; all work and any work.

Called by God

There is precedent for this as we recall the Puritan work ethic. The Puritans had a doctrine of work that rejected any distinction between that which might be conceived as secular over against that which must be identified as sacred. It seems clear that they were consistently as interested in the civil calling of a man as they were in his spiritual undertakings.

7. McKeena, *Theology of Work*, 6.
8. Muggeridge, "Something Beautiful for God," 29.

It was a Puritan belief that both callings were ordained by God and that every man had a responsibility to both and accountability for each. Therefore, for them, little distinction would be made regarding the importance of one job compared to another. All were viewed to be of equal importance before God. For the Puritans, the calling to be a carpenter was not any less "religious" than the calling to be a clergyman. This can be seen in comments made by one of the Puritan's most famous pastors, Cotton Mather, who said in his tract, *A Christian at His Calling*: "Let every Christian walk with God when he works at his calling, and act in his occupation with an eye to God, and act as under the eye of God."[9]

Do we need to recapture a Puritan work ethic? Well, we at least need to recapture a biblical work ethic. And the Puritans had it effectively close. They seemed to realize the danger in dividing life and work between that which is holy and that which is profane. They certainly seemed to embrace the radical statement by the Apostle Paul that, "To the pure, all things are pure" (Tit 1:15).

In our day, Doug Sherman and William Hendricks discuss what they call the "Sacred-Secular Hierarchy" in their book, *Your Work Matters to God*. They rightly identify the problem of living with the tension between "secular" demands and desires and the higher, "sacred" categories of religion, by noting that all of life relates to God. (By the way, can I insert here that this belief that all of life relates to God is something Muslims embrace, why don't we as Christians?) Getting back to Sherman and Hendricks, they write: "Consequently, there is no distinction between the secular and the sacred. At any moment, no matter what we are doing, we are relating to God either properly or improperly. Thus, we need to distinguish, not between secular and sacred, but between sin and righteousness."[10]

For the Christian, everything we do should have a spiritual basis and motivation. Therefore, no work is really "secular." Every job, assuming it is honest employment, has the potential for spiritual investment. And there is a litany of Scriptural support for such a worldview. "And whatever you do, whether in word or deed, do it all in the name of the Lord Jesus, giving thanks to God the Father through him" (Col 3:17 NIV). "Whatever you do, work at it with all your heart, as working for the Lord, not for men" (Col 3:23 NIV). "So whether you eat or drink, or whatever you

9. Mather, *Puritanism and Democracy*, 106.
10. Sherman and Hendricks, *Your Work Matters to God*, 54.

do, do it all for the glory of God" (1 Cor 10:31 NLT). "Everything is pure to those whose hearts are pure" (Tit 1:15 NLT).

Practicing The Presence

Perhaps no one demonstrated this more than Brother Lawrence. Nicholas Herman of Lorraine was born in 1614, he was converted at the age of 18, survived the 30-year war, after which he joined a Carmelite monastery in Paris. His job in the monastery was being assigned to the kitchen, a job he would maintain until his death in 1691. During those years he often counseled with other monks and visitors to the monastery, sharing truths that he experienced in his journey with God. After his death, his letters and maxims were discovered and through the efforts of fellow monks, put into print. They comprised what became the classic book *The Practice of the Presence of God.*

Reading this small book, you quickly discover that even though Brother Lawrence was just a lowly dishwasher, he promised God that he would be the best dishwasher God had on earth. For him, no task, regardless of how small, was outside performing it for the glory of God. He believed that we can do little things for God. For him, as he would describe, just turning the cake that is frying on the pan could be done for the love of God, and in the doing of it, he could worship God for giving him the grace to work. It was Lawrence's conviction that Christians should not get weary of doing little things for the love of God. With keen insight, he believed that God does not regard the greatness of the work, but rather the love by which it is performed.

I have wondered, reading some of the inspirational statements from Martin Luther King, Jr., if Dr. King had Brother Lawrence in mind when he delivered this speech at Barratt Junior High school in South Philadelphia? He was speaking on "What is in your life's blueprint?" and told the students, "If it falls your lot to be a street sweeper, go out and sweep streets like Michelangelo painted pictures. Sweep streets like Beethoven composed music. Sweep streets like Shakespeare wrote poetry. Sweep streets so well that all the hosts of heaven and earth will have to pause and say, here lived a great street sweeper who swept his job well."[11]

The reality is that God would have disciples of Christ who wash dishes and sweep streets. God desires disciples in all walks of life and all

---

11. King, Jr., "What is in your life's blueprint?" (1967).

professions of labor. God is pleased when we convey Kingdom character wherever we are and in whatever we are doing. He wants that of us as employers and employees, as managers and supervisors, and those even in entry-level positions.

There must be a commitment from Blue Collar laborers to White Collar professionals all professing a Christian and biblical lifestyle. He wants Christ-followers who are doctors and nurses, policemen and lawyers, hospital staff, and EMT personal. He wants carpenters that are committed to Christ, and accountants and auto mechanics, and plumbers and painters who are intentionally Christian and act like it.

He wants teachers and professors and principals and administrators who will demonstrate that they want to love the Lord their God with all their heart, with all their soul and all their mind, and love their neighbors as themselves!

In *The Gravedigger File*, Os Guinness seeks to expose a tendency that Christians have, which is a "spare-time faith." Of course, if you have read this book, you know that it is presented as a discussion between two demonic spies seeking to subvert the mission of the church. It is when they discuss Christians at work that the spare-time faith statement emerges. It is preceded by their analysis that: "A Christian's priorities outside the office may be God, family, and business, but once inside the office that order is reversed." They then observe that such "Christians" are of little use to God and pose no threat to them. And then they touch on a profound truth, "The fascinating thing is that their deficiency is so minor. It's not that they aren't where they should be, but that they aren't what they should be where they are."[12]

Did you get that? It is not that we are not *where* we should be, but that we are not *what* we should be where we are! And what are we to be? It might best be illustrated by the young man who was asked by the pastor of a church he was visiting what he did for a living. He replied that he was a disciple of Jesus Christ skillfully disguised as an Electrician.

Work as a Spiritual Task

You will balance and prioritize work when you see your work as a spiritual task as well as a physical demand. Consequently, there are some important "work" factors for us as Christians that should be embraced. The

12. Guinness, *Gravedigger File*, 79–80.

first is to remember that how you do your work is as important as what work you do. Another is to remember that all work, when done for the Lord's glory, is the "Lord's work." And then here is one more to factor into your "life's blueprint," keep in view that your work provides a platform for your witness.

To work efficiently and effectively we need at least three things: motivation (that which impels and incites a person to action), determination (that which keeps a person engaged), and appreciation (which means that whether you like your job or not, you might want to be grateful to God for providing it).

We all need to read again these great verses from Nehemiah. The Book of Nehemiah is the Bible's *Construction Zone*. It is a book about working, about seeing a task, taking on the task, and getting the job done. Here you will read statements like Nehemiah 4:6, "So we built the wall, and the entire wall was joined together, for the people had a mind to work." And in Nehemiah 4:21, where he says, "So we labored in the work." Now that is an interesting statement—they "labored" in the "work." Think about that for a moment. And then, when tempted to stop work, Nehemiah's response to Sanballat was "No way, I am doing a great work and I won't quit!" (Neh 6:3 author paraphrase).

The spirit of Nehemiah speaks directly to those who would embrace a biblical work ethic rather than those who David McKenna refers to as the advocates of the self-development ethic. He writes that they are the ones who "demand a work environment that is guaranteed to be comfortable, cozy and cuddly." But work is not always going to be like that. McKenna writes:

> If the work is hard, they want relief; if the work is routine, they want excitement; if the work is restricted, they want freedom; if the work is lonely, they want help. The truth is that all work has its moments of being hard, routine, restrictive and lonely. Instant gratification is a demand of the self-development ethic that work itself can seldom fulfill. The curse of the ground and the sweat of the brow remain with us. Christians can entertain no illusions about work. Until all creation is redeemed, we must learn to work diligently, patiently, and faithfully on long-term tasks for which the gratification is often deferred. Once we see our work in this perspective, joy will attend our daily tasks.[13]

13. McKenna, *Theology of Work*, 5.

Early twentieth-century historian and philosopher Arnold Toynbee was convinced that any man at work could be happy and spiritually healthy only if he felt that he was working for God's glory through doing what is God's work. Is there a theology of work? As Christians, are we to value our jobs, first, for being provided by God, and second, for being the platform whereby we can glorify God as we work honestly, with dignity, integrity, and honor.

Patrick Morley reminds us in *The Christian Man*, everything we do is for the glory of God and every action we take is an opportunity to bring glory and honor to God. His ultimate challenge to us is that we realize our work is not just a platform for ministry; it is ministry![14]

So, watch out for work! Your work is important, whatever it might be. And you need to know that God has called you to it. You really cannot live a full, free, and meaningful life without it. There is nothing to be gained apart from it. Never forget that there is only one good thing in life that we get without work—and that is salvation!

John S. Hoyland, English Quaker and missionary in India captured the worthiness of work in a poem included in his book *Indian Dawn*. His lines, appear to be part testimony and part prayer. Fittingly, they conclude our thoughts about the dignity of work.

> Idleness is rust and death, but work—hard, exhausting, rigorous labor,
> Is God's good gift of life in action.
> Save us then, Lord, From this shameful disease of sloth,
> From its living death. Grant us the glory of Work,
> Whose weariness is the crown of achievement,
> Whose monotony is solid success,
> Whose end is the end of a soldier,
> Harness on back and face to the foe.
> Use us, Lord, in Thy work: Use us remorselessly:
> Grant us ever the guerdon of Work, of harder and sterner work.
> Use us with pitiless rigor, Wear us out for Thyself,
> Till we pass from this feeble and stumbling activity
> To full sharing at last in Thine own eternal Work.[15]

14. Morley, *The Christian Man*, 158.
15. Hoyland, *Indian Dawn*, 123–124.

Fifteen | Church R Us

THERE IS AN INTERESTING STORY concerning the early years of the Billy Graham crusades. The renowned evangelist did have critics of course, and one of them declared that his type of "fire and brimstone" preaching would set the church back 200 years. Later, at a news conference, a reporter asked Graham if he thought that he was setting the church back 200 years, to which Billy Graham replied, "Actually, I am trying to set the Church back 2000 years!"

I am sure what Billy Graham meant by that ingenious answer was that the church needs to recapture what it had in the beginning, that which made it the irresistible, irrepressible force that it was as it conquered the Mediterranean world of the first century. The Book of Acts attests to the fact that the Church in Jerusalem was "great," as it experienced "great power," "great grace," and had a "great reverence" (Acts 4:33, 5:11).

The modern church it seems is always trying to figure out how to reclaim any of that greatness. As someone said, the early church unleashed on Jerusalem a flood of love while the modern-day church unleashes a flood of resolutions. The greatness and the power and the grace are going to be found at the source, where it all began, and from where it is to continue to this day (Acts 1:8).

In our day, when there are so much confusion and controversy about the church, and now so much uncertainty, given the impact a worldwide pandemic has had on the church, it may be time for us just to get back to some basics concerning the church. And the reason we should do that is that there is little doubt that the church must be part of our Circle of Responsibilities.

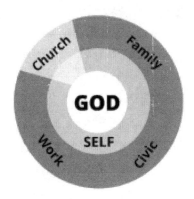

What is the Church?

Who is the Church?

Why is the Church?

Where is the Church?

What exactly does the word mean?

Most commonly, we identify the term with the Greek word *ecclesia* used in the New Testament, although technically our word church does not originate from ecclesia, but rather from *kuriakon*, which means "belonging to the Lord." The Greek word *ecclesia* is a noun derived from the preposition *ek* ("out") and the verb *kaleo* ("to call"). Hence, the most basic idea of the word *ecclesia* refers to "called-out ones." In classical Greek, it was understood to refer to any called out (and therefore, assembled) body of people.

What makes it significant for us, however, is the special sense it is given to refer to those who have been "called out" by Jesus Christ. We can understand this designation both in a universal sense—referring to everyone whom Christ has called out to be part of His body ("I will build my church" Matthew 16:18), as well as in a local sense—referring to those in a given place who have been called out by Christ ("To the church of God which is at Corinth" 1 Cor 1:2, "To the church of the Thessalonians" 1 Thess 1:1).

In the King James Bible, *ecclesia* is translated "church" 112 times out of the 115 times it appears in the New Testament. The three exceptions are Acts 19:32,39,41 where it is translated "assembly," and refers to citizens in Ephesus.

So, what do we gather from this? I suggest this reconstruction, which recognizes the slight difference between the two keywords: the "church" (*kuriakon*, those belonging to the Lord) are the ones "called out," (*ecclesia*) to be the Lord's special assembly.

Called Out!

So, we are called out so that we can be brought in to . . . what? The short answer to this is that we are called out of the "world" and then into his special assembly. There is precedent for this in Scripture. Abraham is called out of Haran to go into a land that God would show him (Gen 12:1) and Israel is called out of Egypt to go into the Promised Land (Judg 2:1). The New Testament sets forth numerous references that provide details as to what it means to be the Lord's ecclesia with that sense of being called "out of and into" involves.

- God has called us to himself: "By his divine power, God has given us everything we need for living a godly life. We have received all of this by coming to know him, the one who *called us to himself* by means of his marvelous glory and excellence" (2 Pet 1:3 NLT).

- We have been called into fellowship with Jesus: "God is faithful, who has *called you into* fellowship with his Son, Jesus Christ our Lord" (1 Cor 1:9 NIV).

- We have been called into life and light: "But you are a chosen people, a royal priesthood, a holy nation, God's special possession, that you may declare the praises of him who *called you out of darkness into* his wonderful light (1 Pet 2:9 NIV).

- We have been called in His Kingdom and Glory: "that you would walk worthy of God who *calls you into* His own kingdom and glory" (1 Thess 2:12).

- We have been called to serve the living and true God: "They tell how you turned to God from idols to serve the living and true God" (1 Thess 1:9 NIV).

- And we are called to love and serve each other: "Finally, all of you should be in agreement, understanding each other, loving each other as family, being kind and humble. Do not do wrong to repay a wrong, and do not insult to repay an insult. But repay with a blessing, because you yourselves were called to do this so that you might receive a blessing" (1 Pet 3:8–9 NCV).

I would offer this definition, that the Church (those belonging to the Lord) is the *ekklesia*, "the called-out ones," who have been spiritually and redemptively united with the living God, made separate from unholiness by his holiness and challenged to make a difference in the world from which they are called. That is an enormous calling and task. And that is why it is worthy of you making it a priority of your life! I intend to focus on the positives of this challenge and calling, but first, we must discuss something else related and timely.

COVID and the Church

As I write this chapter, we are experiencing an unprecedented time in our country (and, in our world) and, in the church. It would be neglectful to fail to address this issue, given its importance and relevance to this chapter. The pandemic that spread worldwide due to the outbreak of the COVID-19 virus has disrupted virtually everyone's lifestyle and livelihood. Infections have affected countries, cities, communities, businesses, groups, teams, families, and, of course, the church.

Christians especially have had mixed reactions to the various lockdowns that have limited involvement in that which is an essential component to our lifestyle—attending regular church services and participating in ongoing ministry activities. For the many churches that were equipped to do so, the alternative was to provide online opportunities of connecting with your church. This "virtual" experience was initially met with skepticism, some reluctance, as well as a sense of temporal support. Eventually, as the lockdowns dragged on, it became embraced and adopted as almost normal (the "new normal").

Now, as we face lockdowns ending and the freedom to meet once again, church leaders are alarmed at how attendance may be significantly altered due to this rather abnormal experience. Will Christians come back to church? It seems almost ridiculous to pose such a question, given the spiritual reality that a "churchless" Christianity makes about as much sense as a Christless Christianity. Neither one will be Christianity.

Carmen Joy Imes explored this question in the blog *Jesus Creed*, "Church after COVID—Why Bother Going Back?" She writes: "It's Sunday morning. I sit by the gas fireplace snuggled up in a warm blanket, relishing the quiet. Before long, the rest of the family will stir, and we'll have a choice to make: Get ready to go to church? Livestream the service at home? Watch it later? Or skip it altogether? Some of these options have emerged in 2020, thanks to the global pandemic. After 6 months of worship at home with church on Zoom or YouTube, rhythms that used to be automatic are no longer a given."[1]

Imes points out what may be a real problem for getting people back into church. We may hate to admit it, but people have grown comfortable not attending physically, as well as allowing for other things to flood into the time vacuum now left open by no longer going to church. In an article discussing the "Five Types of Church Members Who Will Not Return after the Quarantine," Thom S. Rainer reports that many church leaders indicate that somewhere between twenty to thirty percent of church members will not return to church.[2]

This is indeed alarming. And it is not just that people may not be returning to church once in-person gatherings are allowable again, they are not tuning in to the online opportunities as much as before as well. During the early days of the coronavirus lockdowns, online attendance was vibrant and vital, but as time went by, the surge started to slump. Surveys increasingly revealed that many churchgoers were no longer watching online services. This could be the result of any number of things, but the most distressing would be that it is an indication that people are becoming increasingly detached from what was formerly a spiritual discipline. And worse, that they are no longer even concerned about that discipline!

We are, after all, creatures of habit. We form good habits and we also form bad ones. In terms of certain spiritual disciplines, reading the Bible daily is a good habit. Praying consistently is a good habit. Going to church regularly is a good habit. And now, at least concerning the regularity of going to church, that habit has been significantly interrupted. An old friend of mine once told me that once you pick up the Bible, it is hard to put down, but once you put it down, it is hard to pick up. I see something similar happening with church. Once you start going to church regularly, it is hard to stop going, but once you stop going it is hard to start going again.

Due to the COVID restrictions, as well as the fear that has ensued, many Christians seem to be in a rut and do not appear to be very

1. Imes, "Church after COVID" *Jesus Creed*, 2.

2. Rainer, "Five Types of Church Members" *ChurchAnswers.com*, (2020).

intentional about getting out of it. But we have to. We must! Let's remember that the only difference between a rut and a grave is length.

In surveying the current landscape regarding the church, I have formulated two thoughts. The first is that, for many pastors and ministries, it will have to be a "re-boot" process that rivals almost starting over again. It will be the equivalent of a church plant. And, by the way, that may not be an altogether bad thing. Why? Because it should allow some pruning and much-needed trimming. And we know that while pruning may be difficult, it is essential for future growth.

The other impression I have is that hardly in history has one group of Christians in one time period had such a dynamic affinity with another group of Christians in a different time as now. And by that, I mean twenty-first-century Christians with first-century Christians. Think about it. The mirrored dynamics are stunning: the church of the first century existed in a "pre-Christian" environment and we live in a "post-Christian" environment.

The early church had to deal with a hostile government and the church today has to deal with an increasingly hostile government. The first-century church endured censorship and persecution and the church today faces similar scorn from a culture that has embraced "political correctness." The church in the first century was driven into the catacombs and now, with pandemic-driven edicts by politicians, the church was being told to close its doors, lockdown, and forbidden to meet openly.

The similarities are intriguing but do not forget, the comparison also holds out much hope for us, if we endure and employ strategies and tactics from those early Christians. Billy Graham was right, getting back to what made the church great 2000 years ago, will continue to ensure the church's greatness today!

That first-century church grew, but its emphasis was on spiritual health and holiness. We spend a lot of time and effort in trying to *grow* the church, yet we need to focus on the health of the church. There are far too many churches today that are not very healthy, and the subtilty is that they may not know it. Rick Warren is right when he suggested that the key issues for churches in the twenty-first century will be church health and not church growth. In fact, he admits that this distinction is the motivation that drove him (pun intended) to write his best-selling book, *The Purpose Driven Church*.[3]

---

3. Warren, *The Purpose Driven Church*, 17.

So, What's So Great?

The church Jesus built (and continues to build) is great and there are many reasons why that is true. One of them is addressed by Paul in his comments to Timothy. Consider what he says about the church in what some New Testament scholars believe is an ancient hymn of the church embedded in his letter to Timothy:

> These things I write to you, though I hope to come to you shortly; but if I am delayed, I write so that you may know how you ought to conduct yourself in the house of God, which is the church of the living God, the pillar and ground of the truth. And without controversy great is the mystery of godliness: God was manifested in the flesh, Justified in the Spirit, Seen by angels, Preached among the Gentiles, Believed on in the world, Received up in glory (1 Tim 3:14–16).

Six short stanzas. In the first three, note the powerful lyrics relating to such great Scriptural truths like the Incarnation, Crucifixion, and Resurrection? And in the last three, you can see the missional, evangelical, and prophetical importance of each? Next, notice Paul's reference to the Ecclesia (the Church). He is telling Timothy how he is supposed to act "in the house of God, which is the church of the living God, the pillar and ground of the truth."

There is a significant historical backdrop to this statement and one that should elevate our thinking about the church. Paul refers to the church as "the pillar and ground of the truth," and it is the only time he refers to the church this way. Might there be any significance to that? I believe that there is, very much so, especially when you understand the historical context of his statement.

First, Paul is writing to Timothy, and where is he? He is in Ephesus. He is the pastor of the church in Ephesus. During this time, Ephesus was famous but not because of the church, nor because of their young pastor, Timothy. It was famous and known "worldwide" because it was the home of the famous Temple of Diana (Artemis).

The Temple of Diana was one of the seven wonders of the ancient world. The Temple's measurements were colossal—it was 450 feet long by 225 feet wide and 60 feet high. It was twice the size of the famous Parthenon in Athens. But that is not all, it was comprised of 127 pillars, each being sixty feet high and four feet in diameter with intricate figures, mostly depicting the gods of the Greek pantheon, carved in the base.

Each marble pillar was studded with jewels and large sections were also overlaid with gold plating. Antipater of Sidon, who is the one who originally made the list of the *Seven Wonders of the Ancient World*, described the Temple of Diana at Ephesus as being more marvelous than any of the other six wonders!

The citizens of Ephesus all believed that they were entrusted with the protection and upkeep of this great temple, as well as the worship of the goddess Diana. This devotion explains what happens in Acts 19:21–41 as we go back and read about the riot that broke out in Ephesus when Paul first started leading people to Christ. We are told that a merchant named Demetrius worked up the crowd by saying that he feared that "the temple of the great goddess Diana may be despised, and her magnificence destroyed whom all Asia and the world worship!"

Acts 19:28–34 says that when the Ephesians heard that, they were full of wrath and chanted "Great is Diana of the Ephesians" and kept it up for two solid hours! Seizing Paul and some of his companions, they drag him before the city magistrate. And what exactly was his great offense? They said, "you see and hear how this fellow Paul has convinced and led astray large numbers of people here in Ephesus and practically the whole province of Asia. He says that gods made by human hands are no gods at all" (Acts 19:26 NIV).

What they were saying was, "This Paul is saying our gods are dead!" And, of course, that is exactly what he was saying. Every time I read this account, I am reminded of a bumper sticker I saw once on the back of a car that declared: *My God's Alive, Sorry About Yours!* That is what Paul was doing in Ephesus. He was saying, "God is Alive—and Diana is not!"

Now, a few years later, the established *ecclesia* in Ephesus, all those who came to Christ and were called out of Diana worship into the worship of the one true God, are still ministering in a city saturated with idolatry. The church is still overshadowed, in some respects, by the Temple of Diana with its hundreds of pillars. And so, it is at that time, and for that reason, that Paul reminds pastor Timothy that they exist as the "Church of the Living God" and that they are, as the church, the real and only "Pillar of the truth."

All of Diana's 127 pillars could not match just this ONE of God's!

And, do not forget this, within a few centuries Christianity conquered this region, and the Temple of Diana was no more. Book a tour and visit there today (I have), and you know what you will see? Not far from the ruins of ancient Ephesus and the great Roman theater there, to commemorate the site of the Temple of Diana, they have set up a *single* pillar. The marbled sectional pieces restored and laid on top of each other rise to not even half of their original height. A single, dilapidated pillar, forlorn and in disrepair. The day I visited, the glory of the once magnificent, jewel-studded pillar was replaced by the anemic bleak-looking thin column that was unavoidably adorned at the top with a single bird's nest, scraggly, lonely, and empty. It was almost laughable. It certainly was a fitting metaphor for the folly of idolatry.

Our God is alive, sorry about theirs!

Church of the Living God

That is why I love the church! That why the Ecclesia Jesus built is the greatest thing ever built by anyone. There is nothing like it on earth! Scan the pages of the New Testament and you will find that it is the church of the Living God, and it is the church of the Loving God, and it is the church of the Saving God, and it is the church of the Serving God.

The New Testament Scriptures refer to the "Ecclesia" in intriguing ways. For instance, it is referred to as a "flock" (Acts 20:28), as a "family" (Eph 2:19), and as a "fellowship" (Acts 2:42). The New Testament also employs some creative metaphors to help us with the dynamics of the Ecclesia. It is a "building" (Eph 2:19–22), a "body" (Eph 1:22–33), and a "bride" (Eph 5:22–33).

But apart from these unique designations, we need to come back to the initial question of who we are and why we are, and to seek something practical as to why we should allow the church to be part of our circle of responsibilities. Gene Getz reminds us that "The church exists to carry out two functions—evangelism (to make disciples) and edification (to teach them). These two functions in turn answer two questions: First, Why does the church exist in the world? and second, Why does the church exist as a gathered community?"[4]

As Christians, we are the church. As the church, we are to evangelize and edify. Evangelization is our efforts to reach out and edification is our commitment to grow up. Evangelization is our engagement with the world around us, and edification is our encouragement of one another. And that engagement or that encouragement can occur at any time, scheduled or not.

4. Getz, *Sharpening the Focus of the Church*, 232.

As you look back at our circle of responsibilities of which I have suggested as four: Family, Church, Work, and Civic, consider that this is the only one about which you have no choice. Let me explain. If we confess to be a Christian, we are therefore *kuriakon* (someone who belongs to the Lord). Jesus called us. We are the *ecclesia*, his called-out assembly, and as such, we become his Flock, Family, and Fellowship. We are inseparably a part of his Building, we are a member of his Body, and we are irrevocably engaged to him as his Bride.

If you are a Christian, then you are part of his Church. There is no choice about it. There is nothing for you to "join." That is why Christians who say they receive Christ but reject the church have no idea what they are talking about. You cannot have one without the other. I am mystified when I hear someone say, "I like Jesus, but I don't do church!" Really? Jesus would think that strange.

There are rather foolish comments made all the time, like, "I can be a Christian without going to church." Well, granted, *going* to church does not make you a Christian, but becoming a Christian puts you into the church. As I understand it, the Baptism of the Holy Spirit on the Day of Pentecost secured for everyone who comes to Christ their placement in the Body of Christ. It was, in my opinion, a one-time historical event that serves as the entry point for all coming to Christ for salvation and therefore immediately resulting in your placement in the Body of Christ, his church. So, Paul says, "For by one Spirit we were all baptized into one body" (1 Cor 12:13). All of us, with none of us excluded.

Let me repeat, you cannot have a churchless Christianity, any more than you can have a Christ-less Christianity. Once we understand this dynamic, we will realize that ecclesia is *not* something we *do*, it is something we *are*. You can avoid responsibility for something you should do, but you cannot avoid responsibility for someone you are! You can choose whether you want to be married and start a family or not. You can have a choice about whether you want to hold down a job or not. You can reject the responsibility of whether you are going to be a law-abiding citizen or not. But you cannot reject the responsibility of being the church! As a Christian when it comes to church there is no "or not."

As a Christian, you have been called by God *out of* and *in to*. It is an irrevocable calling that carries unavoidable accountability. And that's why Peter said, "you are a chosen people, a royal priesthood, a holy nation, God's special possession" (1 Pet 2:9).

How do you avoid that? The answer is you cannot.

Why Go?

Now, after all this talk about *being* the church rather than just *going* to church, we need to talk about going to church. It is obvious that going to our local churches and enjoying the community of fellow believers, worship, the preaching and teaching of the Word, and the various outlets of service, is not only traditional but theological as well.

Providing Scriptural directive, the writer of the Epistle to the Hebrews wrote, "And let us not neglect our meeting together, as some people do, but encourage one another, especially now that the day of his return is drawing near" (Heb 10:25 NLT).

Just from this one passage alone, we get the idea that being the assembly (remember "ecclesia"), we should not neglect to assemble, and that when we do so it is to encourage and exhort one another and that this is important because of the day in which we live and the impending events of Scriptural prophecy which will occur.

There are forces at work that are unseen to us. We are in a spiritual war, and as an old military maxim states, there is strength in numbers. Jesus would have us function effectively as members of His body. Satan would oppose that and do all in his power to stop that. Early church father, a disciple of the apostle John, and bishop of Antioch, Ignatius, wrote to Christians at the end of the first century, "When ye frequently, and in numbers meet together, the powers of Satan are overthrown, and his mischief is neutralized by your like-mindedness in the faith."[5] His admonition was not only appropriate for the first century, but it is especially so in the twenty-first century.

Drawing some conclusions about the church leads me, first, to acknowledge again that church is something we are, more than someplace we go. But, secondly, it is someplace we go. And it is along these lines that many Christians are having some difficulties as it relates to COVID and the unparalleled lockdowns and inability to meet in person.

Why is that? Why are we confused and struggling? I think it is because we are sensing the frustration of not being able to experience and therefore fulfill the Great Commandment. So much of this book, indeed the thesis of this book, is that "You shall love the Lord your God with all your heart, with all your soul, and with all your mind. This is the first and great commandment. And the second is like it: You shall love your neighbor as yourself" (Matt 22:37–39).

5. JFB, *Commentary, Critical,* Heb 10:25.

Locked in and shut away does not hinder loving God one bit, but it does hinder what should be the necessary and natural by-product of that love for God. It prohibits the personal (in-person), actual ministry to and loving of our neighbor. And do not forget, as we noted earlier, the two commandments of the Great Commandment are one commandment. You cannot fulfill one without doing the other. Carmen Joy Imes was very much on point when she wrote: "My absence (from church) diminishes what Christ can accomplish in and through the church, while my presence is a tangible means of participation in the kingdom. Ultimately, it's not about "what I get out of it." The church cannot fully accomplish her purposes in the world when I withhold my presence. Physical participation matters."[6]

If then I am right about this, we are being "forced" (due to the unprecedented restrictions caused by the pandemic) to not being able to fulfill the Great Commandment. Think about that for a moment. In reality, we are becoming irrelevant. The church is being maneuvered, de facto, to not be a factor.

Now, of course, some of this loving our neighbor and being in fellowship can be accomplished online. But at some point, it must be in-person, up-close, and personal. That is how Christianity thrives. That is the whole idea of the Incarnation, is it not? Can you imagine if God decided to enact a virtual incarnation? No! Listen to John: "That which was from the beginning, which we have heard, which we have seen with our eyes, which we have looked upon, and our hands have handled, concerning the Word of life" (1 John 1:1).

The church is like that. It must be heard, seen, looked upon, handled! Do not confuse your spiritual family with a virtual family. They will never be the same. This is the reason why no in-person gatherings are not normal for the church. Church means "assembly." Only a gathering together gives us the sights and sounds, touch and taste, faith, and feeling that defines the church and has defined the church for over twenty centuries.

I am convinced that one of the emotions that Christians are experiencing due to the forced cloistering brought on by COVID is the absence of ambiance. Ambiance means the feeling and mood of a place. It relates to the character and atmosphere of your surroundings. Even the Christians in Rome in the early centuries of the church, forced into the catacombs, had ambiance down there! Today, sitting around in our

6. Imes, "Church after COVID" *Jesus Creed* 2.

bathrobes and sipping coffee as we listen to some online liturgy, just does not quite have the same ambiance.

Have you ever visited a museum or a historical site and been moved by it, and while there you also videoed the experience? Later, when you watch the video you note that it is good, it is accurate, it provides recall, but it also lacks something. It lacks the original ambiance.

Here is another way to illustrate this. Have you ever watched a cooking show on Television? While you can see it and hear it, TV has not invented a way for you to smell it or taste it. Technology can only do so much. Something is lacking. And we all know it. Think of what we are allowing to happen to our kids, to our youth. It is going to be even harder for them to embrace ecclesia again.

We have got to get back to church. We have got to get back to being the church. We have to taste and see that the Lord is good (Psalm 34:8)!

If We Do Not, the Church Will Not

We are Jesus Christ's ecclesia. He has called us out of the world and put us into service. We are called to turn the world upside down (Acts 17:6), although we know that we are turning a world upside-down right-side up. The church needs to be in the world that God so loved and for whom He gave His only begotten son. We need to engage our world, our countries, our cities, our communities, our neighborhoods. And this has little to do with a building or even a location. It has everything to do with us. It is about who we are—the assembly, the called-out assembly, committed to a new kingdom and our new King.

Being the church always means responding to an opportunity to serve, rather than an occasion to observe. The church involves being participators rather than just spectators. There are no "sidelines" in the church from which the many can cheer on the efforts of the few. Legendary college football coach Bud Wilkenson once described Football as twenty-two people on the field who desperately need rest being watched by 22,000 people in the stands who desperately need exercise. We need to get into the game! In our churches, all too often, we have too few doing too much and too many doing too little!

It is, therefore, up to us. Think of it this way—If we don't, the Church won't. If you will not, the church cannot! Of course, this is just an acknowledgment that we are the church. The "church" is us! We do not share anything that is not the church. The message of the church is the lives we live. The church is a community that communicates. That is why Stanley Hauerwas correctly observes that Jesus did not come just to establish principles to revolutionize society but to create a new community that embodied forgiveness and self-sacrificing love. As such, the church is not just to be the bearer of Christ's message—but to *be* the message!

That is who we are! That is why we are! That is why it is important. That is why it is a priority. This challenge will lead us to our last chapter because we have not always been effective at being the message. We are going to our church services. We are listening to our preachers preach and our teachers teach. We are singing all the inspiring songs, and maybe we are getting all caught up in worshipping worship and praising praise, but how is that impacting the thousands around us heading for a Christless eternity?

Years ago, pastor Daniel Walker wrote a book to challenge the church to revitalize our impact and efforts to connect with our community. He wrote that men would find, "personal dignity in belonging to the church because it is a fellowship that is above making social distinctions, a fellowship that surrounds its members with loving concern, and a fellowship that allows a man to be himself." Furthermore, he wrote, and I love this, that "there is dignity in it because it is a fellowship committed to no lesser purpose than serving the Lord of the universe."[7]

I remember hearing the story of a pastor in the mid-west who visited a disgruntled church member who had stopped coming to church services. It was a cold evening, and the older man had a nice fire going in the fireplace. As the young pastor sat next to him and in front of the fireplace, neither spoke much, they just stared into the fire burning brightly in the fireplace.

Finally, the pastor got up, walked over to the fireplace, took the fireplace tongs, and gently picked out a small burning piece of wood. He then set that small, glowing piece of wood on the hearth away from the main fire and sat back down. They continued to watch, and slowly but surely, the glow of that little piece of wood began to smolder and grow dim, lose its glow, turn grey and become cold. The pastor looked at his old friend, said good night, and left.

The next Sunday, the old man was back in church.

---

7. Walker, *Enemy in the Pew?* 28.

We need each other. We need the glow. We need the heat. We need the flame. We need the fire! That is why we go to church. That is why we are the church. That is why the church matters!

Sixteen | The Foreign Embassy
On Your Street

I THINK ONE OF THE most helpful and influential voices in the church over the last three and half decades has been that of George Barna. In 1984 he founded The Barna Research Group which began surveying and researching the religious beliefs and behavior of American Christians, and mostly with an eye toward how those beliefs and behaviors affected the church and impacted the culture. Over the years he has authored some fifty books and spoken at hundreds of conferences.

Reading a number of his books and attending some of his conferences, I have always come away feeling better equipped to tackle some of the issues confronting us. I have appreciated that he did not just offer survey-driven statistical data but always used that data to probe deeper into the systemic causes of where and how the church and Christians have been succeeding or failing.

An example of this would be in the opening chapter of his book, *The Second Coming of the Church*, in which he sets the stage for the reason he wrote the book. His analysis of where the church is failing is timely due to the growing trend of people in our culture who see the Christian faith as "weak, outdated, and irrelevant." He writes: "The stumbling block for the Church is not its theology but its failure to apply what it believes in compelling ways. The downfall of the Church has not been the content of its message but its failure to practice those truths. Christians have been their own worst enemies when it comes to showing the world what authentic, biblical Christianity looks like – and why it represents a viable alternative to materialism, existentialism, mysticism, and the other doctrines of popular culture."[1]

In *Life-Style Evangelism: Crossing Traditional Boundaries to Reach the Unbelieving World*, Dr. Joseph Aldrich outlined five reasons why Christians were increasingly ineffective at evangelizing the lost. He listed the reasons as:

- Excessive relational demands have crippled our relational capacities.
- The pace of life – too fast and too complicated.
- Exposure to unhealthy evangelism models.
- Perceived cultural barriers and outright theological errors.
- An imbalance between the verbalization and incarnation of the Gospel.

Aldrich decried the seeming fact that many Christians have simply lost their ability to relate significantly to non-Christians. He points out that after knowing the Lord for two years, the average Christian has no significant relationships with non-Christians. This must be remedied, for, as he reminds us, "There is no impact without contact."[2]

Called Out—Called In

As we noted in the previous chapter, as Christians and because we are Christ-followers, we have been called out of the world and called into his service. This being called out of the world does not mean, however, that we have nothing to say to the world. It does not mean that we ignore the world and seek to isolate ourselves from the world. God does not want us isolated from the world, he wants us insulated from the world. The prayer Jesus offered to the Father in John 17 made this abundantly clear:

> Now I am no longer in the world, but these are in the world, and I come to You. Holy Father, keep through Your name those whom You have given Me, that they may be one as We are. While I was with them in the world, I kept them in Your name. Those whom You gave Me I have kept; and none of them is lost except the son of perdition, that the Scripture might be fulfilled. But now I come to You, and these things I speak in the world,

1. Barna, *Second Coming of the Church*, 5.
2. Aldrich, *Life-Style Evangelism*, 16–20.

that they may have My joy fulfilled in themselves. I have given them Your word; and the world has hated them because they are not of the world, just as I am not of the world. I do not pray that You should take them out of the world, but that You should keep them from the evil one. They are not of the world, just as I am not of the world. Sanctify them by Your truth. Your word is truth. As You sent Me into the world, I also have sent them into the world. And for their sakes I sanctify Myself, that they also may be sanctified by the truth (John 17:11–19).

So, we are in the world, but we are no longer of the world. This can get a little confusing. Especially so because so much of the world can get into us. We used to sing an old chorus that said, "This world is not my home, I'm just passing through, my treasures are laid up somewhere beyond the blue. The angels beckon me from Heaven's open door, and I can't feel at home in this world anymore."

The Apostle Paul would agree with that, as he told the Christians in Philippi "our citizenship is in heaven. And we eagerly await a Savior from there, the Lord Jesus Christ" (Phil 3:20 NIV). The word he uses is *politeuma*, which gives us our word "politics." Some of you will remember that the King James Version, as well as many early English translations, translated this word as "conversation." That translation led modern readers to understand this verse a little differently than what Paul would have originally meant.

The translators of the King James Bible had in mind the early etymology of the word "conversation" which came from a Latin verb meaning "to be associated with," and came to be understood as referring to one's conduct and behavior (and not just one's speech).

There has been considerable discussion about why Paul used *politeuma* and what he meant by it. Besides the older word "conversation" and the more common updated word "citizenship," when you look at the various versions, you will find it translated by a host of different (although somewhat related) words, such as *abiding, existence, commonwealth, country, free citizens,* and *homeland,* with most referring to heaven.

I believe, however, that Paul's idea was not so much about "place" as about performance. Because we are associated with heaven, our performance on earth should match the ideals of heaven. We are citizens of heaven and we are supposed to live like it. We represent Jesus Christ and his gospel, so Paul would also say in Philippians 1:27 "Only let your conduct (same word, *politeuma*) be worthy of the gospel of Christ."

Furthermore, the all-important context of Paul's comments in Philippians assists us in determining how we should understand what Paul was talking about. Before his comments about our conversation/citizenship being aligned with heaven, he challenged the Philippian believers to follow his example of how to walk, which certainly implied his conduct (Phil 3:17), as well as to mark how unbelievers and enemies of the cross of Christ walked and conducted themselves (Phil 3:18). Similarly, the same positional emphasis is seen in Paul's comments in Colossians, "If then you were raised with Christ, seek those things which are above, where Christ is, sitting at the right hand of God. Set your mind on things above, not on things on the earth" (Col 3:1–2).

Early Methodist leader Joseph Benson, a contemporary of John Wesley, leaves us an excellent explanation of this important lifestyle challenge and why Paul used this keyword. In his Commentary on Philippians 3:20, he writes:

> We that are true Christians are of a very different spirit, and act in a quite different manner. The original expression, "politeuma" rendered conversation, is a word of a very extensive meaning, implying our citizenship, our thoughts, our affections, are already in heaven; or we think, speak, and act, converse with our fellow-creatures, and conduct ourselves in all our intercourse with them, as citizens of the New Jerusalem, and as being only strangers and pilgrims upon earth. We therefore endeavor to promote the interests of that glorious society to which we belong, to learn its manners, secure a title to its privileges, and behave in a way suitable to, and worthy of our relation to it.[3]

Christian Civic Responsibilities

Our world is full of a lot of things, including the world of politics and the responsibility of being a good citizen. As such, it must be included in our Circle of Responsibilities. There were several words I could have used to describe this fourth area of responsibility, such as community or government or public square, perhaps even the Greek term *agora* (city center or marketplace). But I have settled on the word *Civic*.

---

3. Benson, *Commentary on the Old and New Testaments,* Phil 3:20.

"Civic" is from the Latin *civis*, which simply means "citizen." It is defined as that which is relating to a citizen, a city, or community affairs. It is commonly understood to refer to our activities concerning our community. Some see those activities as a duty, and so we often hear people refer to their *civic duty* or their *civic responsibility*. This area of responsibility and one for which we will have to prioritize relates to our society in general and therefore refers to our sense of, and commitment to, our civic responsibilities.

We should note that in Philippians 3:20, Paul seems to underscore the reality that Christians are *in* the world even though we are not to be part *of* the world. But what does that mean? I believe what it should mean is that we will not be shaped by a worldly system that is morally corrupt and spiritually bankrupt and at enmity with God. That being said, what it does not mean is that you are to be isolated from the world in which you live, and thereby forfeit any possibility of changing that society for good and God.

Before going any further, we should note that our interaction with the "world" involves three areas. There are three aspects of the "world" each different in meaning and application.

The Word of Nature

First, there is the *Natural* World.

This would be the environment and the world of nature. It is the Psalm 8 world—the world of "the sheep and oxen and the beasts of the field, the birds of the air, and the fish in the sea that pass through the paths of the seas." It is also the world that God challenged man to subdue.

The last number of decades has seen a rise in environmentalism, which for some has become the new religion. Global warming and climate change issues dominate agendas on university campuses, corporate board rooms, and political action committees. Evangelicals find themselves often at odds with much of the hysteria.

Cal Beisner writes in *World* magazine about the "Gospel Confusion in Christian Environmentalism." He agrees that many now regard environmentalism as a separate religion and that it is having a growing influence on Christianity. He offers this catalog of the literature of the new religion: "Books like Matthew Sleeth's *The Gospel According to the Earth*, Jonathan Merritt's *Green Like God*, Jim Ball's *Global Warming and the Risen Lord*, and even HarperCollins' *The Green Bible.*"

Beisner admits while there may be some good being offered by so-called Christian environmentalists, he shows concern that they may nonetheless subtly change the gospel. He warns: "We go from 'Christ died for our sins in accordance with the Scriptures, that he was buried, that he was raised on the third day in accordance with the Scriptures,' as the Apostle Paul summarized it in 1 Corinthians 15:3–4, to something like 'If you love God, take good care of the Earth.'"[4]

The World of Things

Then there is the *Material* World.

This is the world of stuff. It is the world of invention and innovation and production and purchase. It is the world of Art, Science, Buildings, Tools, Toys, Machines, and Instruments. It is populated by a plethora of goods and gadgets. It is the world of things.

Joe Magliato's description of these "things" in his book, *The Wall Street Gospel*, is on the mark. He writes, "We live in the age of things. We surround ourselves with things. We sit in expensive things, sleep in expensive things, and drive in expensive things. We have things for the summer, things for the winter, big things, little things, short things, and tall things. We have electrical things, wind-up things, and battery-operated things. Then we need to put locks on these things to secure them against thieves who want our things! Most of these things eventually wind up in the garage and then in a garage sale."[5]

4. Beisner, "Gospel Confusion in Christian Environmentalism," *World*, (2012).

5. Magliato, *Wall Street Gospel*, 17.

Mark Buchanan provides a compelling look into this world in his article *Trapped in the Cult of the Next Thing*. He writes that the Cult of the Next Thing's central message proclaims, "Crave and spend, for the Kingdom of Stuff is here." And then offers this portrait: "Those caught up in the Cult of the Next Thing live endlessly, relentlessly for, well, the Next Thing. For us, the impulse to see the Next Thing is an instinct bred into us so young it seems genetic. It's our paradigm, our way of seeing. It's our unifying Myth. How could the world be otherwise?"[6]

The danger of living in a world of things is that we can be ruled by those things. The more we own, the more we are owned! Jesus warned that we cannot serve both God and Mammon, which would be the clutching, clinging trap of materialistic wealth. Paul tells Timothy that "true godliness with contentment is itself great wealth" (1 Tim 6:6 NLT). The writer of Hebrews exhorts, "Let your conduct be without covetousness; be content with such things as you have" (Heb 13:5). It doesn't seem like we are listening. We continue to buy things we don't need, with money we don't have, to impress neighbors we don't even like!

The World of Man

That brings us, then, to the *Human* World.

It is the third area of our interaction, which then would be with each other. And it is the most important. God has created us as relational beings. We were made to interact with each other. That interaction can be meaningful, or it can be miserable. It can be helpful, or it can be harmful. It can be healthy, or it can be unhealthy.

It is this third area of interacting with our world that relates to our responsibility as disciples of Jesus Christ. Each of us must decide how we are going to intersect and interact with our world? And perhaps it is here that we discover the dilemma of discipleship. That dilemma becomes apparent when we consider two well-known verses of Scripture that seem to be at odds with each other.

How do you reconcile John 3:16, "For God so loved the world that He gave His only begotten Son, that whoever believes in Him should not perish but have everlasting life", with First John 2:15 which states, "Do not love the world or the things in the world. If anyone loves the world, the love of the Father is not in him"?

6. Buchanan, *Trapped in the Cult of the Next Thing*, Christianity Today, (1999).

The seeming contradiction is glaring. God loves the world, but then does he tell us not to love the world? One might ask why is it okay for God to love the world, but not us? Fortunately, it is an understanding of the three areas of the "world" just discussed in the preceding paragraphs that will help us reconcile these two important verses. In John 3:16 the word "world" refers to the world of Humans. This is proven by the use of the word "whosoever" ("everyone who believes" NLT) Which means people. In First John 2:15, John refers to the natural world as well as the materialistic world. The Apostle is therefore exhorting Christians to not love the material world—the world of things. Notice that he makes no mention of humans in his statement.

John 3:16 refers to loving people. Nature is not the focus and we are not called upon to love things. Jesus did not die for *things*! He was not nailed to the Cross for nature! He did not suffer and bleed for climate change, but to change the hearts of people. The purpose of First John 2:15 is that God does not want you to die because you bought into a world's system to own stuff and forgot to own a Savior.

So then, there is no contradiction. We are to love God and love the world of people for whom God sacrificed his Son. Understanding the "world" this way positions us to have a positive impact on people unless you're Linus, who, when Lucy told him he is supposed to love the world, said, "I love the world, it's people I can't stand!" Again, we are in the world, and we are to love people, as does God, but we are not to love the worldly system that long ago declared war on God.

It comes down to love, as we have noted numerous times. We are to love our neighbors as ourselves. Anne Ortland said that one of the greatest failings of Christians is the withholding of biblical love. And why do we do that? Why do we withhold love? That is not an easy question to answer because the answer demands a probing of various levels of context, but generally speaking, it comes down to an unwillingness to commit and be accountable, as well as an inability to manage our time.

Love Costs

To love anyone demands that you are accountable to that person, and accountability always costs something. If we are not willing to pay that cost, then we "withhold" love. But that costs us something as well. The heart-searing comment from C. S. Lewis reminds us of this reality: "There is no safe investment. To love at all is to be vulnerable. Love anything, and your heart will certainly be wrung and possibly be broken. If you want to make sure of keeping it intact, you must give your heart to no one, not even to an animal. Wrap it carefully round with hobbies and little luxuries; avoid all entanglements; lock it up safe in the casket or coffin of your selfishness. But in that casket—safe, dark, motionless, airless—it will change. It will not be broken; it will become unbreakable, impenetrable, irredeemable. The alternative to tragedy, or at least to the risk of tragedy, is damnation. The only place outside Heaven where you can be perfectly safe from all the dangers and perturbations of love is Hell."[7]

Then too, as mentioned above, to love anyone demands time. This brings us back to the beginning of this book. We are already overloaded with time commitments and it is unlikely that we can take on any more (or anyone else!). We are too often just too busy to love the way Jesus wants us to love. I like the way John Ortberg discusses what he refers to as our "hurry sickness." We have discussed these all-important time issues earlier, but Ortberg contributes a startling observation, he says, "The most serious sign of hurry sickness is a diminished capacity to love. Love and hurry are fundamentally incompatible. Love always takes time, and time is one thing hurried people don't have." He warns that hurry is not just a disordered schedule, hurry is a disordered heart."[8]

So, we cannot avoid this issue of loving others and maintain authentic Christian discipleship. Jesus said we will be known by how we love one another (John 13:35). We cannot avoid the responsibility nor the accountability that we are advertising to the world whether we love the world (of people) as God told us to. And that world is watching to see if we even love each other! We are walking billboards for Christ in a broken world.

Sheldon Vanauken, a close friend of C. S. Lewis, wrote, "The best argument for Christianity is Christians; their joy, their certainty, their completeness. But the strongest argument against Christianity is also Christians—when they are somber and joyless, when they are self-righteous and smug in complacent consecration when they are narrow and repressive, then Christianity dies a thousand deaths."[9]

7. Lewis, *The Four Loves*, 111–112.

8. Ortberg, *Life You've Always Wanted*, 84, 87.

9. Vanauken, *Severe Mercy*, 85.

J. Grant Howard saw these three worlds clearly and biblically. He wrote, "The world of nature, people, and things is now enemy-occupied territory. This means that our world is profoundly permeated by satanic influence—a defiling, deceptive scheme that is at work around us and in us; designated to convince us to conform to a mindset and a lifestyle that are essentially anti-God and pro-self."[10]

Ambassadors for Christ

It is for this reason, then, that God expects us to be good and godly citizens, and as such, not to bring reproach upon the Name of Christ before a lost and dying world. The New Testament is loaded with passages exhorting Christians to fulfill civic responsibilities in a spiritually mature way. The Apostle Paul writes, "Let everyone be subject to the governing authorities, for there is no authority except that which God has established. The authorities that exist have been established by God" (Rom 13:1 NIV). "Pray for kings and others in power, so we may live quiet and peaceful lives as we worship and honor God" (1 Tim 2:2). "Remind the believers to submit to the government and its officers. They should be obedient, always ready to do what is good" (Tit 3:1 NLT).

The Apostle Peter joins Paul in exhorting Christians to be good and godly citizens. "Make the Master proud of you by being good citizens. Respect the authorities, whatever their level; they are God's emissaries for keeping order. It is God's will that by doing good, you might cure the ignorance of the fools who think you're a danger to society. Exercise your freedom by serving God, not by breaking the rules. Treat everyone you meet with dignity. Love your spiritual family. Revere God. Respect the government" (1 Pet 2:13–17 MSG).

Ultimately, our civic duties will always be driven by our commitment to God's will and our dedication to being disciples of Jesus Christ. That is why this prayer is ever on our lips "Your Will be done, on earth as it is in heaven." And that is why this command is always before us—to make disciples, teaching them to observe all that Jesus commanded us.

It is Paul, however, that presents to us the most unique way of describing our civic commitment, when he writes, "Now then, we are ambassadors for Christ, as though God were pleading through us: we implore you on Christ's behalf, be reconciled to God" (2 Cor 5:20). The

---

10. Howard, *Balancing Life's Demands*, 134.

word that Paul uses, translated as "ambassadors," is *presbeuomen*, the Greek word from which we derive the word "presbytery," meaning an elder or a trusted statesman. It is understood to mean a representative. And that is what an ambassador is—an official envoy or messenger. In the customary sense, an ambassador is a person representing one government in its dealings with another.

Being an ambassador for Christ is such an amazing appellative that it demands being broken down into applicable components. If we are ambassadors, what does that mean? We should ask first and foremost, who and what do we represent? I found it helpful to think of the task of being an ambassador in the conventional (political) sense and then applying that back into my Christian experience.

Our Country

For example, an ambassador represents a *Place*.

All Ambassadors represent their country, their homeland. Their official residence in their Embassy is the sovereign territory of their country, even though that embassy is on foreign soil. Accordingly, they fly their flag as a sovereign state. My wife is from Washington D.C. and we have driven many times on Massachusetts Avenue where so many foreign embassies are located. As you drive by one embassy after another, you see the various flags of those countries on display.

As Christians, we represent a Sovereign State within a foreign country. As we noted from Philippians 3:20, our true homeland is heaven. It is interesting to note that Peter encourages Christians to "pass the time of your sojourning here in fear" (1 Pet 1:17). The word "sojourning" appearing in this text is *paroikia* which means to dwell in a strange land, a "foreign residence."

Our King

A second thing that is certainly true of an ambassador is that they represent a *Person*.

Be they president, prime ministry, premier, or king, all ambassadors are appointed by the leader of a country to represent them. Who do we, as Christians, represent? Are we not Christ's ambassadors? Does that not mean we represent the Person of Jesus Christ? Consider that this implies, then, that we are acting in his stead!

When Paul says we are ambassadors for Christ he is leaving little doubt as to who we represent and serve. He says, "You serve the Lord Christ" (Col 3:4). He tells Timothy that Jesus Christ is "the blessed and only Ruler, the King of all kings and the Lord of all lords" (1 Tim 6:15 NCV). Jesus is the King of our Kingdom. He is the President of our Country. He is the Ruler of the Redeemed, the Sovereign of the Saved, he is our Head of State.

And then there is one more dimension that is relevant here. Every country has some message to announce about itself. There is some philosophy of government to pronounce, some idealistic system to export, a vision of prosperity to share with someone else.

Our Message

Every ambassador therefore also represents a *Plan*.

America's ambassadors sent abroad by the President of the United States represent America's plan of democracy. American democracy is what we try to export as well as defend around the world. As a political system, it would seem worthy of defending, although I am reminded of a quote often attributed to Winston Churchill that democracy is the worst form of government, except for all the others.

But now we should not forget, our citizenship is in Heaven, and so we are not talking about representing any form of human government, even one as good as we think democracy is. As Christians, we must acknowledge that as good as democracy is, God's will for his world is not a democracy. God's will for his world is a Theocracy. That is exactly what you are praying for every time you pray to God the Father, "Your Kingdom Come, Your Will be Done on earth as it is in heaven." We represent a King, who rules over a different Kingdom. Remember that before Pilate, Jesus said, "My kingdom is not of this world" (John 18:36).

So, what is the Plan of our King? What is the message of this Kingdom? What ideology is being exported? The ideology is theology, and its political platform is called the *Gospel*. The plan is to export the promise as well as the reality that Jesus Christ is "the Way, the Truth, the Life."

It is the message of life in a world of death. It is the message of redemption. It is, as Paul says, the ministry of reconciliation: "Now all things are of God, who has reconciled us to Himself through Jesus Christ and has given us the ministry of reconciliation, that is, that God was in Christ reconciling the world to Himself, not imputing their trespasses to them, and has committed to us the word of reconciliation" (2 Cor 5:18-19). It should be noted that following this comes, "Now then, we are ambassadors for Christ, as though God were pleading through us: we implore you on Christ's behalf, be reconciled to God" (2 Cor 5:20). The importance of this charge cannot be overstated. Do we understand how important this is?

Paul's statement is loaded with important words, one of which is the smallest, but might be the most strategic. Consider the preposition "for" ("we are ambassadors *for* Christ"). It is the Greek word *huper* (hyper) which means "over," or "beyond," and can also mean "on behalf of, for the sake of, or concerning." And then it is placed first in the sentence, which you expect if you wanted to emphasize what follows. Therefore, the actual sentence reads, "*For* Christ therefore we are ambassadors." The emphasis is significant and must not be taken for granted. We represent none other than Jesus Christ, the Son of the Living God!

Martyn Lloyd-Jones, one of the most influential preachers and Christian statesman for much of the twentieth century, who served as the minister of Westminster Chapel in London for almost thirty years and authored almost eighty books, left us an accurate appraisal of being an ambassador for Christ, along with a compelling question. After remarking that an ambassador from any country is always conscious of the fact that they have a tremendous responsibility because they are the representative by whom their country is going to be judged, he then offers this application: "And to us is given the privilege and responsibility of being the representatives of the Son of God in this world. We stand for him, people judge him by what they see in us, and they are perfectly entitled to do so because we are the ones through whom and in whom he is glorified. Do we, I wonder, always realize this?"[11]

So, now do you realize that there is a Foreign Embassy on your street, and it is your house! On my street, it is my house. We should be flying the "Christian" flag over our homes. Whenever someone comes to our homes for a visit, they ought to get a sense that they are stepping into a sovereign "foreign" country. And whether in or out of that home, we should be willing to declare the message of our King and his Kingdom

11. Baker, "Ambassadors: Privilege and Responsibility," Psalm 105.

whenever we get the chance. We are ambassadors for Christ. We represent where he is, who he is, and what he is. That is how we respond to the challenge to be good citizens of heaven.

A Universe in Ruin

In this book, I have talked a lot about the Great Commandment in Matthew 22:36–40. But then there is also the Great Commission: "Jesus came and told his disciples, 'I have been given all authority in heaven and on earth. Therefore, go and make disciples of all the nations, baptizing them in the name of the Father and the Son and the Holy Spirit. Teach these new disciples to obey all the commands I have given you. And be sure of this: I am with you always, even to the end of the age'" (Matt 28:18–20 NLT).

The charge by our Savior to go into all the world with the message of the saving grace of God is repeated in all the Gospels and then in the Book of Acts, just before his ascension, Jesus re-emphasizes those marching orders, "But you will receive power when the Holy Spirit comes upon you. And you will be my witnesses, telling people about me everywhere— in Jerusalem, throughout Judea, in Samaria, and to the ends of the earth" (Acts 1:8 NLT).

As we have noted in our study of Second Corinthians 5:20 and that we are ambassadors for Christ, note further that the verse says that God will be pleading through us as we implore people to be reconciled to God. In the preceding verse, Paul said that God has committed to us this ministry of reconciliation.

The world needs reconciliation. People need to be convinced to turn back to God. And that task is on us, equipped and empowered, thankfully, by God's Spirit. Reconciliation means to be changed back, it means to be reunited, because, as a result of the Fall man has been estranged from God. There occurred a complete fracturing of the relationship between God and man. But now in Christ, there is the possibility of a change from hostility and enmity to harmony and fellowship. As a result of this reconciliation, Paul affirms that we become new creatures, as everything has changed. "Therefore, if anyone is in Christ, he is a new creation; old things have passed away; behold, all things have become new" (2 Cor 5:17).

Of course, the problem is in the convincing. Sin and Satan have blinded the eyes of those who are in desperate need of being reconciled to God. They are lost and wandering and do not often know it. They cannot explain their despair and cannot free themselves from their dilemma. In his critical essay, *A Free Man's Worship*, Bertrand Russell details the dismal view that most people have of life, an attitude that is brewing deep down inside them, and one that does not always surface in expression but that is always there. It is, in Russell's words, the strongest tie that unites all men, the tie of a common doom. "The life of Man is a long march through the night, surrounded by invisible foes, tortured by weariness and pain, towards a goal that few can hope to reach, and where none may tarry long. One by one, as they march, our comrades vanish from our sight, seized by the silent orders of omnipotent Death."[12]

Russell published *A Free Man's Worship*, in December 1903, and it is acknowledged to be his best-known and most reprinted essay. Many, including Russell himself, have tried to explain its mood and language. Russell was certainly a brilliant logician and mathematician, as well as a philosopher and historian. But he was also an atheist and became a scathing social critic. While he was awarded the Nobel Prize in Literature (in 1950) and wrote on numerous subjects including politics, ethics, and religion, his views were jaded by his atheism and his writings often carried the bleak existentialism, pessimism, and despair of a life without God. This is most graphically revealed in his signature essay. And so, he continues: "Brief and powerless is Man's life; on him and all his race the slow, sure doom falls pitiless and dark. Blind to good and evil, reckless of destruction, omnipotent matter rolls on its relentless way; for Man, condemned today to lose his dearest, tomorrow himself to pass through the gate of darkness, it remains only to cherish, ere yet the blow falls, the lofty thoughts that ennoble his little day."[13]

This is the same man who wrote that "we are all orphans and exiles, lost children wandering in the night, with hopes, ideals, aspirations that must not be choked by a heartless world."[14] According to Nicholas Griffin who wrote a journal article entitled, *Bertrand Russell's Crisis of Faith*, like all existentialists, his goal was to establish the absurdity of life. For Russell, the universe is an "accidental collocation of atoms" doomed to

12. Russell, "A Free Man's Worship," (1903).
13. Russell, "A Free Man's Worship," 61.
14. Russell, "The Return to the Cave," 42.

extinction, and human life along with it is the product of purposeless and meaningless processes likewise doomed to "be buried beneath the debris of a universe in ruins."[15]

While I do not think most people have an articulately critical view of life as did Bertrand Russell, the reality is, they do know something is wrong and they are not sure how to fix it. This they do know—that death is inevitable and they cannot stop it. The greatest message we can share with those on that death march, who will find out that the wages of sin is death, is that the gift of God is eternal life, and that life is in His Son, Jesus Christ.

A Day of Good News!

After reading the depressing comments by Bertrand Russell, I ask you, is there any doubt that people need to be reconciled to God? Need we even ask the question of whether we should evangelize and confront our world with the claims of Christ? Why is this not a priority for all Christians? Why does George Barna continue to uncover evidence that so many Christians are not only failing to behave what they profess to believe but that they are also incapable of even presenting what they profess to believe?

Becky Pippert was certainly right when she said that one thing that Christians and Non-Christians have in common is that they are both up-tight about evangelism. And yet, why is that? Why do walk around as if we have the plague when it is the plague we got rid of?

We have all heard the quote by D. T. Niles, that Evangelism is just one beggar telling another beggar where to find bread. Every time I hear that I am reminded of the compelling story found in Second Kings, chapter seven (the story begins in Second Kings 6:24). Ben-Hadad and the Syrian army have besieged Samaria and the ensuing famine is devastatingly perilous to the Israelites. All life is threatened. People are dying. All hope is fading fast, that is until God calls on the prophet Elisha to deliver a message of deliverance and salvation. The Spirit of God causes the Syrians to flee in the night, abandoning their camp in such a hurry that they leave behind all their provisions (2 Kgs 7:6–7). The siege has been miraculously lifted, but no one knows it yet.

---

15. Griffin, "Bertrand Russell's Crisis of Faith," 113.

The scene shifts to four lepers, who without knowing any of this, decide to venture into the Syrian camp in hopes of begging for bread. Imagine their delight and amazement when they arrive at the camp and find it completely abandoned by the soldiers. The text tells us that they go from one tent to another, eating, drinking, and stuffing their pockets with valuables left behind by the frightened Syrian soldiers, they even start to hoard their treasures by hiding all of it.

But then something significant happens. In Second Kings 7:9, we read, "Then they said to one another, 'We are not doing right. This day is a day of good news, and we remain silent.'" They reveled in their good fortune, but then they realized their good fortune was something that they should share. They had been "saved," and now they realized that they could save others. They knew what their duty was. Listen to them! "This is not right, this is wonderful news, and we aren't sharing it with anyone" (NLT). "What we are doing is not right. This is a day of good news and we are keeping it to ourselves" (NEB). "This is a day of glad news, and we do not speak up?" (Amplified). James Moffatt has them saying about their good news, "We are not spreading it!" The New American Standard has them admitting, "We are keeping silent." And Today's English Version has it, "We are keeping quiet."

Would you not agree that Second Kings 7:9 has a legitimate application for us today? Is it not convicting? Especially in our culture where the pressure is increasing to silence all Christian narratives. George Barna reports that in our current environment of political correctness, a "real Christian" is supposed to be "compassionate enough to keep his or her beliefs private." He warns the result will be that "the world's greatest gift is now faced with becoming the world's greatest secret."[16]

We need to be like those poor lepers, having been cleansed of the leprosy of sin, and tell others they too can be cleansed. We need to be like those poor beggars and tell someone else where they can find the bread of Life. It is our duty. It is our responsibility. We cannot hoard this blessing and bounty for ourselves. It is a day of good news and we dare not remain silent.

We are ambassadors for Christ to a lost and dying world. It is a world, a city, a community that is sick and getting sicker, but we have the cure. We know the Great Physician. All we have to do is tell people about him.

16. Barna, *Evangelism That Works*, 24.

This is our privilege, this is our purpose, this is our priority! Your conversion was timely and convenient, and it should never be an inconvenience to tell someone else about it. David Peterson and Becky Pippert authored a powerful book some years ago entitled, *Out of the Saltshaker and Into the World*. They remind us that "Jesus wants us to see that the neighbor next door or the people sitting next to us on a plane or in a classroom are not interruptions to our schedule. They are there by divine appointment. Jesus wants us to see their needs, their loneliness, their longings, and he wants to give us the courage to reach out to them."[17]

In 1953, at the Bob Jones University Lectures on Evangelism, Oswald J. Smith outlined what he believed were the prerequisites for Evangelism. He said they were:

- A vision of the utter bankruptcy of the human race.

- A realization of the adequacy of God's salvation as found in Christ.

- And a life given over to that one great purpose.

The "purpose" of which he spoke was that of declaring with conviction that Jesus Christ is the only hope for a world in ruin as a result of sin. A couple of decades later, Gene Getz echoed a similar challenge to the church: "The evangelical church must recognize with renewed vision that we have the only authoritative answers to our society's deepest needs. We must realize that the pluralisms and the many uncertain voices in our society today provide us with unprecedented and unparalleled opportunities for evangelism. Men everywhere are confused, but they have the potential to differentiate truth from error. The Holy Spirit is still at work in the world, enlightening the hearts of men and honoring the Word of God."[18]

So, there we have it. Do you believe that the world in which we live is languishing in alienation from God? And, if you do, are you convinced that you have a message to share with your world, your city, your community, that will reconcile people back to God?

Patrick Morley, while speaking specifically to Christian men, reminds all Christians that God is ready to use those today who will own the responsibility of being ambassadors for Christ. What he says is a fitting way to conclude this chapter, acknowledging that our interaction with the community around us must be a priority in our circle of

17. Peterson and Manley-Pippert, *Out of the Saltshaker and into the World,*" 104.

18. Getz, *Sharpening the Focus of the Church*, 232.

responsibilities as we affirm God in the center of our lives. He writes: "Here's the challenge for the next generation of Christian men: God is looking for men willing to be sent and to engage with and redeem civic affairs, the education system, public service, commerce manufacturing, service industries, the justice system, education, the trades, and every other arena for the glory of Jesus Christ."[19]

The truth of this could not be timelier and his challenge could not be more relevant in our day when untold millions are still untold. We cannot be silent in our homes, on our jobs, and out and about in our world. With God at the center of your life, are you willing to allow people to see God in you and then to position yourself so that God can touch those people through you?

This must be true of us for the benefit and blessing of our families, our jobs, our church, and our community. And a whole new generation of relationships is waiting for us to do so.

For the glory of Jesus Christ, indeed!

19. Morley, *The Christian Man*, 211.

Last Word

"Well Done!"

I HAVE NEVER FORGOTTEN HOW James Dobson concluded his Focus on the Family video series *Straight Talk to Men and Their Wives*. In a quiet and purposeful tone, he shared his conviction that the accumulation of wealth, even if he could achieve it, would not be a sufficient reason for living. He wanted to know that when he reached the end of his life, he could look back on things more meaningful than the pursuit of houses and land and machines and stocks and bonds. He also rejected the idea that fame was of any lasting benefit. In the final analysis, he knew that his earthly existence would have been wasted unless he could recall a loving family, a consistent investment in the lives of people, and an earnest attempt to serve the God who made him.

His inspiring and insightful critique on his own life challenges my own and compliments so well, I trust, the theme of this book. It is the challenge to pursue a biblically balanced life that places God at the center which then makes everyone around us, be they family, friends, or maybe even foe, a priority in the opportunity of faithfully loving God and loving our neighbor as our self.

The whole premise of this book is to demonstrate that when God is at the center of our lives, we will be fully equipped to meet the needs of the responsibilities that constantly surround us. We will be positioned to love God fully, and then to fulfill our calling to love and serve those around us effectively. When God is the Center of our life, no matter the time or the circumstance, those around us will see Him, and then through us, God can touch them.

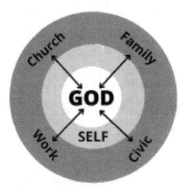

We can only bring a biblical balance to our life by applying biblical principles. It will not just happen on its own. We must intentionally embrace the responsibility to love God and seek his Kingdom only and above all.

We must be willing to love the Lord—constantly, unashamedly, and passionately. Indeed, it demands all of our heart, mind, strength, and soul.

And love our family in a way that they will never doubt that God is in control of who we are, why we are, and how we plan to provide for and lead our families.

And love being the church, the Ecclesia, the "called-out" assembly of Jesus Christ our Lord, knowing it is who and what we are rather than somewhere we attend.

And love our job and invest in it a spiritual value that increases the worthiness of our work, believing that all work done for God is the Lord's work.

And, yes, love the world for whom Jesus died and own the responsibility of being Christ's ambassadors on earth, representing him to a lost and dying world that is in critical need of being reconciled back to God.

Life is demanding and it can certainly be difficult, but with God at the center of your life, it will be balanced with purpose, with promise, and with his power. Paul tells us that God himself will bring forth in you both the desire and the effort to do it, for the sake of his own good pleasure (Phil 2:13 NET).

So, have the desire! Put forth the effort!

Represent the Lord Jesus Christ well. Aspire to hear him say to you in that day, "Well done, good and faithful servant." As James Dobson said, nothing else really matters, nor carries the eternal reward of serving the Lord faithfully. Like him, I have reflected upon my own journey, and I have come to these conclusions:

> I would like to be well-liked, but I do not need to be.
> I would like to be well-groomed, but I may not always be.
> I would like to be well-dressed, but I cannot always be.
> I would like to be well-known, but I probably will never be.
> I would like to be well-read, but I might not always be.
> I would like to be well-thought-of, but that is not up to me.

What is up to me is to serve Jesus Christ faithfully, and represent him well. And having done that, I am trusting that I will hear him say to me, "Well-Done!" And on that day, when he does, that will mean infinitely more to me than being well-liked, well-dressed, or well-known.

And for all of us, on that day, we will fully understand that the key to life was not what we knew but *Who* we knew. That knowing God, and giving him the supreme position in our life, which is at the *Center*, brought balance, blessing, and purpose to our life.

Tozer once said that in every Christian's heart there is a cross and a throne, and the Christian is on the throne till he puts himself on the cross. He is right. And we can infer from this that once we vacate the throne—once we abdicate, the throne is now available to be occupied by its rightful owner.

The throne room of your life is in the center of your being, and when the Lord takes the throne, your life will finally have God at Center.